THE LEGEND OF
MᶜCARTHY

THE LEGEND OF
McCARTHY

JEFFREY L. RODENGEN & RICHARD F. HUBBARD

Edited by Melody Maysonet
Design and layout by Wendy Iverson and Dennis Shockley

Write Stuff Enterprises, Inc.
1001 South Andrews Avenue
Second Floor
Fort Lauderdale, FL 33316
1-800-900-Book (1-800-900-2665)
(954) 462-6657
www.writestuffbooks.com

Publisher's Cataloging in Publication

Rodengen, Jeffrey L.
The legend of McCarthy / Jeffrey L. Rodengen & Richard F. Hubbard; edited by Melody Maysonet; design and layout by Wendy Iverson and Dennis Shockley. — 1st ed.
p. cm.
Includes bibliographical references and index.
LCCN 2001135154
ISBN 0-945903-89-8

1. McCarthy (Firm) 2. Construction industry—United States—History. I. Hubbard, Richard F. II. Title.

HD9715.U54R64 2003   338.7'624'0973
QBI33-1228

Library of Congress
Catalog Card Number 2001135154

ISBN 0-945903-89-8

Completely produced in the
United States of America
10 9 8 7 6 5 4 3 2 1

Also by Jeffrey L. Rodengen

The Legend of Chris-Craft

*IRON FIST: The Lives
of Carl Kiekhaefer*

*Evinrude-Johnson and
The Legend of OMC*

*Serving the Silent Service:
The Legend of Electric Boat*

*The Legend of
Dr Pepper/Seven-Up*

The Legend of Honeywell

The Legend of Briggs & Stratton

The Legend of Ingersoll-Rand

*The Legend of Stanley:
150 Years of The Stanley Works*

The MicroAge Way

The Legend of Halliburton

*The Legend of
York International*

*The Legend of
Nucor Corporation*

*The Legend of Goodyear:
The First 100 Years*

The Legend of AMP

The Legend of Cessna

The Legend of VF Corporation

The Spirit of AMD

The Legend of Rowan

*New Horizons:
The Story of Ashland Inc.*

*The History of
American Standard*

The Legend of Mercury Marine

The Legend of Federal-Mogul

*Against the Odds:
Inter-Tel—The First 30 Years*

*State of the Heart:
The Practical Guide to
Your Heart and Heart Surgery*
with Larry W. Stephenson, M.D.

The Legend of Pfizer

*The Legend of
Worthington Industries*

*The Legend of
Trinity Industries, Inc.*

The Legend of IBP, Inc.

*The Legend of
Cornelius Vanderbilt Whitney*

The Legend of Amdahl

The Legend of Litton Industries

The Legend of Gulfstream

The Legend of Bertram
with David A. Patten

*The Legend of
Ritchie Bros. Auctioneers*

The Legend of ALLTEL
with David A. Patten

*The Yes, you can of
Invacare Corporation*
with Anthony L. Wall

*The Ship in the Balloon:
The Story of Boston Scientific
and the Development of
Less-Invasive Medicine*

*The Legend of
Day & Zimmermann*

The Legend of Noble Drilling

*Fifty Years of Innovation:
Kulicke & Soffa*

*Biomet—From Warsaw
to the World*
with Richard F. Hubbard

NRA: An American Legend

*The Heritage and Values
of RPM, Inc.*

*The Marmon Group:
The First Fifty Years*

The Legend of Grainger

*The Legend of
The Titan Corporation*
with Richard F. Hubbard

The Story of HealthSouth

The Legend of Discount Tire
with Richard F. Hubbard

The Legend of La-Z-Boy
with Richard F. Hubbard

TABLE OF CONTENTS

BUILDING DREAMS

by
Mike McCarthy
Chairman Emeritus, McCarthy Building Companies, Inc.

MCCARTHY IS ALMOST 145 years old. Yet the average life span of a *Fortune* 500 company is 45 years, and building firms, especially privately owned ones like ours, have an even shorter average life. What are the reasons for McCarthy's longevity?

I believe there are specific characteristics that have allowed us to be the exception. First, we share the same values: honesty and integrity, courage in the face of adversity, trust in one another, and a passion for building. Moreover, these shared values create our culture: a commitment of service to our employees and our clients, a desire to make the work fun, and a willingness to take substantial risk that allows us to build the most challenging projects.

McCarthy fosters a climate of inclusion in our extended family; every employee shares the credit for and the financial rewards of our success. We also share the responsibility for recognizing and solving problems. No individual is alone when a difficulty arises. In that same spirit, McCarthy has a culture of forgiveness.

McCarthy people revere our past heroes, and at every get-together there is much retelling of the past glories of our adventurers. We have a wonderfully rich history that gives us our foundation and makes us proud of our roots.

Our company has had legendary leaders—individuals who have lent their significant talents to the pursuit of building excellence: Timothy "Mr. Tim" McCarthy worked diligently during the early 1900s; his son John and nephew Melvin McCarthy hacked it out in the Panama Canal Zone during the 1940s and 1950s; Merryl, Mr. Tim's other son, worked to build up the Midwest; and Paddy and Tim McCarthy, Merryl's sons, made McCarthy the largest builder in the St. Louis market during the 1960s and 1970s. In the 1980s, Roger Burnet, another McCarthy leader, propelled our hospital group from its small beginnings to become the largest hospital builder in the nation. Also in the 1980s, Pat Waters led our foreign efforts in Saudi Arabia and Egypt. Gerry Murphy and Mike Hurst piloted our westward expansion by starting an office in Phoenix. Mike Bolen, the current McCarthy chairman and CEO, spearheaded our explosive growth in California. And Karl Kloster added exciting new business units to grow our Midwest operations, despite a stagnant market.

Throughout all this growth, our goal has not been directed at becoming the biggest. Instead, we strive to be the best builder in America. Each year, we get closer to reaching that target; in some areas we are very close; in others there is much to do, but the passion is there. You can feel it—in every office, in every job, in almost every person. We are growing, learning, committing, and achieving.

Most companies are founded by entrepreneurs who have a passion for a particular line of work, and they do that work with exceptional vigor and creativity. But how rare is the company that continues generating that passion to deliver a truly exceptional result? Even extremely well run companies that lack a compelling, shared passion will eventually die. Business managers do not inspire coworkers to lofty goals; dreamers do. Dreamers make each one of us reach for the stars and demand that we keep getting better.

McCarthy has been blessed with a number of true dreamers. But dreaming isn't enough; you must dream together, work very hard, and trust your partners in business. Since our founding, we have been blessed with an extraordinary level of trust among the principals. I'm sure there were times, even among the family, when questions of competence arose, but there was never a question of trust, and there was never a question of commitment.

In the 1990s, when I decided to eventually sell the company to the employees, I had the full support of the McCarthy family. I felt that McCarthy could not reach its goal of being the best builder in America unless ownership was in the hands of the people who ran the company every day. Every current member of McCarthy's top management was chosen years ago from within the company and trained extensively for the job they would inherit.

We are builders. We are the kinds of people who built the great cathedrals of Europe, the Pyramids, and the Panama Canal. We see ourselves as builders; we love the smell of concrete and lumber, the texture of fine woods and stone, the smell of the earth as it's turned by the great machines of construction. Most of all, we love our craftsmen—men and women who are so talented that they could work for anyone, yet they choose to work with McCarthy.

There are managers of construction who see construction as a business, but McCarthy is a visceral builder. We're deeply devoted to solving problems in pursuit of building the dream. We are not a surrogate; we are the mother!

My grandfather was a stonemason, my father was a carpenter, and I was a carpenter, albeit not a very good one. McCarthy's new chairman, Mike Bolen, was a carpenter, as was his father. We all have engineering degrees, but our sword was forged and tested through hands-on construction.

We are your builder.

If you can dream it, we can build it!

Michael M. McCarthy

ACKNOWLEDGMENTS

A GREAT NUMBER OF PEOPLE ASSISTED IN the research, preparation, and publication of *The Legend of McCarthy.*

This book would not have been possible without the professional skills of our devoted research assistant Barbara Lopez-Lucio. Her efforts went a long way toward making this book a success. Research assistant Michael Renner was a great help in gathering photos. Melody Maysonet, senior editor, oversaw the text and photos from beginning to end, and Wendy Iverson's and Dennis Shockley's graphic design brought the story to vivid life.

Several key people within McCarthy Building Companies lent their invaluable efforts to the book's completion. Mike McCarthy, chairman emeritus, graciously shared his memories and provided valuable oversight for accuracy. Mike Bolen, Chairman and CEO, and Mike Hurst, president, were especially helpful in relating the company's most recent history. And Mike Lenzen, corporate communications manager, helped guide the book's development from outline to final form.

Many other McCarthy executives, employees, retirees, friends, and family members greatly enriched the book by discussing their experiences and lending valued photos from their personal collections. The authors extend particular gratitude to these men and women for their candid recollections and photos: Gary Akin, Gary Amsinger, Kris Anderson, Chuck Avery, Neil Bauer, Ken Bonastia, Dennis Bryan, Harl Buckallew, Roger Burnet, Bo Calbert, Carter Chappell, Frances Choun, Rich Corey, Dan Cummings, Lydia Dawson, April Kemp, Tom Dollar, Jim Faust, Tom Felton, Fran McCarthy Fitzgerald, William Godbey, Andy Greensfelder, Bud Guest, Lloyd Hansen, Laurie Happ, John Heidbreder, Rich Henry, Steve Jennemann, Dennis Katovsich, Karl Kloster, Bob Knochenhauer, Mike Krueger, Kevin Kuntz, Connie Ryan, Chris Brandt, Susan Garritano, Rob Langhoff, Joe Lauer, Mike Lipton, Monsignor Bob McCarthy, Francis "Paddy" McCarthy, Kathy McCarthy, Michael F. McCarthy, Tim McCarthy, Michael McSorley, Mike McWay, Kay Miller, Greg Montgomery, Gerry Murphy, Steve Mynsberge, Catherine O'Brien, Linda Osborn, Mike Oster, Frank Pasztor, Dan Petry, Peggy McCarthy Reynolds, Barb Saey, George Scherer, Bill Schuttler, Jim Staskiel, Sue Stewart, Rod Thayer, Lorrie Tschannen, Dennis Tucker, Jim Ulkus, Rich Vandegrift, Tom Waters, Russ Wenzel, and Lesley Zahn.

As always, special thanks are extended to the dedicated staff at Write Stuff Enterprises, Inc.: Jon VanZile, executive editor; Heather Deeley, associate editor; Bonnie Freeman, copyeditor; Sandy Cruz, senior art director; Rachelle Donley, art director; Mary Aaron, transcriptionist; Barb Koch, indexer; Bruce Borich, production manager; Marianne Roberts, vice president of administration; Sherry Hasso, bookkeeper; Linda Edell, executive assistant to Jeffrey L. Rodengen; Lars Jessen, director of worldwide marketing; Irena Xanthos, manager of sales, promotions, and advertising; Rory Schmer, distribution supervisor; and Jennifer Walter, administrative assistant.

MCCARTHY LEADERSHIP LINEAGE

Michael M. McCarthy
Chairman Emeritus (2002-today)
Chairman (1984–2002)
Fifth President (1976–1984)

Timothy R. McCarthy
Vice Chairman

Francis "Paddy" McCarthy
Vice Chairman
Estimator

J. Melvin McCarthy
Fourth President
(1964–1976)

Merryl L. McCarthy
Secretary/Treasurer
Estimator

John E. McCarthy
Third President
(1950–1964)

John W. McCarthy
First President
Carpenter

Charles M. McCarthy
Bricklayer

Timothy McCarthy, Jr.
Second President
Carpenter, Accountant

Timothy McCarthy
Founded Construction Firm
(1864)
Barn & House Builder

TIME LINE OF MCCARTHY EVENTS

1864: Irish immigrant Timothy McCarthy begins a small business in Ann Arbor, Michigan, building farmhouses and barns.

The 1930s: The company ventures outside the continental United States after winning a contract in the Panama Canal Zone. McCarthy also ventures into the faraway Alaska Territory to build the new federal building in Anchorage.

1951: McCarthy diversifies when Merryl McCarthy leads the purchase of Rock Hill Quarries, an aggregate plant in St. Louis.

1917: After taking on more complex projects such as post offices and commercial buildings, Timothy's sons, John W., Charles, and Timothy Jr. (Mr. Tim), move the now-incorporated McCarthy Brothers Construction to St. Louis, Missouri.

The 1940s: Cousins John E. and Melvin McCarthy continue working in the Panama Canal Zone throughout WWII while Mr. Tim and Merryl McCarthy pursue domestic contracts.

1961: Under Paddy McCarthy's guidance, the company completes the Priory Chapel, which helps establish McCarthy's reputation as a skilled builder with creative solutions. Meanwhile, Melvin, along with brothers John E. and Merryl and Paddy's brother Timothy R., all develop leadership positions in the company.

2002: Mike McCarthy, now chairman emeritus, sells his majority interest in the company to McCarthy employees, making the company 100 percent employee owned.

The 1990s: McCarthy continues its quest to become the best builder in America through excellent customer relations and safety and training programs. It also continues to raise the bar for quality on each and every project.

1976: Mike McCarthy becomes company president upon Melvin's death.

The late 1980s and early 1990s: McCarthy expands into semiconductor, biopharmaceutical, educational, R&D, and general manufacturing markets, becoming a major player in each.

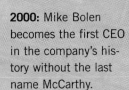

1972: Mike McCarthy founds McBro to continue McCarthy's lucrative parking structure work. McBro also moves the company into construction management for hospitals. That same year, Roger Burnet joins the company as a vice president. (In 1984 Burnet becomes the first president who is not a McCarthy.)

1995: Company president Roger Burnet retires, and Mike Hurst becomes the new president and chief operating officer.

2000: Mike Bolen becomes the first CEO in the company's history without the last name McCarthy.

Timothy McCarthy, father of 10 and patriarch of the family. Like his descendants, he was a builder and a carpenter.

CHAPTER ONE

THE McCARTHY FAMILY

1864–1916

[I] took Martin Naylors job repairing his barn and shed with as many doors and windows as he chose for $110.

—Timothy McCarthy, 1881

LOCKED IN A SAFE IN THE CORporate offices of McCarthy Building Companies, Inc., is a treasured link to the past. The small record book, with its paisley-patterned cover and leather spine, looks curiously modern when closed—but open, the browned pages and faded ink of its entries convey its age. Well over 100 years old, the book contains a wealth of information about the McCarthy family's early days: jobs taken, days worked, material lists, estimates, and payments received. Mundane in its detail, the book has inestimable value as a glimpse at the humble beginnings of a billion-dollar construction company. But for Michael M. McCarthy, the company's chairman emeritus, it provides something even more important and personal—a tangible link to his great-grandfather, the McCarthy patriarch who launched the family into the carpentry and construction business 138 years ago.

In 1864, the Civil War still divided the United States, and the nation's future hung in the balance. That same year, an immigrant from Ireland named Timothy McCarthy moved to Ann Arbor, Michigan, and began to establish himself as a carpenter and builder of farm structures.

Timothy McCarthy had chosen his location well. Ann Arbor, 45 miles west of Detroit, was a thriving community of 5,731 permanent residents and the Washtenaw County seat. Founded in 1824, Ann Arbor had grown slowly until 1837, when it became the site of the University of Michigan. By 1866, several building projects were under way, including eight commercial projects worth $47,000, a church costing $50,000, and residential, school, and small-business jobs worth $86,000.[1] It was a good place for a carpenter like Timothy McCarthy to ply his trade, as evidenced by this classified advertisement that appeared in the Ann Arbor newspaper in July 1866:

WANTED—IMMEDIATELY

FIVE GOOD CARPENTERS & JOINERS
To whom good wages will be paid
and constant employment given.

Apply immediately at the shop of the subscribers East of Cook's Hotel on Huron St.
PLIMLEY & WEBSTER Ann Arbor.[2]

Ellen Curran McCarthy, sitting for a formal portrait. She was just 13 when she immigrated alone to the United States. She married Timothy when she was 15.

Building a Legacy

Little is known of Timothy McCarthy's formative years. He was born in Castle Lyons, County Cork, Ireland, on February 22, 1828.[3] Exactly when he immigrated to the United States is unknown, but by the early 1850s he was living in New York, where he met and married another Irish immigrant, Ellen Curran, some 10 years his junior, of Dungarven, County Waterford, Ireland.[4] Sometime in the mid-1850s, the McCarthys traveled to Michigan, then in 1864 moved to Northfield Township, a rural area of rich, rolling farmland just north of Ann Arbor, where Timothy hung out his shingle as a carpenter and builder.

Northfield Township was a logical place for McCarthy to settle. The area had seen an influx of Irish settlers, who were beginning to replace the English pioneers in the northern half of the township. Many of the Irish families had followed the Reverend Patrick O'Kelly to Northfield Township, where he served as priest of a small church. O'Kelly had established a parish in Rochester, New York, in the 1820s and was later sent to Michigan to minister to the Irish Catholics who were moving there.[5] Within fifty years, most of the township's residents were of Irish descent.[6]

When the McCarthy family moved to Northfield, they settled on a small farm of about 130 acres in the northeastern corner of the township, about eight miles north of Ann Arbor. Figures from the 1870 U.S. census fix the value of the real estate at $1,800, a rather modest holding compared to those of the neighbors, many of whom had property valued above $5,000—and up to $16,000. The value of McCarthy's personal property was put down as $400, which was more in line with his neighbors'.[7]

An 1874 drawing of a farm in Northfield Township in rural Michigan. Timothy and Ellen moved to Northfield in 1864, attracted by growing Ann Arbor and a large Irish immigrant population. *(Photo courtesy Bentley Historical Society, University of Michigan.)*

McCarthy worked hard to support his growing family, which would eventually include 10 children. When he and Ellen moved to Northfield Township, they were already the parents of four daughters. Mary was born in New York around 1854. Alice, Ellen, and Kate followed, all born in Michigan. John W. was born in 1864, and Timothy Jr. followed in 1867.[8] Emma Jane was born soon after, and then Laura and Agnes. Charles, listed as Michael C. in the 1880 census, completed the family in 1878.[9]

Timothy headed a hardworking, close family. Records show that Mary and Maggie worked for a time as waitresses in the restaurant at Cook's Hotel, a well-known Ann Arbor eatery.[10] While it is not certain that these were Timothy's daughters, an entry of "Maggie got married" in one of Timothy's record books indicates that Maggie was someone close to the family.[11] Maggie was most likely a middle name or nickname for one of his daughters, perhaps Alice or Ellen. Nicknames were common in the McCarthy family; the fourth McCarthy daughter—listed as Kate in the 1870 census—lies beneath a headstone inscribed with the name of Kittie.[12]

The McCarthy sons followed in their father's footsteps, working as skilled tradesmen. John W. and Timothy Jr. learned carpentry from their father, while Charles eventually became a bricklayer.

Life on the McCarthy Spread

Besides working hard, Timothy McCarthy kept notes about daily life on the family's small farm. Some of these notes have survived in his book for more than a century, providing a fascinating glimpse into the life of the large family and its business. The first entry was made in 1874. In an elegant hand, Timothy meticulously set down each day's activities, which ranged from work for hire to farming chores. There are references throughout to such farming work as digging potatoes, butchering, picking apples, making cider, and sowing and harvesting wheat. In July 1879, Timothy "commenced Bird Renwick's house,"[13] which he recorded as taking 34 days to complete.

Something of Timothy's character can be inferred from the entries. Only once in the book does he seem to take a workday off for an "escursion."

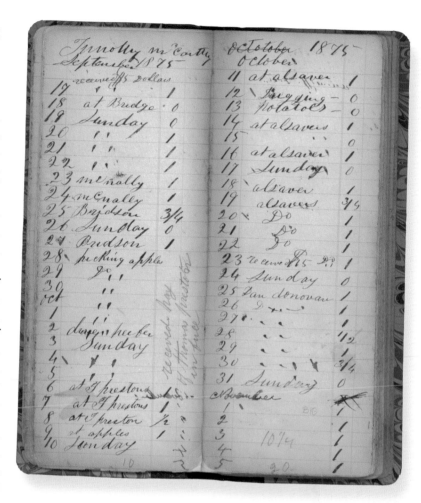

Timothy McCarthy's record book, where he meticulously listed the family's jobs, days worked, material lists, estimates, and payments received

Although he was usually busy six days a week, Timothy never worked on a Sunday.[14]

Timothy's paying jobs included work on barns, houses, and granaries. He also spent time "hewing ties for rail road,"[15] an activity at which he evidently excelled. In a two-day period, he chopped 109 ties.[16] The railroad was most likely the new Toledo, Ann Arbor, and Northern Railroad, an important and long-awaited link for Ann Arbor. Although served by the Michigan Central Railroad, Ann Arbor lacked a link to the growing markets to the south. The dream of an Ann Arbor–Toledo railroad had existed since before the 1840s, but the Civil War and an 1873 depression delayed its construction until 1878. By the early 1880s, the rail line was being built north from Ann Arbor, passing just a few miles from Timothy McCarthy's home.

The completion of the railroad improved economic activity in Ann Arbor over the next few years, but those gains were offset by another recession and dropping enrollment at the University of Michigan. The early 1880s saw Ann Arbor's population shrink. In 1880 the town was home to just over 8,000 residents; four years later that number had declined by nearly 1,000.

Still, there was no lack of work for McCarthy. As early as 1875, he employed a helper named Michael Hayes, whose pay included a pair of boots for $4, a pair of gloves for $1.50, socks for $.30, and two shirts and a set of overalls for $1.95.[17] Timothy tabulated that he had worked away from home in 1881 for 190 days and in 1882 for 185 days. By 1879, his son John W. began showing up in record-book entries, working with his father and on his own.

Timothy's book also includes entries on payments collected for his work. Fees were not always paid in cash. His notations show payment in wheat, corn, tobacco, and hay. One client even included a pencil as part of his payment.[18]

In the spring of 1877, a crisis struck the McCarthys. A series of entries recorded the events. "House Burnt Planting potatoes,"[19] reads the first. The following day, Timothy McCarthy was "at home building Shanty."[20] He spent the next three weeks building a house to replace the old log cabin that had been destroyed. The new house was a two-story farmhouse with a kitchen, sitting room, and bedroom downstairs and a wide porch in front. Up a steep flight of stairs were two more bedrooms, one with a built-in bookcase in which John W. carved his initials.[21] A summer kitchen, barn, and other outbuildings were also on the property. Although most of the outbuildings have fallen under the weight of years, the farmhouse that McCarthy built in 1877 still stands, and under layers of paint the "JM" on the upstairs bookcase is still visible. And while the potato fields and most of the 130 acres have long since passed into other hands, the house has remained in the family and is home to a granddaughter of McCarthy's daughter Emma Jane.

Timothy Jr. made his first appearance in his father's record book when he was 15 years old and

Timothy McCarthy built this two-story house in 1877 after the family's log cabin burned. Smith O'Brien, a grandson of Timothy and Ellen McCarthy, sits on the porch.

went to the city mills to pick up wheat, flour, and bran.[22] The only other family name in the book appears toward the back. Written in pencil in a childlike hand—quite different from the graceful entries of Timothy—is an entry: "Ellen McCarthy went to work for Pete Coldren the 12th of April and quit the 23rd of September. 23 weeks & 2 days. Received Money."[23]

Pete Coldren was not the only Coldren to appear in Timothy's book. The McCarthy family also did some work for a Charley Coldren. Many other names are inscribed, including George Hammonds, Tom Heney, Philo (or Filo) Chubb, James McHugh, Dan Donovan, Thomas Fahey, John Lawton, and Frank Hemingway. It appears that most of McCarthy's work during the 1870s and early 1880s was for neighboring farmers; almost every name mentioned in his record book can be found on the plat map for Northfield or neighboring Salem Township.

It is also likely, given the importance of the church in the McCarthys' tight-knit Irish community, that McCarthy and his sons helped in the construction of a parish church, which was completed in 1878. Named St. Patrick's, the beautiful gothic-revival church was constructed largely by the parishioners, as was the church rectory, built in 1890.[24] The church and rectory are still in use, and the parish is listed as a Michigan Historic Site as the oldest English-speaking Catholic parish in the state.[25] The McCarthy family plot stands proudly in the front of St. Patrick's cemetery.

Several entries in Timothy's record book list materials and their costs, giving some idea of what Timothy's work involved. He built privies for a school, constructed barn frames, doors, and windows, and installed siding, shingles, and floors.

Building a Business

Ann Arbor's stagnation in the early 1880s might have played a role in the next stage of the family's business, but Cupid's arrows are usually credited for bringing the McCarthys to Missouri. Family legend has it that John W. fell in love with a young woman and followed her to Missouri when she moved there with her family. That young woman was Hannah Bently, daughter of John and Sarah Bently, who

owned a farm near the McCarthys. John W. McCarthy and Hannah married around 1890. They settled in Farmington, Missouri, about 60 miles south of St. Louis and the government seat for St. Francois County.

Farmington, with a population of more than 1,000 in 1900, was not merely the agrarian community implied by its name. It was also a shipping, trading, and financial center that served the mining district to the west. An old plank road, built in the mid-1800s to transport iron ore and supplies between the mines and the Mississippi River at Ste. Genevieve, ran through Farmington. The road was later replaced by the St. Louis and Iron Mountain Railroad, which ran a few miles west of Farmington.

In December 1896, a daughter, Bernice, was born to John W. and Hannah. Four years later, the family was living in a rented house in Farmington with Hannah's widowed mother. Listed as a carpenter, John W. had experienced a rough year; he had been unemployed for eight of the preceding 12 months.[26]

His trials were not over. In December 1901, Hannah took ill and died. The *St. Francois Herald* reported her death:

> *MRS. JOHN MCCARTHY DIED AT HER HOME IN FARMINGTON—ABOUT EIGHT O'CLOCK YESTERDAY MORNING. SHE HAD BEEN UNWELL FOR A FEW DAYS, BUT NO SERIOUS RESULTS WERE THOUGHT PROBABLE. EVEN ON YESTERDAY MORNING SHE SEEMED IMPROVED; AND ATE SOME BREAKFAST. MR. MCCARTHY, WHO IS A CARPENTER, HAD GONE TO HIS WORK, NEAR HOME, WHEN HIS WIFE BEGAN SINKING AND NEVER REVIVED.[27]*

A widower with a five-year-old daughter, John W. finally prevailed in his business. By 1903, he had built the administration building at State Hospital Number 4, beginning a relationship that would continue for years. Still in use in the 21st century, that administration building is part of a large complex of structures (many of which are

John W. McCarthy, the eldest son of Timothy and Ellen, with his first wife, Hannah, and their daughter, Bernice. John W. would later found McCarthy Construction Company.

McCarthy-built) that later made up the Southeast Missouri Mental Health Center. In 1904, John W. was building in downtown Farmington at the corner of Jackson and Columbia Streets. Nearly a century later, the brick, two-story building was restored and became home to a specialty store.

In 1905, John W. and three partners—R. Fugate, S. R. Turley, and J. S. Clay—each put up $2,500 and created the St. Francois Real Estate Company. Formed "to buy and sell real estate, erect hotels, halls, business houses, dwellings, and other buildings," the company wasted no time.[28] The articles of incorporation were accompanied by a report on the company's first activity: "The shareholders in this company have purchased the old Rucker mansion, paying nearly $10,000 for the same, and will probably erect thereon a large business house in the near future."[29]

McCarthy Construction Company

John W. was living in a time of booming prosperity and expansion in the United States. The early 1900s saw a huge population explosion, caused by births, an influx of immigrants, and continued westward migration. At the same time, the country was going through a dizzying period of technological advancement. Automobiles, airplanes, radio, and telephones would all come in the near future. But in 1900, America still moved to a quieter rhythm, one that evoked the just-passed days of pioneers and frontiers. "America presented to the eye the picture of a country that was still mostly frontier of one sort or another, the torn edges of civilization's first contact with nature, man in his invasion of the primeval," wrote Mark Sullivan, a famous journalist of the early 20th century, in his landmark book *Our Times*.[30]

St. Louis enjoyed a reputation as a thriving, modern city poised on the great eastern edge of the United States' inevitable expansion across the Rocky Mountains. In 1900 the city had electric lights and trolley cars, more than half a million residents, and even downtown skyscrapers. It was this level of comparative sophistication that earned St. Louis one of the greatest distinctions of the new century. In 1904 it was chosen as the site of the Louisiana Purchase Exposition, also known as the St. Louis World's Fair—the largest and

MAC CÁRTAIȝ

THE McCARTHY NAME

THE FAMILY NAME OF McCARTHY has an old and proud lineage. Its origins can be traced to a third-century Irish King of Munster, Oilioll Olum. The king had three sons, Cormac Cas, Eoghan, and Cian. The descendants of Eoghan were known as the Eoghanacht and ruled in south Munster. By the early 11th century, the Eoghanacht were led by Cárthach, whose name means "the loving one." His descendants took the name McCárthach, meaning "sons of Cárthach." Different branches of the family evolved. The McCarthy Mór were found in Kerry while the McCarthy Reagh were centered about Carbery, in West Cork.

The traditional McCarthy coat of arms

grandest of all world's fairs. Over the course of the World's Fair, about 20 million visitors descended on St. Louis, sparking a building boom that lasted until World War I. New hotels, office buildings, factories, and homes sprang up throughout the city, which was the world's foremost producer of such products as beer, shoes, stoves, and wagons.[31]

John W., already a partner in the St. Francois Real Estate Company, was anxious to join the rush. In early 1907 he sent for his brothers, Timothy Jr. and Charles, who relocated from Ann Arbor to St. Louis. On March 16, 1907, the brothers incorporated their new business, McCarthy Construction Company, with John W. listed as the company president. The articles of incorporation list the company's original subscribers as J. W. McCarthy, 77 shares; Timothy McCarthy, nine shares; Charles McCarthy, one share; John W.'s second wife, Minnie M. McCarthy, 10 shares; and Tillman Rock, presumably an employee, three shares; for a total of 100 shares, with a par value of $100 each. At its first official stockholders meeting two days later, all five stockholders were named directors, Timothy was voted vice president, and Minnie, secretary. As president, John W. was voted a salary of $100 per month; Minnie was to receive $25 per month as the company's secretary.[32] All votes were unanimous.

The directors' next move was to purchase John W.'s existing carpentry business. The lot on which the shop was located was valued at $200. It was purchased, along with machinery, lumber sheds,

Left: Timothy "Mr. Tim" McCarthy, the middle son of Timothy and Ellen, with several women in his family. From left: Mr. Tim; Nell; Emma Jane; Agnes; Mr. Tim's wife, Mame; and Jessie, wife of Charles McCarthy Sr.

Right: Charles McCarthy, born in 1878 and the youngest of the McCarthy clan, became a master bricklayer and a partner in the family construction company.

lumber, and the interest as it appeared in unfinished contracts, for $5,330.[33]

In its first year, McCarthy Construction borrowed more than $8,000 from John W. at an interest rate of 6 percent. At its first annual stockholders meeting, with John W., Minnie, Timothy, and Rock present, "a correction was made in the list of original Stockholders, as there appeared to be an error in this list." The corrected list shifted the single share held by Charles to Timothy, giving him a total of ten shares.[34] It would be 1912 before Charles once again owned McCarthy stock.

In these early years of McCarthy Construction, several people outside the family also occasionally held stock. In addition to Tillman Rock, Lee Huff and W. H. Agnew, also presumably employees, are listed in the company records with small amounts of stock.

In 1910, the capital stock in the company was increased to $30,000 (300 shares at $100 each), and the company was renamed McCarthy Lumber & Construction Company. "This change was necessary in order to carry a stock of lumber, and the increase in capital was necessary to take care of the vast increasing business," the minutes reported. John W. now held 204 shares and Minnie 30. Timothy had 45 shares, and the three employees held a total of 21.[35]

In 1911, the company authorized the purchase of property behind and next to its shop "to erect thereon a planing mill of suitable size and also lumber sheds for the storage of materials."[36] The planing mill was expanded the following year.

The financial statements from the early years unfortunately do not include any mention of particular projects. They are a simple balance sheet of the company's assets and liabilities. Still, they show a corporation that nearly tripled in size in its first decade. McCarthy paid its bills, quickly built up a healthy surplus, and had plenty of cash.

Headquartered in Farmington, the McCarthy lumberyard would soon become a local fixture. It provided material for everything from culverts and tiling for local roads and bridges to labor and materials for repairs, remodeling, and additions to the jail, infirmary, and old county courthouse.[37] But the company also had a greater vision; its construction arm focused on building commercial and government structures both locally and throughout the state. John W., Timothy, and Charles were on their way to turning the skills and hard-work habits learned from their father into a company that would carry the family name around the world.

Back in Michigan, the elder McCarthy had long since given up his building business; the 1900 census lists his occupation simply as a farmer. It should be no surprise that the hard-working Timothy had retired from construction work by the age of 72. On August 20, 1909, Timothy McCarthy died. Ellen Curran McCarthy joined him seven years later. They are buried in the cemetery of St. Patrick's Church in Northfield Township, Washtenaw County, Michigan.

From Missouri to the Pacific

Eagerly pursuing building projects throughout Missouri, McCarthy Lumber & Construction Company soon won its first opportunities. In 1911, officials in Scott County, Missouri, decided to build a new courthouse to replace the county's outdated building. Architect Henry H. Hohenschild, who designed many of Missouri's courthouses, was appointed by the court to design the new structure.

The Scott County Courthouse in Benton, Missouri, in 1913. This was the first of four courthouses McCarthy built in Missouri. (Used by permission, State Historical Society of Missouri, Columbia.)

A gang of McCarthy construction workers in the first decade of the 20th century. By this time, John W. had relocated McCarthy to Farmington, Missouri.

Hohenschild's plans were for a three-story, T-shaped structure. The base of the T measured 56 by 122 feet; the wings were 52 by 55 feet. The building was to be faced with brick and trimmed with terra cotta and would have four entrances. Columns graced the main facade. Construction on the new courthouse was to proceed in stages, and McCarthy Lumber & Construction won the contract to erect the shell of the building in October 1912.[38]

Originally, the courthouse was to be paid for out of the county's general revenue funds, and $50,000 had been reserved for this purpose. But proponents of the new courthouse, impatient with the slow pace that the financing plan allowed, pushed for a $40,000 bond issue, even sponsoring an essay contest on the topic. Their strategy was successful. In March 1913, voters approved the bond issue, which allowed completion of the building's interior. By December 1913, the new courthouse was finished at an estimated cost of between $100,000 and $140,000. Nearly 90 years later, that McCarthy-built courthouse is still in use.

Around the time McCarthy was building the Scott County Courthouse, the company bid on and won the contract to erect the Missouri Building at the 1915 Panama-Pacific International Exposition in San Francisco, California. It was the company's most distant contract to date, and according to company legend, McCarthy sent its entire construction crew to San Francisco by train. This willingness to take risks, to pursue far-flung projects, and to devote whatever resources were necessary to the successful completion of a project would become a McCarthy trademark in the decades ahead.

John W., left, and Timothy "Mr. Tim" Jr., right. Two of Timothy McCarthy's three sons, they formed McCarthy Construction Company with their brother, Charles, in 1907.

CHAPTER TWO

MOVING TO THE CITY

1917–1940

My mother's side of the family were artists, and my dad's side were singers and musicians. So you wonder how we got in the construction business. You couldn't make any money singing and playing instruments back in the 1930s. My grandfather [Charles McCarthy] played clarinet for Benny Goodman, and he was really good, but he was a bricklayer.

—Michael M. McCarthy, 2001

BY 1910, WITH A POPULATION approaching 700,000, St. Louis was the fourth-largest city in the country. Although World War I, which lasted from 1914 to 1918, slowed construction in the city, building activity resumed immediately after the war ended in Allied victory.[1]

The opportunities available in a growing city like St. Louis must have been a powerful lure for McCarthy Lumber & Construction Company, which was still headquartered in the bucolic town of Farmington, Missouri. Or perhaps the growing company found itself hampered by Farmington's remoteness. Whatever the reason, in 1917, John W., Timothy Jr., and Charles moved the firm to St. Louis. The company's first St. Louis address was at 604½ Chestnut, in St. Louis's central business district.

Good Citizens

Although the company moved to St. Louis, the McCarthy brothers kept residences in Farmington for several years. The family ties were strong. There John W. met and married his second wife, Minnie Dunn; their two children, John D. and Margaret Ellen, were born in Farmington and raised with their half-sister, Bernice, John W.'s daughter by his first wife. In 1906 Charles also married a Farmington woman, Jessie E. Murphy, a great-granddaughter of one of Farmington's founders. Their children, Melvin and Charles Jr., soon joined the growing clan, which also included Timothy Jr.; Timothy's wife, Mary E. Donovan (called "Mame"); and their children, Merryl, John E., Katherine, and Agnes.

Besides having familial ties, McCarthy had done a lot of work in Farmington and the surrounding areas. John W. was known as a good citizen, a "friend of our people while a resident here," wrote the Farmington paper in 1936. He remained active in community affairs even after moving to St. Louis.[2]

A 1917 St. Louis city directory listed John W. as the company's president; Timothy as vice president; and John W.'s wife, Minnie, as secretary.[3] The company disappeared from the city directories of 1918 and 1919, only to reappear in 1920 as McCarthy Construction Company, with an address at 816 Olive.[4] By 1921, McCarthy was headquartered at 721 Olive, and John W. and Timothy had both moved with their families to St. Louis.[5] Charles apparently remained in Farmington.

Charles McCarthy Sr., pictured in the 1930s. Charles was a master bricklayer but not involved in the day-to-day management of the company.

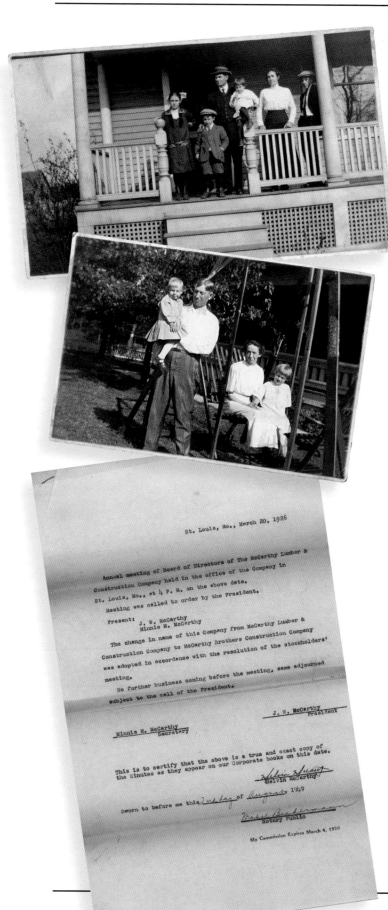

A new generation of McCarthys was reaching adulthood. Some entered the family business while others followed different pursuits. Bernice went to work for the St. Louis Public Library, where she remained for many years. Merryl attended the Missouri School of Mines, later the University of Missouri—Rolla, and was honored as the university's first-ever "St. Patrick." (The university's annual tradition continues to the present day.) After graduating, Merryl worked as a civil engineer, presumably for the family business, and became a McCarthy superintendent.[6] In 1924 he was living in Cape Girardeau, Missouri,[7] no doubt supervising a building project there.

A Specialty in Courthouses

By 1925, McCarthy had once again moved, this time to the Roosevelt Hotel building at 4908 Delmar Boulevard.[8] The following year, the name was changed to McCarthy Brothers Construction Company[9] and would not change again for many years.

Although McCarthy had relocated to St. Louis, the company continued to build county courthouses in far-flung corners of Missouri. On October 30, 1922, fire destroyed the Osage County Courthouse, which had been built in 1874, remodeled in 1881, and had "one of the finest-furnished and best-planned courtrooms in Missouri."[10] After much debate over a year's time, the court decided to build a new courthouse rather than try to rebuild the burnt one. McCarthy won the contract for the first stage of the building, worth around $45,000. The new courthouse was completed in October 1925 at an estimated cost of $85,000.

Top: Mr. Tim's family, pictured in the early 1900s. From left to right are Katherine, John E., Mr. Tim, Agnes, Mary "Mame," and Merryl. Both Merryl and John E. would become directors in the family construction company.

Center: John W. with his second wife, Minnie, and their children, John D. (being held by his father) and Margaret Ellen.

Left: The minutes from the 1926 board meeting at which McCarthy Lumber & Construction Company was named McCarthy Brothers Construction Company.

As in Scott County, the architect was Henry H. Hohenschild, who designed a three-story red brick structure with white trim. Although McCarthy's company records do not date back that far, it is tempting to imagine Charles, the bricklayer, laying those courses of brick, using his art to fulfill Hohenschild's design.

Architect Hohenschild and McCarthy worked together on at least one other courthouse in 1924, this one for Pemiscot County in the town of Caruthersville, which is located in the Missouri bootheel, hard on the Mississippi River. Officials there planned to build a school and courthouse, both designed by Hohenschild. The simultaneous construction was designed to save money and ensure adequate supervision of both projects by the architect. McCarthy was awarded the courthouse contract in June 1924. The contract amount of $114,000 was lower than originally estimated because of declining prices.[11]

The design of the Pemiscot County Courthouse was similar to the one in Scott County, built by

A McCarthy construction crew poses in front of Osage County's partially built courthouse, which replaced the courthouse that had burned down. The new courthouse was designed by noted Missouri architect Henry Hohenschild, who designed several courthouses around the state.

St. Francois County Court House and   Public Square, Farmington, Missouri

Above: The St. Francois County Courthouse on the public square in Farmington, Missouri. McCarthy-built, it remains in use today. *(Used by permission, State Historical Society of Missouri, Columbia.)*

Below: A group of McCarthy workers in the 1930s in Farmington, Missouri. Active all over the state, McCarthy was a hard-working, family-oriented company.

McCarthy from a Hohenschild design more than a decade before. But in Pemiscot County, the brick structure was trimmed in stone rather than terra cotta. The courthouse was finished in the autumn of 1925.

As in Scott County, both the Osage County and Pemiscot County Courthouses remained in use beyond the millennium, a tribute to the skills of the builder and a fact of which McCarthy can be proud. But McCarthy's proudest monument to courthouse construction can be found back in Farmington, presiding over its central business district like a beloved matriarch.

The Courthouse in Farmington

In May 1926, McCarthy was awarded the contract for a new St. Francois County Courthouse. Coincidentally, in 1823 the ancestors of Jessie Murphy McCarthy—Charles's wife—had donated 52 acres of land in what would become the heart of Farmington for the establishment of a county seat.[12]

The courthouse McCarthy built was the fourth to occupy the site; its predecessors were built in

1823, 1848, and 1885. In 1925, county voters authorized a $250,000 bond issue for a new courthouse. The court met with several architects but had a difficult time agreeing on which to hire, taking 18 ballots before a decision emerged. Norman B. Howard, of the St. Louis firm of Bonsack and Pearce, was the architect finally chosen. Picking McCarthy as the builder was an easier decision, given the company's strong ties to Farmington.

Howard's first design, which was similar to one he had worked on for nearby Franklin County, was criticized as unoriginal and out of proportion. The plans ultimately used called for a stately structure in the Italian Renaissance style, clad in Carthage marble and Bedford limestone, although strong sentiment had arisen for the local red granite. The entrances on each side of the courthouse were to look alike, with loggias, or open porches, and Corinthian columns. The interior was to be similarly elegant, with marble floors, steps, and wainscoting. An elevator was included to carry passengers to the third-floor courtroom.[13]

Problems plagued the project almost from the start. After the dissatisfaction with Howard's initial design, questionable procedures on the architect's part led to talk of fraud and brought about a grand jury investigation. Closer supervision of the architect by the court resolved the procedural questions, but the ceremony for setting the cornerstone was delayed and finally canceled because the cornerstone Howard provided was not acceptable to the court.

These problems seem to have been laid at the doorstep of the architect rather than McCarthy, which finished the building in September 1927, just 18 months after it received the contract. The courthouse, which cost St. Francois County taxpayers close to the $250,000 approved and appropriated, was dedicated on October 13, 1927. The lovely building, called "one of the finest courthouses in Missouri,"[14] still graces downtown Farmington and houses St. Francois County offices.

Finding Work

On October 29, 1929, a day since known as "Black Tuesday," the U.S. stock market collapsed, sparking an economic depression that would persist for nearly a decade. The nation's income dropped by more than half between 1930 and 1933. Unemployment was rampant, and construction activity ground to a near halt. The effects of the Great Depression were somewhat ameliorated in St. Louis by work remaining from a 1923 civic improvement bond issue and from another passed in 1934, but jobs were still hard to come by.

Forced to look farther afield for work, McCarthy soon began bidding on government contracts, and in February 1933 the company won a $24,684 contract from the Navy Department for extension of the Aircraft Overhaul Shop at the Fleet Air Base in Coco Solo in the Panama Canal Zone.[15] This job would mark the first time McCarthy went outside the boundaries of the continental United States, entering into a tropical and remote area full of adventure. The Panama Canal Zone work would loom large in McCarthy's future.

McCarthy also found work closer to home. In 1935, the company won a $146,625 contract to erect the administration building at Algoa Intermediate Reformatory for Young Men, located near the state capital of Jefferson City, Missouri.[16] That same year, McCarthy built a new post office in Farmington. And in 1938 the War Department awarded McCarthy a $48,925 contract to erect a

McCarthy was respected for its brick work. Here, workers take a break from building a brick schoolhouse in Farmington.

new Post Exchange at Scott Field on the Illinois side of the Mississippi River. That structure was a one-story brick building that held a restaurant, offices, a tailor shop, and a beauty parlor.[17]

In 1940, the company won a second Navy contract in the Canal Zone, this one for a whopping $859,529 for apartment buildings at the Naval Submarine Base at Coco Solo.[18]

Family Losses

Besides the hardships brought on by the Great Depression, the McCarthys faced losses of a more personal kind during the 1930s. On March 11, 1934, Charles's wife, Jessie Murphy McCarthy, died at the age of 50, leaving behind her husband and two sons, Melvin and Charles Jr. Jessie was laid to rest in her hometown of Farmington. Nearly 70 years later, "Mama Jessie" was credited by two granddaughters she never knew for instilling in their father, Melvin, the virtues of commitment to quality, perseverance, and caring that became a McCarthy tradition.

"The most important thing my father taught was the value of human beings," said Melvin's daughter Peggy Reynolds. "People were extremely valuable and almost sacred. You treated them correctly, and that was taught to us from day one."[19]

Her sister, Fran Fitzgerald, remembered their father's commitment to quality. "There are businessmen to whom it is more important to do a good job than make a lot of money," she said, "and he was one of them."[20]

Then in 1936, John W. McCarthy, president of McCarthy since its incorporation in 1907, died at his home in St. Louis at the age of 72. After a brief funeral service in St. Louis, his body was taken to the Carleton M.E. Church in Farmington, "his old home church," said his obituary, "which he loved and had served so well."[21]

The funeral service in Farmington was an elaborate event, conducted by the pastors from John W.'s St. Louis and Farmington churches and attended by a host of friends and relatives. A quartet of singers and an organist provided the music, and nephews Merryl, John E., Melvin, and Charles, along with two McCarthy employees, served as pallbearers. A host of honorary pallbearers also volunteered.

There is little doubt that John W. was well loved in his adopted hometown, a fact evidenced by his obituary, which ran in the Farmington newspaper:

In spite of 17 years of absence from here, he had always considered Farmington his hometown. He was delighted when his company received the contracts for the buildings which are now in the process of construction here, because it offered him the opportunity of returning frequently to this town, which he loved so much. Unfortunately his recent illness kept him from realizing this desire. He was known by all with whom he came in contact, both in a business and a personal way, for his kindly helpfulness, his sincere honesty, and his consistent loyalty to his friends.[22]

Above: Timothy "Mr. Tim" McCarthy, shown here in 1936, became the company's new president when his brother John W. died in 1936. He was accompanied in the business by his surviving brother, Charles, his sons, Merryl and John E., and his nephew Melvin.

Above right: Charles McCarthy Sr. in 1940. Charles McCarthy married into a prominent family in Farmington, Missouri, and did not relocate to St. Louis when the company headquarters moved.

Opposite: John W. McCarthy was the eldest son of family patriarch Timothy McCarthy. John W. was responsible for moving the family business to Missouri and, along with his brothers, founding the modern McCarthy Construction Company.

The Farmington work referred to was for five new cottages at State Hospital Number 4 (later called the Southeast Missouri Mental Health Center). At the time of John W.'s death, McCarthy had a contract for almost $1 million worth of work at the hospital, building on a legacy that reached back to 1903, when John W. built the facility's administration building. In the years since, McCarthy had erected nearly all of the hospital's buildings.[23]

After John W.'s death, Timothy McCarthy, who became known as Mr. Tim, became the company's president. Charles, his son Melvin, and Mr. Tim's son John E. were vice presidents, and Mr. Tim's son Merryl was secretary. These five men also made up McCarthy's board of directors.

Developing the Alaska Territory

In 1939, McCarthy, already working in the faraway Panama Canal Zone, took on another distant project, the construction of the new federal building in Anchorage, Alaska Territory.

A new federal building was a long time coming for Anchorage. In 1922 the Anchorage Chamber of Commerce asked the federal government for money to build a replacement for the city's old post office and territorial jail. But it was not until 1937 that the money was finally appropriated, with the understanding that there would be a three-year delay before construction began. But pressure from the community convinced Washington that an immediate start was critical, and construction got under way a year later. The outbreak of World War II in 1939 turned Anchorage into a boomtown with a soaring population and a new military base on its outskirts. It became obvious that the partially constructed federal building would not be adequate for its larger role, and an annex was added to the plans.

Designed by architect Gilbert Stanley Underwood, the Anchorage Federal Building was considered a definitive expression of modern architecture and quickly came to symbolize the federal government's commitment to Alaska. The U.S.

Above: John E. McCarthy working in Anchorage, Alaska. Daughter Kay watches him smile for the photo, circa 1939.
(Photo courtesy Kay Miller.)

Right: Mr. Tim stands next to a McCarthy truck in 1939. Emblazoned with a banner reading "Enroute to Alaska," the truck and McCarthy were about to build a post office and courthouse in Anchorage. By this time, the company was already active in the Canal Zone in Panama.

Above: McCarthy expanded its footprint well beyond Missouri when it built the Anchorage Federal Building in the Alaska Territory. Alaska wasn't yet a state, and the building was symbolic of the federal government's commitment to Alaska. *(Photo courtesy Anchorage Museum of History and Art.)*

Above right: (From left) John E. McCarthy; his wife, Eleanor; his mother, Mary "Mame"; and his father, Mr. Tim, in Anchorage, Alaska, circa 1939 *(Photo courtesy Kay Miller.)*

General Services Administration detailed the building's significance.

Devoid of the typically elaborate detail of the classical revival architecture popular at the end of the 1930s, the simple rectilinear form of this poured-in-place concrete building has been characterized as "New Deal Concrete." The Federal Building was constructed in an era of economic depression, yet its stable, classical proportions were symbolic to the citizens of Anchorage of the Federal Government's commitment to strengthen-ing the economy and continued development of the Alaska Territory.[24]

Over the years, the Anchorage Federal Building played a major role in Alaska's development. Parades passed by its front doors, the world-famous Iditarod dogsled race begins in its shadow, and when Alaska became the nation's 49th state, the building was wrapped in a flag to which Miss Anchorage fastened a 49th star.

While most of its federal offices have since moved to other quarters, the building itself remains a beloved part of downtown Anchorage. Its inclusion on the National Register of Historic Places ensures that it will remain a fixture in that city.

The Alaskan job signaled a change for McCarthy. Because of the United States' looming entry into World War II, construction business was drying up across the country. In June 1940, McCarthy decided to withdraw from bidding on domestic jobs and concentrate on its government work in the Canal Zone, a possible war zone with great potential for heavy development.

During World War II, Melvin McCarthy, son of Charles, worked in the Panama Canal Zone with his cousin John E. McCarthy.

CHAPTER THREE

UNCOMMON ENDURANCE

1941–1946

There was that...sensation of being about as close as a civilian can come to the war itself; of being in that part of all the Americas that might some day become an active War Zone.

—John E. and Melvin McCarthy,
on working in the Panama Canal Zone during World War II

ON OCTOBER 14, 1941, THREE OF the five directors of McCarthy Brothers Construction Company gathered in the firm's office at Delmar Boulevard and Euclid Avenue in St. Louis to chart the company's course through the uncertainty of World War II.

Present were Timothy "Mr. Tim" McCarthy, the company's president, now a well-seasoned 74; Mr. Tim's younger son, John E. McCarthy, 34, a company vice president and veteran of the Canal Zone work; and company secretary Merryl McCarthy, 43, Mr. Tim's elder son and the corporate heir apparent. Merryl held the proxies for the two missing directors: Mr. Tim's 63-year-old brother, Charles, and Charles's son Melvin. Although Charles rarely appears in the few surviving pre–World War II company documents, Melvin, at the age of 32, was a company vice president and McCarthy's legal representative in the Canal Zone.[1]

The triumvirate of Mr. Tim and his sons owed a duty to both McCarthy Brothers Construction and the various McCarthy relatives. They undoubtedly took that duty seriously. They must have known that the decisions they made would determine the company's direction and the potential fortunes of the McCarthy family. What they could not have foreseen was how important the decisions they made that autumn day would prove to be.

Conditions at home and in the Canal Zone had changed in the 16 months since the directors had ceased bidding on local jobs to concentrate on pursuing opportunities in the Canal Zone. With the United States gearing up for entry into the war, business on the domestic front had markedly improved, and Mr. Tim and Merryl wanted to take advantage of "the improvements of competitive conditions in the domestic market that have appeared."[2] They wanted to resume bidding for local projects and to stop working in the Canal Zone once the current contracts had been completed.[3]

John E., however, wanted to remain in the Canal Zone and noted that his cousin Melvin McCarthy was "like minded."[4] John E. "pointed out the large number of small offerings appearing constantly in the Canal Zone market and spoke of his and Melvin's confidence in their competence to handle them." The two young men "had aspired for some time to undertake a contracting venture as individuals or partners."[5] The opportunity to carry on the Canal Zone work independently was just what they were looking for.

Although the board remained "firmly convinced of the desirability of concentrating its efforts on the

Michael M. "Mike" McCarthy, Melvin's son, about age four, wearing a navy uniform in Panama in the mid-1940s. Mike spent his early childhood in the Canal Zone.

John E. McCarthy, younger son of Mr. Tim and Mame, circa 1927. He joined Melvin in the successful Canal Zone operation.

immense war construction program at home, [it] looked kindly upon the aspirations of its junior members"[6] and gave its blessing to the venture. Splitting its resources was a risk the company was willing to take. John E. and Melvin could keep the lucrative Canal Zone work flowing while Mr. Tim and Merryl built the core business close to home.

McCarthy Brothers Construction gave the fledgling entrepreneurs more than its blessing; it gave them access to the resources they would need to succeed. Papers were drawn up immediately allowing John E. and Melvin "to withdraw [from active participation in the company's affairs], without prejudice, for the purpose of undertaking ventures of their own responsibility."[7]

Less than two weeks later, John E. and Melvin made their venture official, signing a partnership agreement forming McCarthy Builders Company. The papers, appropriately enough, were signed at Cristobal, in the Canal Zone, on October 27, 1941. McCarthy Builders was established for the purpose of "general contracting and building of frame and masonry buildings or shelters, concrete and earth improvements, cartage and delivery of raw or manufactured items, rental and sale of supplies, machinery and other real property."[8]

Melvin and John E. each put up $25,000 in working capital and agreed to a 50-50 split of any profits or losses. They also agreed "that the duties of each partner will be manifold; and that both shall share in the management and production end of the business."[9]

The partners quickly put their two-pronged strategy into action. In St. Louis on December 6, 1941, Mr. Tim and Merryl, on behalf of McCarthy Brothers, signed an agreement with McCarthy Builders. In two pages containing six sections written in straightforward language, the agreement defined the relationship between the two business entities. The first section halted the corporate salaries and other remuneration of John E. and Melvin, effective December 31, 1941.

The second offered "[e]quipment, tools, vehicles, and mess and camp facilities owned by the corporation and not required in the conduct of its operations" to the partnership "at rental, lease, or sale prices not lower than sufficient to yield the corporation a fair return on its investment, or higher than such facilities can be obtained from other sources."[10] The partnership would not be forced to take unneeded equipment or that which could "be obtained at more advantageous rates elsewhere."

The corporation agreed to immediately accept the return of leased or rented equipment and to "assume all responsibility for the customary insurance coverage on its property at all times." The partnership agreed to "take all ordinary or special precautions customarily regarded as necessary to protect the leased property from all damage beyond ordinary wear and tear."[11]

The third section of the agreement required the partnership to pay "fair remuneration" for services provided by the corporation. "Due allowance" was made for the exchange of services between corporate officers and the partners. "The time spent by any officer of the corporation on behalf of the partnership will be considered the equivalent of equal time spent by either of the partners on affairs of the corporation." Good-faith acts by either side were held harmless of liability.[12]

The fourth section dealt with money. The partners were instructed not to withdraw from the partnership income "for their personal use any sums in excess of their customary living and traveling expenses until they shall have completely discharged all financial obligations to the corporation."

The fifth section released the workers employed in the Canal Zone by the corporation to the partnership "upon assumption of repatriation and return passage obligations." The corporation also promised not to pressure workers to return to the United States if the partnership wanted those workers to remain in the Canal Zone. The final section of the agreement was a good-faith statement.[13]

After the agreement was signed, it was sent to the Canal Zone for the partners' signatures. It took nearly a week for the agreement to reach Melvin and John E. in Cristobal; by then the Japanese had attacked Pearl Harbor. The United States was at war on two fronts, and the Panama Canal provided a vital economic and military link between the Atlantic and Pacific Oceans. When the cousins signed the agreement on December 12, they were in a war zone.

Life in the Canal Zone

McCarthy Brothers had been working on various projects in the Canal Zone for seven years, and both Melvin and John E. spent a great deal of time there. "[S]ome measure of credit must be reserved for the skill, ingenuity, and know-how of Tropical contracting learned painfully, commencing in 1934," they said in a 1944 summary of the advantages and disadvantages of Canal Zone operations.[14] John E. and Melvin worked day and

The Fleet Air Base in Coco Solo, Panama. The Fleet Air Base project took place in the 1930s, leading Melvin and John E. to military and government contracts throughout World War II.

night for the success of their venture. They spent their days on the job sites, supervising "the active conduct of the contracts," and their evenings planning the following day's work and attending to an endless stream of administrative detail "and all tasks that could be postponed until such times."[15]

The cousins would have had no illusions about the formidable working conditions they were taking on. Although they mentioned the discomfort of the "heat, rain, [and] sand fleas,"[16] their greater concerns were on the practical side of operating a business so far from home.

Logistics could be a nightmare. The partnership's "utter dependence upon shipping for the delivery of all materials of construction, machine parts, and personnel" often made for long delays. The attack on Pearl Harbor and the subsequent declaration of war disrupted shipping schedules. In April and May of 1942, everything the partnership had en route to the Canal Zone from St. Louis was diverted to stateside warehouses, where it sat until December. Since the only construction

DeVERE
SAINT LOUIS

of the early 1940s, labor was usually 20–30 percent of a general contractor's budget, materials cost about 25 percent, and subcontracts accounted for 50 percent or more. Contractors in the Canal Zone, the partnership said, faced the greatest financial risk in the labor portion of their contracts.

The risk of material cost exceeding the budget is slight if the quantity survey was accurate. The risk on subcontractors is limited to their default, and can be covered by bond at insignificant cost, but there is no insurance against labor overruns and in the Canal Zone labor is more than normally unpredictable.[19]

The partners didn't consider the threat of attack in the strategically important Canal Zone as one of the disadvantages of doing business there. Rather, it was specifically listed as one of the advantages. "There was that pleasant sensation of being about as close as a civilian can come to the war itself; of being in that part of all the Americas that might some day become an active War Zone." Other advantages noted were the freedom from strict trade-union rules and the opportunity to make money. The latter was especially important for those "contractors persuaded to leave the comfort and security of their homes for ventures into foreign lands." The higher risks should be balanced by the chance for higher profits, the partners believed.[20]

The quest for reliable workers, or even enough less-than-reliable ones to get the work done, took some bizarre turns for John E. and Melvin.

Spanish is the native tongue and we didn't know any Spanish. We imported many American

materials originating in the Canal Zone were sand and gravel, "There was always the disturbing possibility that some vitally needed material or machine part would arrive late or not at all." Although German submarines were a real danger to shipping between the Canal Zone and ports in the United States, McCarthy Builders considered itself lucky to have lost "only small shipments of minor cost and importance" to submarines.[17]

Labor costs were of particular concern to the partnership since their contracts were "almost exclusively labor contracts."[18] In their summary, the partners explained that "in normal States' practice"

This page: Margaret "Dusty" Rhoads, Mike McCarthy's mother, in a formal portrait. Mike remembered that his mother served as a surrogate mother for the lonely workers during their time in the zone.

Opposite: Dusty's diary and picture collection provide interesting glimpses of her life in the Canal Zone. From top are the post office in Cristobal, Dusty surrounded by a group of her friends, and the Cristobal high school, attended by many children from McCarthy.

July 7, 1940
Hotel Washington
...tobol, R.P.

The voy...
though...
had an...
along an...
squalls...
The even...
marvelo...
would...
sicky sen...
would be fast a...
bunk and wat...
free to have a...
It was so t...
able to stand o...
with nothing but the sea and
sky and heading out to parts

Dusty kept a scrapbook of her time in Panama. These pictures show Panama when it was an active war zone. Counterclockwise from top right are a statue of Christopher Columbus at the end of Bolivar Street; another view of Bolivar Street, which "contains honky tonks," according to Dusty; a U.S. naval ship in dry dock; and a reminder of the war: a German train station on the left side of the street flying a swastika and the British Royal Mail station on the right side of the street flying a Union Jack.

in the Canal Zone became too large for the available labor supply we went into Colombia, Costa Rica, Honduras, Jamaica and Venezuela for help and even tried for a while the savage Darian [sic] Indians and the San Blas Indians who spoke neither English nor Spanish and whom we could instruct only by example and pantomime.[21]

The Canal Zone's heat and humidity were brutal on equipment, accelerating "the disintegration of all paint and the rusting of all metals." An auto fender "receiving ordinary care and no extraordinary abuse rusted through in six months."[22]

The near-constant rain meant near-constant mud, "and the strain of operating in the mud materially shortened the life of all equipment." Heavy use, careless operators, and the lack of replacement vehicles all contributed to the equipment

mechanics at the beginning but few stayed long enough to justify our outlay for their travel. For some, we paid round trip passage for less than a week's production. When the volume of work

Left and below: McCarthy trucks in Panama. Since equipment was hard to come by and the environment was so harsh, McCarthy did anything possible to keep its fleet running.

Bottom: Melvin, far right, on a job site in Panama around 1940. By this time, the company had six years' experience in the tropical environment and had learned to deal with its challenges.

Left: The view from Melvin McCarthy's front porch, across the job site. Note the company barracks on stilts. McCarthy workers were not allowed to live in the more developed military zone and had to carve their own space from the jungle.

Below left: A young Mike plays with some friends. The sandbox is surrounded by chicken wire to protect the children from the iguanas and snakes that could pose deadly dangers.

Below right: Melvin and Dusty sit on the steps of their "first real home" in Panama. The McCarthy homestead was sometimes visited by local tribesmen hoping to sell such curios as two-headed boa constrictors and human heads.

headaches. "Equipment was worked long hours, seven days a week, and for about twenty per cent of the time was worked two shifts daily" by workers characterized as "without mechanical aptitude or any sense of responsibility for the care of their machines." After their first year, many vehicles were so used up that it would have made better financial sense to scrap them, but since replacements were unavailable, the trucks "were kept running by welding, buying parts and borrowing parts from other trucks." Parts for repairs eventually totaled more than $16,000, more than 45 percent of the trucks' original cost.[23]

Living in the Canal Zone was a challenge for the workers and their families. Michael M. "Mike"

McCarthy, who moved to the Canal Zone with his father, Melvin, when he was one year old and would later become chairman and CEO of McCarthy Building Companies, Inc., spent some of his early years in the Zone. "The men came down by steamship," he said. "There wasn't any airline travel. They would be housed in a bunkhouse, and they were lonely."[24] Communications were difficult for the expatriate workers. There was postal or telegraph service, but no telephone calls home. Since the partnership's employees were civilians, they were not allowed to live on the military bases, where they worked.

"We lived in the jungle because there was nowhere else to live," said Mike McCarthy. "The first thing we had to do was build our houses in the jungle. Then we built the lodging for the men. My mother's job was to sort of run the commissary and take care of the men in the bunkhouse and all of the lonely hearts."[25]

Melvin supervised projects on one side of the Canal while John E. handled those on the other, but the families and the imported workers and their families all lived together in a community carved from the jungle. "It became kind of a family venture even then because we had a lot of young men working and lots of problems," remembered Mike McCarthy. "And then the holidays would come. That was very difficult on the workmen because they were away from their families. So we built a culture of caring. I think that was probably the beginning of McCarthy's caring kind of culture."[26]

The exotic Canal Zone and its denizens made a lasting impression on the child who would one day become McCarthy's most progressive leader.

I remember there was a tribe of Indians who were headhunters. They'd bring shrunken skulls right into the village, right where we lived, and try to sell them. They'd bring in gold. They'd bring in arrows and bows strung with human hair, human teeth. They'd bring in some

odd things like two-headed boa constrictors. It's hard to believe what it was like back then living in the Canal Zone. There was the military part of it, which was fairly established and controlled, but the other part of it was not controlled at all.[27]

With a scant four months—from January 15 to mid-May—"favorable for outdoor work," the partners had a limited time to make their fortunes. They were also hampered by their "isolation and immobility" in the Canal Zone. Early in 1942, the partnership bought "a completely modern paving plant" for use on a major airfield runway contract. In June 1942, with less than half the work done, the government canceled the contract. The partnership was stuck with a plant that stood idle for

Above: The first family Christmas in Panama (1940). Mike McCarthy later remembered that holidays were an especially hard time on the workers, who missed their families.

Left: An Easter egg hunt in the Canal Zone. Mike McCarthy is on the right. His friends are "Mikio Bear" and J. E.

Although they endured a hard life, workers in the Canal Zone did have some luxuries. They were allowed to shop in the commissary area, pictured on the left, and relaxed at the Gold Country Club, right. The receipt in the background is from the commissary.

two years "because there was no more work of this nature awarded in the Canal Zone."[28]

In the Zone: Successful Operations

By the end of 1942, their first year in operation, the partners were working on nearly $700,000 in government contracts, including work on truck sheds, a telephone building, and two warehouses.[29] Contract earnings were not the only or even the major source of the partnership's bottom line. Income from the rental of owned equipment netted the partners more than three times the return generated by their general contracting work in 1942. McCarthy Builders ended its first year with a net income of $133,128.[30]

The following year brought even more work for John E. and Melvin. They held contracts totaling $976,613. Again, the partnership self-performed on the largest contract, which was for "igloos," or concrete storage structures. They also worked on an officers' club and several other buildings. An adjustment of 1942 income bumped the partnership's contract operations into the red, but the money flowing in from equipment rentals more than made up the difference.[31]

By 1944, the partners were winding down their work in the Canal Zone. They began selling off equipment that was no longer needed. Although several major projects were still incomplete, many smaller contracts for work on recreational facilities, roads, docks, and ammunition niches were finished. McCarthy Builders grossed $88,806 on contracts of $465,180 and managed to earn more on the sale of equipment and interest income.[32] In 1945, however, the partnership suffered its first net loss due to cost overruns on a major contract for gun casements and adjustments to the previous year's figures.[33]

In 1946, McCarthy Builders finished its last projects, sold off its remaining equipment and construction materials, and sent its workers and their families home. The partnership was able to leave the Canal Zone on a high note; thanks to the profits generated by the sale of the equipment and material, McCarthy Builders finished 1946 with a net profit of $81,915.[34] Although McCarthy Builders existed for many more years, it was never again an active construction company.

The Prisoner of War Camp

While John E. and Melvin were busy in Panama, McCarthy Brothers concentrated on rebuilding its Missouri-based business. After returning to domestic bidding late in 1941, McCarthy quickly landed several contracts to build prisoner-of-war camps in Missouri. In August 1942, the army announced that McCarthy had been chosen to build a $1.5 million "enemy alien internment camp" at Weingarten, Missouri, a few short miles from the McCarthy stronghold of Farmington. McCarthy was already working on a similar camp across the state in

The McCarthy Builders construction oversight crew in Panama in 1945. Melvin is in the middle of the back row holding daughter Peggy, who was born there. By this time, Canal Zone work was winding down.

Three generations of McCarthys in 1940: from left, Melvin, Mike, and Charles Sr. All three would play important leadership roles in the family company.

Nevada, Missouri.[35] With its experience building military facilities in the Canal Zone and at Scott Field in Illinois, McCarthy must have been an easy choice for these new projects.

The plans for the Weingarten camp included 200 frame buildings, barracks, mess halls, and guard towers on 790 acres about 90 miles south of St. Louis. The camp was to be ready for occupancy in four months and completed in five.[36]

A description of a typical army prisoner-of-war camp built at nearby Fort Leonard Wood, Missouri, provides an idea of what McCarthy built at Weingarten and Nevada:

[The camp] was divided by barbed-wire fence into three compounds, with each compound designed to hold 100 prisoners. Following the Geneva Convention of 1929, these compounds were built according to American military camp standards. Standard facilities included barracks, latrines, and showers, all of which were single-story, tarpaper covered buildings with tent roofs. The structures were erected on concrete slab foundations or elevated on concrete posts.[37]

Thomas P. Waters Jr., the son of McCarthy superintendent Tom Waters, was 15 years old when McCarthy built the prison camps; it was his first job experience with the company. Six decades later, Waters clearly remembered an episode at the prisoner-of-war camp.

"We were still working on the hospital portion of the camp when a whole trainload of Germans and Italians came in with the army," Waters said. "As I remember, there were about five or 10 Italians for every one German, but they put them all together. They started to riot. The Germans were fighting the Italians and they set some of the barracks on fire. It went on all day long, and several of them were dead when the army got back in and separated them. They never put Germans and Italians in the same prison camp anymore."[38]

With work available close to home, it is easy to see why the company was so eager to return to domestic bidding. McCarthy's net income for 1942 came to only $154,560.[39]

Numbers dropped in 1943, and in 1944, McCarthy lost $587 on a measly $56,155 of completed contracts.[40] The situation was worse in 1945, when the company posted a net loss of $69,764.[41]

A summary of completed contracts for 1946 showed reason to hope the company was getting back on its feet. Melvin and John E. were finished with the Canal Zone work and could offer their experience and expertise to local clients. The contracts completed during the year presented a nice mix of locales and clients: three jobs for the Missouri School of Mines (now the University of Missouri—Rolla); painting and maintenance at Scott Field; a warehouse job in Vichy, Missouri; and a soybean mill in Mexico, Missouri. These contracts were overshadowed, however, by a power plant job in Poplar Bluff, Missouri, which had a number of cost overruns, and once again the company suffered a loss for the year.[42]

The struggling McCarthy Brothers Construction Company was finding plenty of work; it just wasn't making any money.

TIM McCARTHY

A CHRISTMAS LETTER FROM MISTER TIM TO ALL MEMBERS AND EMPLOYEES OF THE McCARTHY BROTHERS CONSTRUCTION COMPANY

My dear folks:

Although I am far away in Florida this winter, I feel very close to all of you in spirit, and I want to share with you some of the memories I treasure from my 86 years.

I have been a builder since I was a boy. My father before me was a builder. My brothers were builders. My sons are builders, my grandsons are builders, and I am happy to think on this Christmas Day that some of my great-grandsons are probably going to be builders. As long as there is anything left in this world to build, there are going to be McCarthy Brothers and McCarthy Cousins to build it.

In my 70 years of building experience, I have seen hundreds of construction companies come and go. We are one of the oldest firms now in the Middle West, and as the oldest President of any construction company, I am going to tell you the good reasons why we have continued to build, through all these years.

The first quality that has made the McCarthy Brothers and their co-workers strong is their fine family feeling, their loyalty to one another and to me, and their ability to work well together in mutual trust and helpfulness, without any of the dissension that has ruined other firms. Our friendly feeling extends from the top management all through the firm to every laborer on the job, and I want this spirit of harmony and cooperation to continue always, in the family and in the firm.

Another reason why McCarthy Brothers is recognized and respected throughout the United States is that we have always done the very best possible work on every contract we got. Sometimes we have lost big money on our contracts, but nobody can say that we ever did a skimpy, jack-leg job. We always leave our clients satisfied and happy, even if we have to sacrifice part of our profits to do it. That is why people are asking for us now and giving us big jobs without competitive bidding, whenever that is legally possible.

I want every one of you, young and old, to be proud of these big institutions that prefer to have us do their building, not because we are cheapest, but because they trust us, because they know that no matter what difficulties may come up on the job, everybody connected with our firm will always be fair, good-natured, and easy to get along with. I have always said that a person's disposition has more to do with the success of his life than education or other advantages. The happiest memory of my life is being out on the job when I was past 80 years of age, and having the men I had been hiring for the past 30 years crowd around my car and ask for me and wish me well. I wonder how many other big employers can say the same, and this simple message of being good to work for, and good to work with, is the message I want to give all of you to remember your Mister Tim by. God bless you all.

MISTER TIM

Christmas, 1953
803 West Druid Road
Clearwater, Florida

Mr. Tim summed up his strong sense of integrity in a 1953 Christmas letter to McCarthy employees: "This simple message of being good to work for, and good to work with, is the message I want to give all of you to remember your Mr. Tim by," he concluded.

CHAPTER FOUR

BUILDING A REPUTATION

1947–1959

We have always done the very best possible work on every contract we got. Sometimes we have lost big money on our contracts, but nobody can say that we ever did a skimpy, jack-leg job.

—Timothy "Mr. Tim" McCarthy, 1953

IN 1947, TIMOTHY "MR. Tim" McCarthy turned 80. Although he still held the title of president of McCarthy Brothers Construction Company, it was his son Merryl who, as secretary-treasurer, ran the day-to-day operations. Merryl's oldest son, Francis F. McCarthy, better known by the nickname Paddy, remembered his father as a consummate operations man. "He was kind of a one-man gang," Paddy said during a mid-1980s presentation on McCarthy's history. "He did all of the paperwork, did all the estimating, all the work you see in operations." Merryl also supervised longtime bookkeeper Martha Struckmeyer, who had worked for McCarthy Brothers since at least 1936. With Mr. Tim as president, Merryl was aided by Charles, Melvin, and John E., all vice presidents; young Paddy, a nonofficer; and (later) Timothy R. McCarthy, Merryl's second son. But because McCarthy Brothers was "a very adventuresome outfit," as Paddy put it, the others were often away at far-flung job sites, leaving Merryl to keep the office running smoothly.[1]

Merryl McCarthy

Merryl was much more than a paper pusher, however. At the age of 16, he had gone to San Francisco to help his father erect the Missouri Building for the 1915 Panama-Pacific International Exposition. He had been managing McCarthy Brothers jobs since his graduation from the Missouri School of Mines in 1921. His first job was to build the city public library at Cape Girardeau, where he quickly proved his worth by cutting labor costs in half. From there, Merryl went on to build schools, courthouses, and other structures, working sometimes with his father and sometimes on his own. Merryl supervised the construction of the Farmington Courthouse in 1928. In 1934, he worked on a bridge in Paris, Missouri, and the State Teachers' College, in Jonesboro, Arkansas, where he received a $4,000 bonus for early job completion. By the late 1930s, Merryl was spending most of his time in the office rather than in the field, although he did oversee a 1939 job at Scott Field.[2]

Robert Louis "Father Bob" McCarthy poses with his brothers and mother after his ordination as a Catholic priest in 1958. From left: Timothy R.; Father Bob; Gertrude; Father Bob's twin brother, John; and Paddy.

Rock Hill Quarries

Merryl proved his value to McCarthy in many ways, but perhaps his most important company decision was the purchase of the Rock Hill Quarries Company.

The owner of Rock Hill had three daughters but no sons. His sons-in-law didn't get along, so, perhaps worried about the fate of his business when he was no longer around to run it, he decided to sell the company. A local cement salesman told Merryl the place was a gold mine and Merryl should look into it. Although skeptical about the sons-in-law story, Merryl was curious. He took the cement salesman's advice and began investigating the quarry.[3]

Most of Rock Hill's income came from selling crushed rock. It also had a concrete block plant department and one for building material.[4]

Merryl's son Timothy R., known simply as Tim during his long career at McCarthy, later acknowledged that Merryl "didn't know about quarrying" but couldn't find anything wrong with Rock Hill. "[He] couldn't find . . . the catch," Tim said, "and finally went ahead and bought it." As it turned out, the investment paid for itself in only a few years.[5]

Merryl purchased enough shares of Rock Hill in April 1945 to have a controlling interest and became the company's secretary-treasurer. McCarthy Brothers bought 402 more shares in 1951.[6] McCarthy Builders, the partnership originally formed by Melvin and John E. for Canal Zone work, purchased another 103 shares that year, giving the McCarthys just over a third of the 1,500 shares issued.[7]

As its previous owner had indicated, Rock Hill was indeed a gold mine for McCarthy. From 1945

Above and below: Rock Hill Quarries as it looked in 1934. Merryl McCarthy oversaw the purchase of the quarry in 1951. Later, McCarthy's corporate headquarters would be located on the site.

through 1951, sales nearly tripled, to almost $775,000. Earnings also took a jump under Merryl's management, from some $12,000 in 1945 to just under $120,000 by 1951.

All that growth did not come without investment. By the end of 1946, Rock Hill had added plants in Piedmont and Elsberry, Missouri, in addition to crushed rock, concrete block, and building material departments.[8] The Piedmont plant was the only department to lose money; after three years of red ink, Rock Hill cut its losses and leased the plant.[9] By the end of 1949, the quarry had paid off all the debt it had accumulated from expansion.[10]

Rock Hill's deep pockets were instrumental in helping McCarthy Brothers survive depressions in the construction industry in the 1950s. Rock Hill loaned McCarthy some of its surplus cash on "favorable terms" to tide the builder over during rough times. "It played a big part in the history of McCarthy Brothers," Tim said.[11]

McCarthy-Pohl Contractors

Rock Hill Quarries was not the only outside venture pursued by Merryl. In September 1946 he formed a partnership with Joseph L. Pohl to create McCarthy-Pohl Contractors, Inc. Pohl owned 50 percent of the partnership, and the triumvirate of Merryl, Mr. Tim, and Charles owned the other half.[12]

McCarthy-Pohl was an earth-moving contractor specializing in levees and other flood-control projects along the Mississippi River drainage. Projects included the Kaskaskia River levee and the million-dollar-plus Clear Creek levee in Illinois. On the Missouri side of the river, McCarthy-Pohl

completed a flood control project at New Madrid. Other contracts included highway work and a $1.7 million contract for runways at Lambert Airport in St. Louis.[13]

Building Up Contracts

While Rock Hill would prove to be a vital asset and McCarthy-Pohl provided complementary services, the McCarthys and McCarthy Brothers were, before anything else, builders—and the building business kept growing.

As the 1940s waned, McCarthy Brothers continued to rely heavily on government and military work. In 1947, the company worked several jobs at Scott Field in Illinois, including one for housing. McCarthy Brothers had also done heating facilities and five classrooms in Rolla for the School of Mines and Minerals, which would later become the University of Missouri—Rolla. In addition, the company performed site work for the University of Missouri; the Greater Mexico Realty Company, in which McCarthy Brothers and McCarthy Builders owned shares; and the Wappapello Forestry Camp.[14]

The company's revenues took a big leap in 1948 with the completion of $1.6 million in contracts. Leading the way was the Delta Community Hospital, in Sikeston, Missouri, at more than $660,000, and a dormitory in Warrensburg, Missouri. That year McCarthy Brothers completed the chemical building at the university in Rolla and a nurses' home for the Sisters of St. Joseph in Wichita, Kansas.[15] The Wichita job, unremarkable at the time, would prove to be one of the company's most important—not just for the building, but for the friendship forged between the Irish builders and the Catholic sisters.

Tim McCarthy remembered the unsolicited act of generosity that helped cement the friendship. The job had gone well for McCarthy, and the company had realized a larger profit than anticipated. "So that money was just given back to the sisters," Tim said. "Believe me, they never forgot it."[16] The generous donation was in the neighborhood of $5,500, a considerable gift by itself but even more generous considering McCarthy Brothers ended 1948 with income of just under $6,000.[17] Mother Mary Ann of the Sisters of St. Joseph never forgot McCarthy Brothers and would call on the company in future years, opening doors of opportunity that might have otherwise remained closed.

Paddy McCarthy

In 1946, Francis F. "Paddy" McCarthy—the 22-year-old son of Merryl and grandson of Mr. Tim—already had four years at the University of Notre Dame and a hitch in the U.S. Navy under his belt. Paddy had just graduated at the head of his class, but honesty compelled him to add a disclaimer. "I always hesitate to tell the kids I was the only one in the civil class that year," he joked years later. "But I still can say I was number one."[18] Three days after graduation, Paddy was sent to the Sisters of St. Joseph job in what he remembered as the "bitter cold" Kansas weather.

Despite his youth, in 1946 Paddy was already an eight-year veteran in the family business. When he was 14 years old, he spent the summer working on one of Mr. Tim's projects, St. Francis of Assisi Hospital in Cape Girardeau, Missouri. Although technically a laborer, he was actually a self-proclaimed "kid that was getting in the way all the time." Still, he treasured the time he got to spend with his grandfather.

Left: Mr. Tim, a hands-on builder, was also an avid reader.

Opposite: During World War II, Paddy McCarthy served in the U.S. Navy.

The following summer, Mr. Tim was again working in Cape Girardeau, this time building Kent Library. Mr. Tim decided to put the 15-year-old Paddy to work as his driver. "He detested driving," Paddy remembered, "so one afternoon he had a laborer take me out for a half hour, teach me how to drive, and I was to drive back to St. Louis that weekend. Well, he immediately went to sleep. We came down a huge hill, got halfway up, and the car slipped into neutral and I didn't understand it until I started rolling backward. I finally had to wake him up."[19]

Not all of young Paddy's training was so dramatic, and he did gain experience on many McCarthy job sites while still in high school. The level of trust the company and his family had in him was demonstrated his senior year of high school. Paddy led a team of eight high school boys—including his three brothers, 16-year-old Tim and 14-year-old twins Robert and John—on a four-truck convoy from St. Louis to Los Angeles. The trucks were loaded with equipment and material for the company's work in the Panama Canal Zone.

This circuitous route was dictated by the times. After the United States entered World War II, ships leaving New Orleans were being sunk as soon as they were out of the harbor, so McCarthy "took a chance with a bunch of kids," according to Paddy, and sent them to Los Angeles, where the equipment could be shipped to the Canal Zone.

One piece of the equipment was a 5,000-pound wrecking ball. Trying to keep that heavy orb under control "was like trying to lash King Kong in a cage," Paddy said. The boys nevertheless completed the delivery, and everything, including the wrecking ball, made it safely to the Canal Zone. Paddy and the boys had accomplished their mission, but "King Kong" had the last word. "When they finally got it down to Panama after all the trouble we had, it dropped and went through the bed of our truck, through the dock, and down to the bottom of the bay," Paddy said.[20]

A Tragic Loss

After his graduation from Notre Dame, Paddy spent several years moving from job to job as McCarthy Brothers' needs dictated. Early in 1949, he was in Columbia, Missouri, working on a dormitory project for the University of Missouri

when bad news arrived. His father, Merryl, McCarthy's 51-year-old "one-man gang" and the company's only estimator, was gravely ill. There was little the family could do but wait. Paddy was called home and began training as an estimator.[21] Sadly, he had only three weeks of his father's tutelage; on February 27, 1949, Merryl McCarthy succumbed to cancer.[22]

The morning after Merryl was laid to rest in St. Louis's Calvary Cemetery, the McCarthy board met at the Roosevelt Hotel. Mr. Tim, Charles, John E., and Melvin had but one order of business for this special meeting—to elect a new corporate secretary and treasurer to fill Merryl's shoes. Melvin was elected by unanimous vote.[23] They also agreed to continue paying Merryl's salary to his widow, Gertrude, "in recognition of the loyal and effective services of Merryl McCarthy."[24] Gertrude McCarthy took Merryl's place on the board of directors in 1951.

Merryl's death proved a devastating blow for McCarthy-Pohl Contractors. McCarthy-Pohl had become one of the biggest earth-moving companies in Missouri. With its size and excellent concrete people, the company seemed ideally positioned to benefit from the dawning era of the interstate highway system. The big, blustery, outgoing Pohl and the quiet, reserved Merryl had formed a close friendship over the years, but a hopeless personality clash divided John E. and Pohl, and the two men decided to go their separate ways.[25] Other than a small job worth about $7,000, McCarthy-Pohl took on no more new work.[26] By 1953, the earth-moving firm had completed all its outstanding work;[27] its income after that came from equipment rentals and sales of assets. By 1958 all McCarthy-Pohl's equipment had been sold,[28] and in September 1965, the stockholders of McCarthy-Pohl voted "to dissolve the corporation as soon as possible."[29]

Merryl's son Tim ruminated on what might have been if only John E. and Joe Pohl had been able to

Opposite: At the January 30, 1956, board meeting, the directors amended the company's original articles of incorporation to extend McCarthy's duration from 50 years to "perpetual duration" and to extend its purpose to include engineering, design work, and real estate investment.

SPECIAL MEETING OF THE BOARD OF DIRECTORS
OF
McCARTHY BROTHERS CONSTRUCTION COMPANY

The undersigned directors, constituting the full membership
of the Board of Directors of McCarthy Brothers Construction Company,
being present this 30th day of January, 1956, at 10:00 o'clock A.M. at
the offices of the company at 4903 Delmar Boulevard, St. Louis, Missouri,
and waiving all requirements as to notice of time, place and purposes of a
directors' meeting, do hereby convene in special meeting to consider
amendment of the Sixth and Seventh Articles of the Articles of Incorporation.

The following resolutions are presented to the members of the

Board for vote:

RESOLVED, that the Sixth Article of the Articles of
Incorporation which provides "The Company shall continue
for a term of fifty years" be amended to provide as follows:
"The Company shall have perpetual duration."

BE IT FURTHER RESOLVED, that the Seventh Article
of the Articles of Incorporation, which provides "The Company
is formed for the following purposes. To erect hotels, halls,
business houses, dwellings and other buildings; and to do
general contract and construction business." be amended as
follows: "The Company is formed for the following purposes:
To erect hotels, halls, business houses, dwellings and other
buildings, to engage in any and all general engineering and
design work, to do a general contracting and construction
business, to purchase or, otherwise, acquire and hold real
and personal property for investment or otherwise and to
mortgage, sell and convey the same and to do all things
necessary and incidental to engaging in connection with any
and all of such businesses."

BE IT FURTHER RESOLVED, that these proposed
amendments to the Articles of Incorporation be submitted
to the stockholders of the corporation for their vote of
acceptance or rejection and

BE IT FURTHER RESOLVED, that a special meeting
of the stockholders be called to convene at   one   o'clock
P. M., this day at the offices of the company at 4903
Delmar Boulevard, St. Louis, Missouri, providing that all
stockholders waive notice and publication of notice as required
by law.

A vote being taken, each of the above resolutions is passed

nd all of the undersigned directors who

f the Board of Directors.

ng before the Board, the meeting is

-1-

Paddy McCarthy (working in rear corner) built his family home in St. Louis County in 1953. "He built it during the Cold War with lots of concrete," related his son Thomas in 1994. "It's made it through eight rowdy kids."

get along. In 1956, President Dwight D. Eisenhower signed the Federal Aid Highway Act, which set up the Highway Trust Fund and began the era of the interstate highway system. The original act authorized the construction of some 42,500 miles of high-speed, limited-access highways connecting the nation's major cities. The federal government was to pay 90 percent of the estimated $33.5 billion price tag, with the states picking up the balance for highways solely within their borders. The first section of interstate highway was built in the heart of McCarthy-Pohl's home territory of St. Louis, but by then the company was no more than some numbers on a balance sheet. Other firms would go on to reap the billions of federal and state dollars that poured into road building over the next several decades.

"At that time, Fred Weber was a little tiny two-bit contractor, and you've seen what happened to Fred Weber," Tim McCarthy would moan years later. "That just as well could have been McCarthy-Pohl, but that's hindsight talking."[30]

John E. McCarthy

Although Melvin was elected to fill both of Merryl's offices, John E., by then a vice president, stepped in to help fill the void left by Merryl's death.[31]

John E. was the de facto president, as Merryl had been, although Mr. Tim didn't relinquish the official title until 1959.[32]

Though nine years Merryl's junior, by 1949 John E. was a seasoned and well-traveled builder. He worked his first official job in 1932, when he built the post office in Centralia, Missouri. From there he went to Mexico, Missouri, and built several commercial buildings. After that he worked on various projects, including post offices and the Algoa Reformatory for Boys, in Jefferson City, Missouri. The Algoa job was won after 14 months of unsuccessful biddings.[33]

John E. also oversaw the 1939 construction of the Federal Building in Anchorage, Alaska, where crews "worked the 16 hours of sunlight each day." From there, he went to the Panama Canal Zone with Melvin.[34]

Ups and Downs

McCarthy Brothers was doing a lot of work for Missouri universities. In 1949, nearly all of the $1.6 million in completed contracts came from building dormitories and a gymnasium at three Missouri campuses.[35] The trend continued into 1950, with more dormitories, a mechanical engineering building, and an elementary school. Total contracts took another jump that year to almost $2.5 million.[36]

The year 1951 saw McCarthy Brothers back at work in familiar territory, building housing at Scott Air Base (formerly Scott Field) and barracks at nearby Belleville, Illinois. That year the company suffered a rare loss on gross costs over contract price.[37]

Tim McCarthy

In 1951, Tim McCarthy graduated from Washington University in St. Louis with a degree in civil engineering. Like so many men of his generation, he had put off college to go to war. During World War II, he had served with the U.S. Army's 110th Combat Engineers, which was attached to the Seventh Infantry and marked beaches in the Philippines for the infantry landing during the naval battle of Leyte Gulf. Tim's basic training was in tanks, which he loved. He wrangled a transfer out of the engineers and into a tank company but, along with nearly everyone else in the company, came down with schistosomiasis japonicum, an unusual tropical disease.

"I really wasn't all that sick," Tim remembered, "but they loaded me on a hospital ship to ship me back to the United States."[38] Tim's war was over. The engineering and tank companies he had been a part of went on to Okinawa, but he was sent to a hospital in New Guinea and finally back home on a hospital ship.[39]

After the war, Tim applied to Notre Dame, where Paddy had gone. He was accepted but was told he would have to wait a year to enroll because of the number of returning veterans applying to the university. While he waited, he took classes at St. Louis University that he knew would be transferable. The next year, Notre Dame told him he would have to wait yet another year, so he decided to enroll at Washington University, which was within walking distance of his St. Louis home.

After graduation, Tim was sent to Dodge City, Kansas, where McCarthy Brothers was building the St. Mary of the Plains Academy, a job that Mother Mary Ann of the Sisters of St. Joseph had helped to secure. While on the job, Tim particularly liked to watch the company's veteran bricklayers at work. Superintendent T. P. Waters Jr.

had other ideas for Tim, however. "I was a young engineer on the job," Tim said, "but Tom didn't believe in nonproductive people, so I was a carpenter." Waters was more than glad to instruct Tim at the Waters's home after hours. "He'd talk job all night long," Tim said, "and he taught me a whole lot, but he wanted me with my nose to the grindstone all day long. I didn't mind the work, but I wanted to learn something."[40]

Tim felt he had some catching up to do since he was 26 years old and just out of college. He didn't waste any time. In Dodge City he met his wife, Theresa. From there, it was on to Rochester, Minnesota, where he spent five years working on several McCarthy projects. He was project engineer for the Motherhouse for St. Clare Novitiate School, a "magnificent building" of stone, slate, and marble.[41]

McCarthy Brothers did all of the masonry work on the St. Clare Novitiate School. Tim characterized the company of that era as an excellent masonry contractor forced to do most of its masonry jobs outside the St. Louis area. A very strong bricklayers union allowed only St. Louis bricklayers to work in St. Louis. According to Tim, only three St. Louis contractors were allowed to do their own masonry work in St. Louis, and McCarthy Brothers was not on that short list. The company gradually got out of the masonry business largely because of this issue.[42]

Tim's next project was at St. Mary's Hospital, also in Rochester. This was his first assignment as a project superintendent, but he was already on familiar terms with the client, the Sisters of St. Francis, for whom McCarthy Brothers built the St. Clare Novitiate School. The sisters had long been affiliated with the Mayo brothers, and before long McCarthy Brothers was building for the Mayo Clinic.[43]

Building a Local Presence

McCarthy's 1952 contracts were considerably lower than those of previous years. The company's projects that year included enlarging St. Joseph Hospital in Wichita, Kansas; working for St. Mary of the Plains Academy, in Dodge City, Kansas; building the Motherhouse at St. Clare Novitiate School in Rochester, Minnesota; and building the library at St. Mary's Seminary, in Perryville, Missouri. It rented out equipment for projects in Dodge City, Rochester, and Perryville.[44]

Although McCarthy Brothers had been in St. Louis for more than 30 years, the company had done remarkably little work in the immediate St. Louis area. Mr. Tim's list, compiled in 1949, mentioned a scant four projects in the St. Louis suburbs: apartment and high school buildings in Clayton, a Lutheran church in Ferguson, and a college dormitory in St. Charles. In St. Louis proper, McCarthy had done only two jobs, an apartment building and the Bird House at the St. Louis Zoo. All had been completed before 1930.[45]

That dearth of local work changed in a big way in 1952, when McCarthy Brothers won the contract for the U.S. Army's Adjutant General Publication Center in suburban St. Louis. The Publication Center was to be a one-story steel and masonry structure covering more than seven acres and was to house a printing plant, office, and warehouse. The job ended a 20-year drought in local work.[46]

Building from the Base

In 1956, the year it billed over $7.4 million in St. Louis–area work, McCarthy Brothers amended its articles of incorporation. Engineering, design work, and real estate investment were added to the company's original function of erecting "hotels, halls, business houses, dwellings and other buildings; and to do general contract and construction business."[47] Over the years, the company's scope would continue to expand as it discovered new areas of profit and repositioned itself in fluctuating markets.

As the 1950s progressed, McCarthy Brothers continued to build hospitals—some profitably, others not so profitably. The company built hospitals in Cairo, Illinois (losing over $50,000);[48] Evansville, Indiana; Centralia, Illinois; and Cincinnati, Ohio. In addition to this bid-based hospital work, which tended to be insecure for the company since costs could easily overrun original estimates, McCarthy Brothers established long-running relationships with several hospitals. In this way it gained much more secure fee-basis work for St. Mary's Hospital in Rochester from 1953 through 1958. The company also did fee work for St. Joseph's Hospital in Wichita, Kansas, and for the Mayo Clinic.

McCarthy did more projects for religious institutions too. Besides continuing work in Dodge City and Rochester, the company built a library for St.

Mary's Seminary. In 1958, much to Paddy's delight, the firm won the contract to construct the Moreau Seminary on the Notre Dame campus. "Paddy was such a strong Notre Dame man," said his brother Tim. "[For Paddy] there was only one school in the country, and that was Notre Dame."[49]

The builders also continued their long relationship with the University of Missouri, building apartments, dormitories, and other structures at campuses in Columbia, St. Louis, and Rolla. In 1958, the firm won a $1 million contract for general construction of a fine arts building at the Columbia campus.[50]

The company continued doing work for the military as well. In 1955 it won a $4 million contract

Mr. Tim circulated this Christmas card in the early 1950s.

Tim McCarthy

from the Army Corps of Engineers for rehabilitation work at the St. Louis Ordnance Plant, a $2.3 million job for the Atomic Energy Commission's Weldon Spring uranium processing plant, and a $440,000 Corps of Engineers rehabilitation of a World War II tank parts plant in St. Louis.[51] (In the mid-1990s, McCarthy would do a lot of work cleaning up toxic atomic waste at the Weldon Spring site through the Environmental Protection Agency's Superfund.)

In 1958 and 1959, McCarthy Brothers won two contracts to build public housing projects: a 100-unit development in suburban Kinloch for nearly $1 million and the Anthony M. Webbe Apartments in St. Louis for $6.7 million.[52]

Embodiment of Success

In 1959 Mr. Tim finally relinquished the title of president to his son John E. The old gentleman spent his final years on the go while keeping in touch with family and the company he had helped build. He spent winters at his daughter's Florida home. In the summer, he traveled to Michigan to visit his three surviving sisters in Ann Arbor and the family farm in Northfield Township. Spring and fall brought him back to St. Louis to spend time with John E.

Although he no longer ran the company, Mr. Tim maintained a keen interest in McCarthy Brothers. "Mr. Tim, as he got older, never lost his love for the company," said Paddy, who served as his grandfather's inside informant. "He always called me every two or three weeks, and if I failed to keep him posted, I would get an angry call."[53]

Looking back over his decades as a builder, Mr. Tim once credited the continuing success of McCarthy Brothers to the company's reputation for "being good to work for, and good to work with." The "fine family feeling" spread from top management to the workers in the field. Mr. Tim believed that

The five youngest children of Timothy and Ellen McCarthy at the family farm in Michigan, circa late 1950s. From left: Laura, Emma Jane, Charles Sr., Agnes, and "Mr. Tim."

"loyalty to one another... and [the] ability to work well together in mutual trust and helpfulness" made the company strong.

"I want this spirit of harmony and cooperation to continue always, in the family and in the firm," he said. He also attributed the company's success to its determination to perform work of the highest quality. "We have always done the very best possible work on every contract we got," Mr. Tim said. "Sometimes we have lost big money on our contracts, but nobody can say that we ever did a skimpy, jack-leg job."[54]

McCarthy Brothers would continue to build because that's what the McCarthys did, Mr. Tim believed. "As long as there is anything left in this world to build, there are going to be McCarthy Brothers and McCarthy Cousins to build it."[55]

John E. McCarthy (right) was president of the Associated General Contractors (AGC) of St. Louis.

CHAPTER FIVE

TRANSITIONS

1960–1965

*The successful completion of a project . . . requires the utmost cooperation
of all parties involved. It requires practical specifications and a great
amount of flexibility on the part of the designers, as well as the builders.*

—Francis F. "Paddy" McCarthy

FOR MCCARTHY BROTHERS and the McCarthy family, the first half of the 1960s was a period of transition. The company had grown rapidly in the post–World War II years and had established a reputation as a top builder. The family, too, had grown, and more McCarthys had become involved in the family business. By the turn of the decade, the company's rapid growth was slowing somewhat, but its projects tended to be larger, which meant each one was more vital to the company.

McCarthy Brothers learned, sometimes painfully, that it needed to refine its skills if it were to continue its rapid rise. At the same time, the circle of life continued—the older generation of McCarthys was making way for the younger generation. And one family member in particular, Michael M. McCarthy, was climbing the McCarthy career ladder.

The Priory Chapel

In August 1960, McCarthy Brothers began construction of a chapel for the St. Louis Priory School for Boys, a project that would help cement the company's reputation as a skilled and innovative builder and establish the firm as one of St. Louis's leading construction companies. Designed by Gyo Obata of the St. Louis architectural firm of Hellmuth, Obata & Kassabaum, the Priory Chapel gained national notice for its "bold architectural form" even before construction began.[1]

Hailed as a "unique house of worship" by the well-known construction publication *Building Construction,* the chapel was a reinforced concrete building with "two sets of thin concrete parabolic shells on two levels, set in 20 identical bays tapering toward the center of a circular plan." It also featured a 32-foot-high bell tower and a 40-foot-high dome.[2] Preservation historian Esley Hamilton described the chapel somewhat more poetically: "From a distance, its tiers of parabolic arches seem to be lifting off from its green ridge, and from inside, the sense of soaring is even more pronounced."[3]

The chapel's complex design made bidding on the project a challenge, for none of the bidding contractors seemed to know how best to approach the unique construction. McCarthy Brothers won the bid at $538,000; its nearest competitor was $50,000 higher, and the high bid was more than $260,000 above McCarthy's figure.[4]

"Needless to say, this indicated a considerable difference of opinion as to what would constitute

---

Standing in the middle of the Priory Chapel and looking straight up gives one the impression of looking to the heavens.

the most economical method of construction for the particular project," Paddy McCarthy remarked years later. "There is no reason to be critical of any of the estimators who prepared bids on this project since each was compelled to rely upon his imagination to a great extent rather than upon past experience as is most often the case. The estimator had to study the project in sufficient detail to develop a feasible method of doing the work, as well as cost of performing the various necessary operations. Fortunately, our estimate was reasonably accurate, and we do not have any unhappy memories concerning this project."[5]

Of course, McCarthy Brothers did not rely solely upon imagination to envision how the Priory Chapel would be constructed. Design engineers provided descriptions of shoring and placement methods in the structure's specifications, giving McCarthy and the other bidders an accurate picture of the construction loads they would need to deal with. The design itself was also helpful: the shape of the shells and ribs conformed to the

mathematical formula for a parabola, and the identical shape of the arches would save time in planning and actual construction. The bidders were given the formula and a detailed diagram of a building section. Armed with such information, Paddy's job of estimating became one of painstaking computation. As *Building Construction* noted, "Careful and thorough geometric calculations gave [Paddy McCarthy] his competitive edge."[6]

Paddy did indeed take great care in estimating the Priory Chapel job. He drew page after page of preliminary sketches with calculations on shell-forming frames. Later, photostatic copies of his sketches transferred the carpentry data to the job site, where carpenters used them to build a platform with grid lines on which the complicated elements of the concrete forms were laid out.

Michael F. McCarthy, Paddy's son and a McCarthy productivity and cost analyst, was a boy when McCarthy built the Priory Chapel, but he fondly remembered visiting the job site and walking between the soaring arches. He recalled his father's "real passion" for the project and the pains Paddy took bidding on such a complicated job. "He designed the formwork for the Priory Chapel, and they had the darnedest time figuring out how they were going to build it," Michael said many years later. "It was one of his favorite projects."[7]

The architect's specifications originally allowed two methods of concrete placement. One was to pour the concrete; the other was to apply the concrete with a pressure gun. McCarthy applied the concrete for the first section with a pressure gun but found the method took too much time. With the architect's approval, the company performed the work in a more timely and economical manner by blending the two methods: The ribs were poured, and the shells were applied with the pressure gun.

The architect also allowed McCarthy to modify the sequence of pouring the shells. The original plan called for form work in three bays and would have meant construction of more forms to meet construction schedules. Instead, after consulting with the architect, McCarthy began with five bays of shell forms. One was left in place to serve as an anchor; the other four were moved in jumps. As the concrete was poured in one section, ironworkers were busy on the next while carpenters worked a step ahead on the concrete forms for the shells.

Well into the Priory Chapel project, workers attach metal lath over the parabolic shells. This was the most technically challenging structure McCarthy had built.

The finished Priory Chapel in 1962. "From a distance, its tiers of parabolic arches seem to be lifting off from its green ridge," wrote one historian, "and from inside, the sense of soaring is even more pronounced."

The construction of the concrete shells and ribs was completed in three months using this assembly-line method.

In a 1963 presentation to the Midwest Concrete Industry Board, Paddy noted that the flexibility and cooperation between the architect and the builders was instrumental in the successful and profitable completion of the Priory Chapel, adding that all parties involved were "most cooperative," especially the owner, "whose ability to understand the problems being discussed and resolved was of the greatest importance to all concerned."[8]

The Priory Chapel project was a success for everyone involved. McCarthy earned more than $33,000[9] and gained recognition both locally and nationwide. The Midwest Concrete Industry Board, the Portland Cement Association, the American Concrete Institute, and the University of Missouri School of Mines and Metallurgy all invited

McCarthy Brothers to give presentations on the project. Hellmuth, Obata & Kassabaum, the architectural firm that designed the chapel, would eventually become one of the biggest and most prestigious architectural firms in the world, and images of the chapel would grace magazine covers and architectural publications.[10] Most importantly, the St. Louis Priory School for Boys gained a house of worship that *Building Construction* described as a "meaningfully strong and eloquent statement" that was built "out of such simple materials as steel, concrete, Georgia granite stone altars, bronze candlesticks and altar appointments, ceramic tile floors and red oak wood pews."[11]

Floodwalls for St. Louis

St. Louis is located on the Mississippi River a few miles downstream from its confluence with the Missouri River. Although the founders had wisely settled on the high river bluffs, the city had long since spread into the floodplain. Floodwater periodically inundated parts of the city, causing millions of dollars in damage. Despite its location in such a flood-vulnerable area, St. Louis was, at midcentury, the nation's only major city abutting a navigable river but lacking flood protection.[12]

In 1955, Congress authorized the St. Louis Flood Protection Project, budgeted at over $130 million. The plans called for 11 miles of earthen levees and concrete floodwalls that would stretch along some 20 miles of the St. Louis riverfront to protect the city from the unpredictable Mississippi River. The system was designed to contain floodwater of up to 52 feet, a full 10 feet above the highest estimated flood, which occurred in 1785.[13]

Ground was broken for the project on February 24, 1959, a day designated by the city as Flood Protection Day. Plans for the ground-breaking ceremony at first included the detonation of a mock "atomic bomb," made principally of photographer's flash powder, that would send a 40-story mushroom cloud looming over the riverfront.[14] The mock bomb was supposed to attract the public to the ceremony, but, concerned that its detonation might instead instill shock or fear (this being a time when many Americans had bomb shelters in their basements), officials dropped plans for the mock bomb, and the ceremony proceeded along more conventional lines.

The first stage of the flood-control project was construction of earthen levees (a project for which the by-then-defunct McCarthy-Pohl Contractors would have been ideally suited), so it is unlikely that McCarthy Brothers bid on those jobs. But in June 1961 the company began building a three-quarter-mile section of floodwall along St. Louis's northern riverfront.[15] This was only one of many sections of floodwall McCarthy would build in the 1960s as part of the St. Louis Flood Protection Project. In November 1962, the company won out over seven other bidders for a $2.4 million contract to build 4,350 feet of concrete floodwall.[16] In 1965, McCarthy won another flood-protection contract for $2.1 million,[17] and two years later it was awarded two more floodwall contracts totaling more than $5.28 million.[18]

Although much of the floodwall work was routine, McCarthy Brothers did have some engineering challenges to deal with. On one section, built on a narrow strip of land between the Mississippi River and existing railroad tracks, subterranean features prevented the construction of the typical concrete base that would support the floodwall. An article in a local newspaper described how the floodwall would be secured.

Engineers determined that the floodwall could be attached to a horizontal layer of rock extending far below the surface. Holes must be drilled into the sides of the bed of rock at depths of as much as 70 feet. Anchors will be extended from these sockets through the floodwall to hold it firmly in a vertical position. The holes are 16 inches in diameter and from 2 to 18 feet deep.[19]

The St. Louis Flood Protection Project, announced in 1955, was originally slated to take six years. But as with any massive project dependent on government funding, numerous delays obtruded, and it wasn't until 1973 that the complex system of levees, floodwalls, pumping stations, and altered sewer systems neared completion.

Despite missing its timetable by years, the project proved its value upon completion. In April 1973, the middle reaches of the Mississippi River broke flood-level records. During previous floods, the river had reached an estimated 42 feet (in 1785) and 41.3 feet (in 1944). But on April 30, 1973, the river level rose to 43.3 feet. Many nearby communities suffered severe damage from the floodwater, but St. Louis escaped the ravages of the river, thanks in part to the floodwalls constructed by McCarthy Brothers.

During the Great Flood of 1993, the raging waters of the Mississippi stayed above flood level for two months and, on August 2, 1993, crested at 49.6 feet—19 feet above flood level and a scant 2.5 feet below the top of the floodwalls and levees. Once again the floodwalls protected St. Louis from the flood's devastation, just as McCarthy had built them to do 20 years before.

Michael M. McCarthy

In 1962 another scion of the McCarthy family graduated from the engineering school at Washington University in St. Louis. If ever a boy was born with a silver hammer in his mouth, it was Melvin and Dusty's son, Michael M. "Mike" McCarthy (not to be confused with Michael F. McCarthy, son of Paddy and Nadine). Although Mike needed a little convincing as to his true calling, he developed a love for the people working for his family's company, and the same independence that made him resist the family business made him work all the harder to become a success once involved in it. Ultimately his affection for McCarthy's people and his determination and hard work made him the ideal leader for the family business, which, in later years, he would convert from a family-owned company to an employee-owned company.

Mike's toddler years were spent in the Panama Canal Zone, where his father was building airstrips and gun emplacements for the United States. The remote location and the shared camaraderie made an impression on the young Mike. "It was just like a family," he said. "Whether you drove a tractor or you were the boss in charge of everything, we were all together, all equal."[20]

When the family moved back to St. Louis, Melvin took him to many of the job sites. "So I got to know all the superintendents and all the people who worked for us," Mike said. "We had a nice traveling group of labor force, many of whom I knew personally. So I was really brought up in the business that way."[21]

During his high school years, the athletic Mike, who played baseball and football and was an avid

swimmer, had dreams of a pleasant summer gig as a lifeguard. But Melvin had other plans for his son, and despite Mike's druthers, he was sent to work as a driller at Rock Hill Quarries.

Mike's first job was certainly memorable but not necessarily in a pleasant way. "It was about 120 to 130 degrees in the quarry," he said. "We were drilling holes in the rock to set the dynamite, using an 80-pound jackhammer. We drilled to make the hole, then set the dynamite, then put the fuse in the dynamite. Then we would all run around with little clickers, light the dynamite, and dive under a big dump truck. That was our safety precaution."[22]

At first, Mike figured the job would be a great way to get in shape for the football team at John Burroughs School, the private St. Louis–area prep school he attended. "I thought I would work at the quarry to bulk up, get some muscle, because I wanted to ram it through the line," he said. "But all these quarry guys were so skinny. After a week, I was amazed that they could even live through this, and I wasn't sure I was going to make it. But I survived the summer, and it made me pretty lean. Football was nothing compared to running that damn jackhammer."[23]

Despite the hardships, Mike thrived on the friendships he developed with the quarry workers. After work, Mike hung out with the older men, who liked to rib the company's youngest family-member-in-training by giving him cigars or making jokes at his expense—all in fun, of course. Mike developed true affection for the hard-working men, and those experiences made a lasting impression on him.[24]

"I love the horny hands of toil," he said, years after becoming the company's chairman. "The biggest joy I've had is being able to work with our field people. I love the guys who really do the work, and you'll find that same affection throughout McCarthy's leadership. I mean, that's really what we're all about."[25]

After that first summer in the quarry, there was no more talk of being a lifeguard. Mike worked on McCarthy jobs each summer, first as a laborer and later as an apprentice carpenter. While in high school, he worked jobs in St. Louis, but as he grew older and gained more experience Melvin sent him farther from home. "I would go out of town to work and have to find a place to live," Mike said.

Mike McCarthy was an active child as well as a diligent one.

"The money was always good, but I've worked some places where you wouldn't want to go. I've worked in some river towns where, come Saturday night, the major sport was fighting."[26]

Mike showed early signs of another trademark characteristic: a deep caring for the well-being of others. After Melvin and his young family returned from Panama, they lived for a time in Farmington. Melvin would commute to work in St. Louis during the week, returning to Farmington on weekends to be with his growing family. Mike had been joined by a baby sister, born while the family was in the Canal Zone. Christened Margaret after her mother, the baby was called Peggy.

Mike was a doting brother to his little sister, as he proved when he was eight years old. The house caught fire one night when Melvin was away in St. Louis. Peggy recalled the story that could have ended in tragedy.

My mother got out, and my brother got out, but I didn't get out. I was in a crib in the front room, and of course the firemen were not going to let anybody go in. But my brother got down on his hands and knees and got away from them. He crawled underneath the smoke into the house and brought me out.[27]

Peggy also remembered how Mike looked out for her at school. Mike was in fifth grade when Peggy entered kindergarten. He was able to watch his sister at recess from his classroom. "I was so shy that I stayed back and wasn't making any friends," Peggy said. "He'd watch me and couldn't concentrate on his studies because he was worrying about his baby sister. So the teacher finally had to move him to the other side of the room so he wasn't constantly worrying about whether I was making friends or not."[28]

Mike also admitted to having a "rambunctious style" and remembered that his high school "continued to attempt to refine me." Years later he jokingly admitted that the school was only partially successful in its attempts.[29]

Mike's rambunctious side was not of the rebellious sort; rather it was the quest of an energetic and outgoing boy looking for fun. "He was a fun kind of kid," said Peggy. "He got into some difficulty, too, because he likes a lot of fun."[30]

Peggy remembered Mike taking her to a local orchard to filch some apples. "Now this is what I'm going to do," Peggy remembered him saying. "I'm going to drive up there, and I want you to jump out of the car and grab these apples and get back in the car really quick if the farmer comes because he's got a shotgun and he'll shoot at you." Not surprisingly, the farmer did come out (sans shotgun). With her heart in her throat, Peggy jumped in the car, and her big brother "peeled out of there." Peggy fondly remembered the incident as one of the most exciting things she had ever done.[31]

Mike was Peggy's protector, but his other sister, Frances, 10 years his junior, became the little brother he never had. "I got to learn how to detail cars," Fran said decades later. "And to this day, I'm a great boxer. As a matter of fact, I knocked him out once, but it was with the help of a doorstop. He would box me while on his knees."[32]

As all good big brothers do, Mike taught Fran some of the finer points of being a man. Although Mike "swears this isn't true," Fran well recalled a three-day train trip the family took to Phoenix when she was seven years old. "During that time, my brother taught me how to smoke, how to drink liquor, and how to play poker—five-card stud and seven-card draw."[33]

When it came time for Mike to make his college plans, the easygoing son and his quiet, gentle father had a major disagreement. Melvin wanted Mike to get an engineering degree to help prepare him for a role in the family business. "It wasn't as though any of us could be in the company just because our last name was McCarthy," Fran said.[34] Mike, it seemed, had other ideas. He thought perhaps he might like to study law.

"I don't remember any major fights between kids and parents except for Dad in my brother's room and them yelling at one another over what Mike would do in college," said Fran. Although Mike had "a very strong personality" and was stubborn, Fran said their father "never, ever gave up—and he got his way."[35]

So it was off to Washington University's engineering school for Mike. He graduated in 1962 with an engineering degree, but rather than joining McCarthy, he went to work for another building

contractor, Hathman Construction Company, of Columbia, Missouri.

"I went to work for another contractor because McCarthy Brothers, at that time, was doing what I considered to be boring stuff, which was floodwalls along the Mississippi," Mike said. "One floodwall was like any other floodwall, and I didn't want to do that."[36]

Hathman Construction was partially owned by Thomas P. "Pat" Waters Jr., who had worked for McCarthy for many years before buying into Hathman Construction and had stayed with Paddy's family while working in St. Louis. His father, Tom Waters, worked for McCarthy Brothers as well.

Pat Waters recalled a story his father had told him about the teenage Mike. "According to my dad, Mike was running all over this job site, and he ran off the end of one of the stairs that wasn't built yet and fell on the rough concrete about half a story below. Banged him up something awful. My dad said the kid jumped up and didn't cry a bit, said he's going to be one tough kid."[37]

In 1962, when that "tough kid" was looking for an alternative to building floodwalls for McCarthy, he found a place among familiar faces at Hathman.

Family Losses

Merryl's widow, Gertrude, the mother of Tim and Paddy, passed away in 1961. Then in May 1963, McCarthy family patriarch Timothy, the beloved Mr. Tim, died just a month short of his 96th birthday. Minnie McCarthy, John W.'s widow and the company's longtime secretary, died in 1964 at the age of 84.

While the passing of the old guard was a personal loss for the close-knit McCarthy family, control of McCarthy Brothers had long since passed to younger generations. In the 50-plus years since McCarthy's incorporation, one trend had held true: those who did the work ran the company. When McCarthy's first president, John W., died, the presidency and control of the company's future went, not to his son, but to his brother Mr. Tim, who had done so much to grow the company. As Mr. Tim retired, the presidency passed to his son Merryl, another hands-on builder. At Merryl's untimely death, Mr. Tim's second son, John E., assumed the

leadership role, assisted by Melvin, son of Mr. Tim's brother Charles.

John E. and Melvin's working relationship had begun before World War II, when the cousins formed their successful partnership to continue McCarthy Brothers' work in the Panama Canal Zone, allowing the parent company to focus on stateside work. The successful association between the cousins came to an abrupt end on July 13, 1964, when John E. died of an apparent heart attack while at home. He was 57.

Less than a week after John E.'s death, McCarthy's board held a special meeting chaired by Charles, the last of the original McCarthy brothers. The board quickly passed a resolution of mourning for John E.

The McCarthys had always been a close family. Here Mike McCarthy poses with his sisters, Fran (left) and Peggy, in the mid-1960s. *(Photo courtesy Peggy McCarthy Reynolds.)*

Resolved, that in the passing of its President, John E. McCarthy, the Company has suffered a severe loss; that record thereof be made of such loss, and that a proper memorial be prepared, and presented to his widow on behalf of the company.[38]

The board also voted to continue paying John E.'s annual salary to his widow, the former Eleanor Mason.

Taking Stock

As they had after the deaths of John W., Merryl, and Mr. Tim, the directors combined their mourning with the pragmatic details of running the business. Mike was elected to the board to fill John E.'s vacant seat and became a company vice president. Melvin was voted president, and Paddy traded in his vice president's hat to take on the duties of secretary-treasurer, the post vacated by Melvin. Eleanor was elected assistant secretary-treasurer. As was customary with McCarthy's board, all votes were unanimous.

Eventually the board's discussion turned to the 366 shares of McCarthy Brothers stock owned by Mr. Tim's estate. The stock in question "had been bequeathed to certain individuals, subject to a provision that they pay the entire death taxes imposed on the Estate of Timothy McCarthy."[39] Since those taxes were greater than the value of the stock, those "certain individuals" sensibly refused the bequest, and Mr. Tim's estate offered to sell the shares to McCarthy to raise funds for the taxes. The stock buyback would be a good move for the company, Melvin said. The board agreed, approved the purchase, and later bought the shares to be held as treasury stock.[40]

Mr. Tim's 366 shares didn't remain in McCarthy's treasury for long. The following year, the directors allowed Paddy, Tim, and Mike to buy a third of those shares at par value, payable in three annual installments of $4,066.66. Immediately after authorizing the sale, the board praised Paddy, Tim, and Mike for their "untiring efforts in behalf of the Company during the year 1965" and voted them bonuses "in recognition of their tireless efforts in their service to the company during the year." The bonuses came to exactly $4,066.66 each.[41]

Queeny Tower

At the same time its leadership was shifting, the company was in the midst of a large job that turned out to be especially significant for Mike. The construction of Queeny Tower at the Barnes Hospital complex in St. Louis was a pivotal project for McCarthy Brothers in the early 1960s. McCarthy was by that time an experienced builder of hospitals and had a well-established reputation

Mike and his father, Melvin, cooking out in the summer of 1965 *(Photo courtesy Peggy McCarthy Reynolds.)*

for quality. If there was an area where the company had problems, it was in getting projects finished on schedule.

Queeny Tower was designed to be something new in hospital buildings, according to the *St. Louis Globe-Democrat.*

> They took a hospital and wrapped a dream around it. . . . From clinical halls and marble floors that magnify the footstep and hold the smell of surgical cleanliness, they thought of flowered panels and thick carpets that cushion the step. They thought of the patient's family and where it could stay. They thought of not a hospital by itself, but a hospital as an integral part of a medical complex. They even thought of the skyline of west St. Louis. What they came up with was the Queeny Tower Building, an 18-story, completely air-conditioned monument to medical security.[42]

The tower was named for Edgar Monsanto Queeny, son of the founder of Monsanto Chemical Works and former chairman of the board of that corporate giant. Queeny also was chairman of the Barnes Hospital board and contributed half of the $9 million price tag for the building. He had a reputation for being a tough businessman and was keenly interested in the construction of the building that would bear his name.

Paddy McCarthy remembered the crisis that erupted at a meeting—on the very day McCarthy was awarded the Queeny Tower job—when Queeny insisted on a stiff penalty for late completion. "Mr. Queeny was there sitting in a slouched position," Paddy said. "He was not in good health; you could barely see his chin above the table. One of his bright assistants told him that the penalty was only $250 a day, and he said, 'That's got to be at least $1,000.'"[43]

The McCarthy team made some quick adjustments. They asked for and received permission to build the tower first and add an included parking garage afterwards. They assigned their best project manager, Tom Waters, to oversee the work. The firm was determined to finish the project in the allotted time. "We pushed the living hell out of that project," Paddy said.[44]

When Mike McCarthy learned of the Queeny Tower project, he approached Melvin about coming back to work for McCarthy under the elder Waters. "I petitioned my father to see if I could work for this gentleman because I wanted to learn from him," Mike said.[45] Melvin was undoubtedly delighted to have his son back in the family fold. Mike was hired as an engineer for the project.

Mike formed fond memories working under Tom Waters. "He was a wonderfully tough guy and a nice guy, but a very disciplined guy in the Vince Lombardi style," Mike said. "I learned a lot, fast."

One of Mike's duties was to figure quantities and order concrete. When ordering concrete to be placed behind a retaining wall, he overordered by five yards. Waters was not pleased. "He came up to me and he said, 'How much concrete can you eat?'" But, Mike amended, "He was a wonderful guy."[46]

Unfortunately, Mike's tutelage under Waters would be short. When the building was no more than one-third complete, Waters was diagnosed with cancer. Within weeks, and just two months before the death of John E., Tom Waters died.

Construction Challenges

As president of McCarthy Brothers, one of Melvin's most pressing issues was ensuring the timely completion of Queeny Tower. Although the company had other experienced project managers, "they were unable to get the project moving," Mike said, so Melvin put his 26-year-old son in charge.

As project manager, Mike had to work closely with Edgar Queeny and soon learned that rough, tough men could be found in places far from the river towns and Saturday night brawls of his college days. Queeny often invited Mike to lunch, usually at the very upscale Racquet Club, where he regularly ordered the "Queeny special," one ice cube in a tall tumbler filled with straight gin.

"Whatever I wanted to accomplish, I had to accomplish before Mr. Queeny had his second special," Mike recalled, "and once he had his second special, he would lay into me. There's no way to describe the words that he used or what he said he was going to do to us. He was going to ruin our company. He had legions of attorneys. He'd just get on me and nearly scare me to death. I couldn't eat my lunch. Then we'd get into his limo and go back to the project site, and I'd go back to trying to get the damned thing built."[47]

Despite such intimidating rhetoric, Mike and the irascible Queeny became "great friends," Mike said. "I didn't back down to him. I just told him what I could and couldn't do."[48] In later years, Mike would visit Queeny during the holidays at Queeny's home, where they would reminisce over tea and cookies.

Dealing with Queeny wasn't the only challenge Mike had to face. He also had to deal with the labor unions, which, during the 1960s, had a well-deserved reputation for rough tactics. Mike told how his youth and inexperience actually worked in his favor.

I was going to finish this job on schedule, come hell or high water, and, frankly, the unions realized how stupid I was and decided they were going to help me—because I was young and stupid, but I was a nice guy. They felt a little sorry for me, which they should have, because I just didn't understand the ways of the world.[49]

This page and opposite: In 1963 McCarthy began constructing Queeny Tower, the 17-story ambulatory care center at Barnes Hospital in St. Louis. The tower was named for Edgar M. Queeny, who furnished the equity capital for the structure, which was completed in 1965. *(Photos courtesy Becker Medical Library, Washington University School of Medicine.)*

With the help of such unlikely allies, Mike accomplished his goal, finishing the project ahead of schedule and at a tidy profit for the company. The long-term benefits derived from the Queeny Tower project, however, proved far more valuable to McCarthy than the dollars. McCarthy showed it could complete a major project in a timely manner, despite considerable setbacks.

"We made it go, and it helped to turn this company around, and we did very, very well thereafter," said Paddy.

Perhaps more important, the project brought Mike McCarthy into the company for good and kindled his interest in finding a better way of building hospitals.

Mike and his father, Melvin McCarthy, circa 1968. After McCarthy Brothers reorganized in November 1971, Melvin and Mike had more of a stake in the company and therefore had more input into its direction. *(Photo courtesy Kathy McCarthy.)*

CHAPTER SIX

CREATING A FAMILY

1966–1971

The main value in a construction company is the people who operate it and are capable of making a living from it. The only other values it has are: a mortgaged building, and used equipment which would not bring a third of its value on the market.

—Melvin McCarthy, 1970

McCarthy Brothers Construction Company
announces the removal of their headquarters
to new and larger offices
effective June 24, 1966
1341 North Rock Hill Rd.
Ladue
St. Louis County, Missouri 63124

S INCE 1957, MCCARTHY Brothers had been considering moving from its offices in the Roosevelt Hotel in St. Louis, but it wasn't until January 1966 that the company bought two acres of land near Rock Hill Quarries and hired an architect, Keith Underwood, to design its new office building.[1]

The move to be closer to the quarry had many advantages. The neighborhood surrounding the Roosevelt Hotel was, like so many big-city neighborhoods of the time, rapidly deteriorating, and moving closer to the quarry allowed better supervision of the shop's operations and a closer check on inventory of equipment and materials that were stored at the yard. With the headquarters so close to the quarry, pickup trucks were readily available for visits to local job sites. The move also strengthened the ties between the quarry's operations and McCarthy's top executives. Moreover, the move saved considerable money.[2]

On June 24, 1966, the company celebrated its move to 1341 North Rock Hill Road in suburban St. Louis. McCarthy had taken the next step to becoming one of the nation's leading builders, but there were more steps to come, and some of them would prove quite challenging.

Pensions and Bonuses

As the need for a new headquarters indicated, the company's volume of work was continuing to increase. If the burgeoning construction firm were to continue growing, it needed to retain quality personnel and recruit good people. One way to do so, Paddy told the directors at a special meeting of the board in January 1966, was to establish a pension plan.[3]

After careful consideration, the company decided on a profit-based plan administered by its bank, with the pension funds invested in a mix of stock and bonds. The plan was open to full-time salaried employees. Current employees were immediately eligible to join; future employees would become eligible after a year of employment. Company contributions were set at a minimum of 5 percent of McCarthy's net taxable income, and interest on the contributions was vested at a rate of 10 percent annually.[4]

In 1967 the directors established another benefit, a regular bonus program for McCarthy's officers. In profitable years, 10 percent of McCarthy's

In June 1966, McCarthy Brothers moved to its new headquarters in Ladue, a suburb of St. Louis.

net pretax income would go into a bonus pool, with the directors deciding the amounts of the officers' individual bonuses. The directors also voted bonuses for several other key employees.[5]

The family ambience that had been a company characteristic since McCarthy's founding was extending its embrace to nonfamily employees.

One Big Family

Starting a company pension plan wasn't the only step Paddy initiated to update the company's policies. Over the years, his willingness to embrace new ideas and his belief in giving people oppor-

tunities to develop their skills proved immensely valuable and did much to uphold the company's family-like traditions.

Sue Stewart, senior vice president of estimating for the Midwest division, was hired in 1980 with Paddy McCarthy as her immediate supervisor. "Paddy was very studious, hard working, and a very good man to work for," she said. "He gave me every opportunity, and I think he really opened the door for women to have a real presence in the company."[6]

It was Paddy who started the company's maternity leave policy and Paddy who initiated the office's first blood donation drive. He also improved the company's estimating system by setting up a way to recover data from past jobs for use in current estimates.

"A lot of people from his generation were afraid to use computers," said Jim Ulkus, project manager. "But Paddy was very open-minded about computers and trying new software programs."[7]

"Paddy is, without a doubt, the most wonderful person you could ever meet," said Jim Faust, vice president of human resources. "He's the type of person who would give you the shirt off his back if he thought it would help you. He's very typical of the family atmosphere that has always existed at McCarthy."[8]

"He was always so sincere and always had the time to stop and say hi and ask about the family," said Barb Saey, who has held a variety of roles within McCarthy. "Paddy was always worried about people's families."[9]

Dollar's Reward

Even in the 1960s, McCarthy Brothers had a knack for attracting good employees—and not just because of its pension and bonus plans. The company had a reputation for being a good place to work, and that attracted the assets held most dear by ongoing generations of McCarthys: the best hands-on, hard-hat construction men in the business. Tom Dollar's experience with

Francis "Paddy" McCarthy set an example of diligence and hard work, and his willingness to embrace new ideas guided the company toward new policies and technologies.

McCarthy exemplifies some of the company's ongoing traditions—that it cares about its employees and that hard work definitely pays off. Dollar ultimately became the company's first senior vice president who did not have the last name McCarthy.

Although he was not yet 30 years old, Dollar was already an experienced project superintendent (the equivalent of today's project director) when he walked into McCarthy's office looking for work in 1965. A native of St. Louis, Dollar had begun working, at age 16, as an itinerant apprentice carpenter, but he soon signed on with RK&A Jones, a local contractor, where he worked his way up to foreman and then superintendent. By the time he was 23, Dollar was married and traveling the country with his wife while he worked at building hotels.[10]

In 1965 Dollar was finishing up a long-term job in Syracuse, New York, where his first son had been born. His boss wanted him to move the family to Montana for yet another hotel job, but this time Dollar balked. His daughter was about to enroll in school, and the family wanted to settle in one place. Dollar returned to St. Louis and began looking for a job.[11]

He had been away from St. Louis for some time, but what he had heard about McCarthy had aroused his interest. McCarthy Brothers was said to be "an old-line company" that cared about its employees.[12]

Dollar had heard that Tim McCarthy was the man to see, but Tim wasn't there, so his first interview was with Paddy. "I was so impressed," Dollar said many years later. "Paddy was the kind of guy who wrote everything down no matter what you said. He wrote very tiny, and he constantly wrote while you were talking to him. He asked a lot of nice questions and probing questions about what I was all about, and so it looked to me like McCarthy was interested in its people."[13]

When Dollar returned to McCarthy Brothers the following day to talk with Tim, he was ready to do whatever he could to get on board.[14] His eagerness is no surprise considering Paddy's and Tim's magnetism and sincerity.

"Tim McCarthy is a quiet person, but he has always very quickly established excellent personal relationships with people, especially people who

Even outside of the company, the McCarthys were recognized for their altruism. Here Paddy poses with his wife, Nadine, after the Khoury League of Kirkwood, Missouri, named a sports field in his honor to recognize his many years of coaching little-league sports. *(Photo courtesy Paddy McCarthy.)*

work in the field," said Mike Hurst, who began at the company in 1974 as a project engineer and rose to become president of McCarthy in 1996.[15]

"Tim McCarthy was just an extraordinarily fine gentleman and a good businessman," said Jim Ulkus, who was hired by Tim in 1981. "I could not have asked for a better boss."[16]

Decades after meeting Tim, Dan Cummings was still impressed by his sincerity.

I had been with the company for a couple of years, and I had seen Tim on the job, and he had seen me, but he was too busy, and I was in a carpenter's position where he really didn't have any reason to talk to me, even though I'm sure he would have if the opportunity had presented itself. By this time I was a superintendent on the project, and I remember Tim coming out, and it was almost like he was relieved to have finally met me. I mean he was just so sincere in his concern for me and how things were going for me personally. It was funny how much he knew about me because he asked me several questions that he couldn't have possibly known to ask without going to someone to get information on me.[17]

At RK&A Jones, Dollar had had seven or eight superintendents under his direction and was in charge of all of his company's commercial work in St. Louis. At McCarthy Brothers, no general superintendent jobs were available, but because Paddy and Tim had made such an impression on him, he decided to take what he could get. Having to take orders rather than give them did not unduly bother Dollar. "The field force tried to muscle me out because I wasn't an insider," he said. "I ignored it and just kept working, but I did take flak for a couple of years. Eventually, most of those guys either left or ended up working for me."[18]

Over the next half-dozen years, Dollar would oversee work on some of McCarthy's biggest and most important projects, including major expansion work at Barnes Hospital, where McCarthy Brothers had built Queeny Tower, and construction of the Bissell Point Water Treatment Plant.

Pollution Cleanup

The Bissell Point Water Treatment Plant was part of the Metropolitan St. Louis Sewer District's $95 million Mississippi River Pollution Abatement Project. The project was created to treat sewage and industrial waste for a 190-square-mile area

including St. Louis and some 70 surrounding municipalities in St. Louis County. Never before had the area had such treatment.[19]

The need for a regional sewage treatment system had become obvious as the post–World War II housing boom exploded into farmers' fields and small villages. Raw sewage and dangerous industrial waste flowed through numerous open creeks, posing a health threat of epidemic proportions. In 1954 voters approved formation of the Metropolitan St. Louis Sewer District (MSD) to oversee wastewater treatment in St. Louis and much of adjacent St. Louis County.[20]

In the mid-1950s, MSD built the spider's web network of sewer trunks and laterals that would someday connect to a treatment plant. Then in 1958, the United States Public Health Service and the Missouri Water Pollution Board ordered a cleanup of the polluted waters in the St. Louis area. A scramble for federal dollars ensued. In November 1962, voters approved the bond issue funding by a five-to-one margin. It was the "largest single water pollution abatement project ever submitted to voters in the United States." Preconstruction engineering took another 18 months, and it wasn't until May 1964 that construction began.[21]

In all, 36 construction contracts were awarded.[22] McCarthy became one of a handful of principal builders on both the Bissell Point Treatment Plant and the Lemay Treatment Plant.

Business as Usual

Building on its reputation for quality construction and client satisfaction, McCarthy continued to win plenty of work. By August 1966, it had $28 million worth of contracts.[23] Melvin was happy to report to stockholders in December that the company's work load was at its highest volume ever.[24]

Unfortunately, all that work worried McCarthy's bonding company, Travelers Indemnity. Though Travelers agreed that the work in progress

Known company wide for his sincerity and problem-solving skills, Tim McCarthy had a knack for developing personal relationships with McCarthy employees.

Above: Tom Dollar oversaw construction of the Bissell Water Treatment Plant, which treated sewage and industrial waste in St. Louis County.

Left: Tom Dollar began at McCarthy in 1965. He worked his way up the ranks, overseeing many projects, and in 1972 he became the company's first senior vice president who did not have the last name McCarthy.

appeared to be profitable, it would not underwrite future bid bonds unless McCarthy doubled its outstanding capital stock, which stood at $150,000. With $15 million in planned fall bids on the line, the directors complied. McCarthy's bidding schedule, vital to maintaining a consistent flow of work, seemed safe.[25]

Parking Structure Venture

McCarthy entered a new market in 1969 that would expand its presence nationwide, make substantial money, and steer the company into other areas. The new market was parking structures, and McCarthy entered it in May via a joint venture with California-based Portable Parking Structures International (PPSI).

McCarthy's involvement with PPSI began with Melvin's gesture of professional courtesy to William H. Godbey, one of PPSI's owners. Godbey had spent 10 years as a fighter pilot in the Marine Corps and had seen active duty in both World War II and the Korean War. He began his parking structure company in 1965 when he partnered with a man from Hungary who had invented an iron device that could be inserted into lightweight concrete slabs. The business proved successful, and soon the company was looking to expand outside California.

PPSI and McCarthy both had bid on jobs for parking garages for the University of Missouri. Although McCarthy lost the bids to PPSI, Melvin sent Godbey a note offering PPSI help in dealing with local conditions that might be unfamiliar to an outsider.[26]

Godbey took Melvin up on the offer when he returned to St. Louis to sign the contracts for the University of Missouri jobs. "Melvin was a super guy," Godbey said, remembering his first impression of the man. "He was a great big gregarious guy. Everybody loved him."[27]

Melvin confided to Godbey his fear that PPSI's bid was too low and that the out-of-towners might have gotten themselves into trouble. Godbey, however, was sure PPSI had put in a good bid. Melvin offered to have Paddy look over the estimates just to make sure.[28]

The next day Godbey was having coffee with Melvin when Paddy walked into the office. Godbey remembered the conversation.

"I think Godbey did make a mistake," Paddy told Melvin. "He thought he had a 20 percent profit in this job, and it looks to me like he's got 25 percent profit."

"Are you sure?" Melvin asked.

"I checked and rechecked all the numbers," Paddy said. "They're using a new concept that we're not familiar with, and I think it's going to be good."[29]

The new parking structure concept that Paddy was referring to involved a steel framework with lightweight prefabricated concrete slabs attached via special fasteners rather than the traditional poured-concrete methods. The frame-and-slab structures were cheaper to build and could be erected more quickly than the all-concrete structures. They could even be dismantled and moved. The *St. Louis Globe-Democrat* later reported that PPSI had "pioneered the world's first portable, demountable concrete and steel parking structures."[30]

Melvin agreed that the pioneering concept was sound and soon began negotiating with PPSI to form a partnership to build more parking structures. On May 20, 1969, McCarthy and PPSI formed Portable Parking Structures Midwest (PPSI-Midwest), which would have exclusive rights to market and build in Missouri, Illinois, Indiana, Wisconsin, Minnesota, and Iowa.[31]

"Joint venturing with Bill Godbey was, in essence, our first shot at expansion throughout the country," said Ken Bonastia, who was hired in 1971 as the self-described "controller, bookkeeper, accountant, and dishwasher" for PPSI-Midwest.[32] Bonastia later became controller of McCarthy's Midwest division.

McCarthy and PPSI would each receive 2 percent of each job's direct cost to cover indirect costs and overhead. PPSI would receive, "from the first monies available of each contract performed," 6 percent of the gross contract amount for design costs. The first $365,000 of earnings would go to PPSI. Thereafter, earnings would be divided: 60 percent for PPSI and 40 percent for McCarthy. The initial stock distribution was to be 600 shares for PPSI and 400 for McCarthy.[33]

A provision of the agreement stipulated that, once the $365,000 had been paid to PPSI, either PPSI or McCarthy could require that any further work be done by a separate corporation formed to handle the work. The agreement also required McCarthy Brothers to provide its bonding capacity and credit to the enterprise until the joint venture was in a position to bond its own jobs on its own credit.[34]

Marketing Construction

At the corporate level, Mike McCarthy presided over the joint venture. Donald Shank, a McCarthy project director, became PPSI-Midwest's general manager. Barry Hayden, another McCarthy employee, was hired as estimator, and Richard Vandegrift was recruited to handle the marketing.[35]

Vandegrift and Mike McCarthy had been classmates in the civil engineering department at Washington University in St. Louis. Vandegrift had been involved with marketing and business development in Ingersoll-Rand's Mining and Construction Group. Both Rock Hill Quarries and McCarthy Brothers were potential Ingersoll-Rand clients, and when Vandegrift came calling, he became reacquainted with Mike. Although he never sold any equipment to McCarthy, Vandegrift made a sale of another sort on those visits to Rock Hill Road. When Mike needed someone to handle sales, marketing, and business development for PPSI-Midwest, he knew just whom to call.

Vandegrift began work at PPSI-Midwest on November 15, 1969. In the late 1960s, Vandegrift

Richard A. Vandegrift came on board in 1969 to handle the marketing of McCarthy's new parking structures venture. He went on to become a McCarthy senior vice president and was a major player in the company's growth.

said, construction companies did not generally market themselves to potential clients. They usually obtained work either by hard bid or via a network of relationships with owners and architects. Vandegrift and PPSI-Midwest did something different.

"We had a product in this system we were trying to promote," Vandegrift said, "and McCarthy didn't have anybody to go out on the sidewalk. So I was the first one to ever do that, and through the course of 1970 and 1971, we probably obtained a dozen projects in the Midwest."[36]

By the end of 1970, PPSI-Midwest had paid the required $365,000 to PPSI. The joint venture had projects going in St. Louis, Tulsa, and Cincinnati and was working with several prospective clients in pursuit of future work. But cracks were beginning to appear in the joint venture. Because McCarthy was performing all the construction work, furnishing the performance bonds, charging the costs against its own bonding capacity, and doing a major share of the marketing, the company felt that it should receive more than 40 percent of the earnings.[37] Or, as Vandegrift said years later, "It was a sweetheart deal for PPSI. McCarthy did almost all the work while they sat back and collected the cash."[38]

The directors were quickly becoming disenchanted with their California partners. It was agreed that Mike would bring up the issue of the percentages at PPSI's next board meeting.[39] Whatever was discussed there, the outcome was not to McCarthy's liking. As Mike reported to McCarthy's board in 1971, "[I]t is our feeling that we are doing most of the work and not getting our full share of the profits."[40]

PPSI-Midwest was also having problems getting its bids low enough to be competitive, and with few new projects coming in, the company's future looked doubtful.

And there was yet another reason McCarthy Brothers was concerned about its California partners.

We further feel that it is the intention of the new majority owners [of PPSI] to go public with a glamour stock and recover their investment and perhaps to let the company die on the vine, which it certainly will do unless more effort is made sales-wise. Therefore, we must protect ourselves.[41]

The board ultimately decided that, because McCarthy's people were doing all the work and had improved McCarthy's design capabilities, it would set up its own parking structure group, independent of PPSI. McCarthy would finish up pending jobs and was not averse to possible future projects with PPSI, but it was obvious that the partnership was over.[42]

Indemnity and Bonding

Disgruntlement with the PPSI joint venture was only one problem faced by McCarthy Brothers in the late 1960s and early 1970s. During those years, a different kind of crisis was brewing, one that hit much closer to home.

Melvin called a special meeting of the board in September 1968 to discuss the company's dilemma. Travelers Indemnity, McCarthy's bonding company, had requested that the principal officers—Melvin, Paddy, Tim, and Mike—personally indemnify McCarthy's bonds. Melvin had been able to hold the bonding company at bay by arguing that "in the face of the considerable amount of stock that was held by persons not employed by the construction company, it was not equitable to expect the four officers to give their personal indemnifications."[43]

But Travelers Indemnity would no longer be put off. If McCarthy Brothers wanted to keep bidding on new work, it should buy out all the "outside ownership" so the principal officers could personally indemnify the corporate bonds with the corporation's full value.[44] Complicating the issue, Mercantile Trust, McCarthy's bank, began demanding, instead of the indemnification of the four principal officers, indemnification from all of the company's stockholders.

All but one of McCarthy's stockholders at that time bore the last name McCarthy. Of the original McCarthy brothers, only Charles remained. The other stockholders came from his and Mr. Tim's lineage. Since Mr. Tim and his two sons had died, the shares they had once controlled were now held by six additional stockholders: John E.'s widow, Eleanor; John E.'s estate as represented by coexecutor John H. Hendren (Melvin was the other coexecutor); and Merryl's sons, Paddy, Tim, Dr. John M. McCarthy, and Monsignor Robert "Father Bob" McCarthy.[45] Melvin, Michael, Paddy, and Tim were the only stockholders actually working for the company. Eleanor continued to draw an honorary "salary," though she wasn't actually working for McCarthy. Charles also drew a salary as a vice president.

Reluctantly, the directors voted to arrange for the fair purchase of all outstanding stock from Eleanor, John E.'s estate, Dr. John, and Father Bob and to then sign indemnification agreements with Travelers Indemnity and Mercantile Trust. However, payment for the stock would be made over a five- to ten-year period, and aside from this agreement, no further action was immediately taken.[46]

At the end of 1968, Melvin warned that Travelers Indemnity "is still pushing us hard." Melvin had explained to the bonding company that an independent appraisal of the stock's value could not be made until the company's 1968 financial statements were completed and promised he would move quickly once the financial statements became available. Melvin had managed to buy some time, but he worried that time was running out, as he expressed in the minutes of the company's December 1968 board meeting.

So far, with this assurance, the bonding company has permitted us to continue bidding, however we must proceed with the purchase of the

McCarthy Brothers Construction Company Stock Ownership as of December 31, 1969

Name	Number of Shares	Percentage of Total Shares**
Charles McCarthy	318	10.6
Melvin McCarthy*	222	7.4
Michael M. McCarthy*	244	8.0
Subtotal	**784**	**26.2**
Francis F. McCarthy*	589	19.6
Timothy R. McCarthy*	587	19.5
Rev. Robert McCarthy	155	5.2
Dr. John McCarthy	155	5.2
Subtotal	**1,486**	**49.5**
Eleanor McCarthy	50	1.5
John Hendren, trustee for John E. McCarthy estate (2 daughters)	680	22.5
Subtotal	**730**	**24.3**
TOTAL	**3,000**	**100.0**

* Works for McCarthy Brothers Construction Company
** Subtotals and totals may not add exactly due to rounding

At the end of 1969, Eleanor McCarthy and the John E. McCarthy estate together owned 24.3 percent of McCarthy Brothers' stock, which led to numerous complications concerning the company's future.

stock in question as quickly as possible or we will be in trouble with our bonding company. . . . With the large volume of work under contract, each time we want to bid a large job we have to enter into long discussion with them before we can get a bid bond.[47]

Somehow, the company got through 1969 without the bonding company pulling the plug. At that year's annual meeting, Melvin was able to report contract volume of $88 million,[48] yet another record, although the company suffered a net loss on the year of almost $145,000.[49] The losses were attributed to a four-month Ironworkers' strike that had delayed completion of some projects and increased the costs on others.[50]

Melvin also reported on a promising meeting he had attended that August with Travelers Indemnity. He had been seeking increased bonding capability for McCarthy Brothers and new bonding capacity for the joint venture with PPSI. The bonding company had agreed to do both, "taking each job on its merits."[51]

Then on July 5, 1970, Charles McCarthy passed away. Charles, described by the other directors as "an officer and a director of the corporation since its incorporation in 1907," had been the youngest of the original McCarthy brothers.[52] With him, he took the last living memory of the company's origins in far away Michigan and the Irish immigrant father who had taught his three sons to be builders. Now his son Melvin had to either guide the firm through its current impasse or risk presiding over its demise.

The Impasse Breaks Open

In 1970 a successful bid on a job at St. John's Hospital in Springfield, Illinois, finally forced the bonding issue when Travelers Indemnity refused to provide the performance bond. McCarthy reminded Travelers that without the performance bond, it would forfeit the $600,000 bid bond. But the bonding company was unsympathetic. "They said that this was our problem," Melvin told the directors in December 1970.[53]

Melvin, Paddy, Tim, and Mike signed the agreement to personally indemnify McCarthy's bonds. The alternative would have been "the complete dissolution of McCarthy Brothers," and the four principal officers were determined not to let that happen. The directors pointed out that the company had more than $107 million worth of work under contract. "Therefore, these four officers have used all of their financial holdings on behalf of McCarthy Brothers Construction Company." All four expressed apprehension about taking on the full burden of financial risk.[54]

The personal indemnity and ownership issues posed a serious threat to McCarthy's future and reflected a deeper split within the company. Both Travelers Indemnity and Mercantile Trust required personal indemnity agreements with all company stockholders, but Eleanor and the trustee for John E.'s estate, John Hendren, had refused to sell their stock or sign an agreement. Melvin, Paddy, Tim, and Mike were not only actively running the construction company but personally indemnifying its obligations to the tune of millions of dollars. Eleanor

and the estate were apparently not willing to accept the same risk.

The Great Divide

In the wake of John E.'s death in 1964, McCarthy's stock was held by or on behalf of 10 different McCarthys. On one side of a growing chasm was Mike, young and flush with the success he'd had with his parking structure venture. Mike had big ideas and wanted to try new things. Mike, his father, Melvin, and grandfather Charles, who had died in July 1970, held slightly more than 26 percent of McCarthy's stock.

On the other side, holding 24 percent of McCarthy's stock, were John E.'s heirs: widow Eleanor and John Hendren, cotrustee for John E.'s estate on behalf of daughters Katherine "Kay" McCarthy Miller and Ellen McCarthy Miller. Neither Eleanor nor her daughters worked for McCarthy, though Eleanor drew an honorary salary.

The remaining McCarthy stock, just less than 50 percent of the total, was held by Merryl's four sons, with Paddy and Tim, the two builders, owning by far the largest share. Their brothers, Dr. John and Father Bob, left the running of the company to those who had chosen to go into the business.

Melvin's Plan

Clearly McCarthy needed to regain control of its stock to move forward, in its own interest and in the interest of the minority shareholders. Melvin's plan had two basic objectives: to acquire all of John E.'s heirs' stock and to balance the company's ownership among its four active stockholders: Melvin, Mike, Paddy, and Tim.

As the trustee for John E. McCarthy's estate on behalf of John's daughters, Katherine and Ellen, John Hendren was a major player in the wrangle over McCarthy's stock ownership.

A handwritten list entitled "Melvin's Reasons for Purchase" detailed Melvin's thinking on the matter. As pressing as the issue of indemnification was, it was not the only reason Melvin was so determined to reorganize. "I want to see McCarthy Brothers continue for future generations of McCarthys," he wrote. He was, no doubt, thinking about his son. Mike had some innovative ideas and was eager to give them a try.

If Mike couldn't flex his muscles at McCarthy, the golden state of California was beckoning, for Bill Godbey had tried to lure Mike away to work for PPSI. "I had built a golf course in La Quiñada, and I had a house on the second tee, and Mike used to come back and visit me all the time," Godbey said. "I told him, 'Mike, if you come back and go to work for the parking structure company, I'll buy you a brand new Cadillac, and I'll give you my house to live in. I'll pay you double whatever you're making.'"[55]

When Mike told his father of Godbey's tempting offer, Melvin was understandably unhappy. According to Godbey, father and son struck a deal: If Melvin could obtain a voting majority of McCarthy's stock, and with it, control of the company, Mike would stay.[56]

Melvin was not enthusiastic about his latest mission. "Were it not for the indemnification it would be just as well for me to let things remain as they are, keep my present job and retire when the time comes," he wrote. "I am 63 years old. This kind of problem I do not need." Investing his own money in the company would be "foolish," he wrote, because "it will be hard to get out." That being said, he noted that "the only way" the company could go forward would be if it were wholly owned by the four active McCarthys, who could then indemnify the bonds and bank loans. Melvin was willing to provide his personal indemnification only if he controlled 50 percent of the company. The equation seemed as simple as it was inexorable. "The stock sale must be accomplished and we will have to take steps to see that it is accomplished," he wrote.[57]

Melvin and Mike knew they had a difficult task. After all, they would be trying to buy stock from people who were not only family, but family who had every right to consider the company their own. The shareholders descended from Mr. Tim far outnumbered the slender line of descent from Charles, and they owned more stock. "You can imagine what

it was like for these guys," Mike said many years later. "Tim and Paddy's family really had the strongest ownership position in the company."[58]

In late 1969 and early 1970, Melvin gathered proposals, tax advice, and appraisals. Finally, in May 1970, he presented a proposal to Hendren. Melvin's plan called for Eleanor and the trust to sell their shares of McCarthy Brothers to Melvin in exchange for Melvin's 50 percent interest in McCarthy Supply Company, cancellation of a debt that company owed Melvin, and cash.

McCarthy Supply had been formed in 1954 by John E. and Melvin as the parent corporation for two lumber supply businesses in southern Illinois. Its 5,000 shares were evenly split between John E.'s and Melvin's families. The company's officers received no salaries or bonuses from McCarthy Supply; the business was run by a salaried general manager.[59] McCarthy Supply earned a steady profit and was well positioned for future growth.

Eleanor, the trust, and "other outside stockholders" would be better off selling their McCarthy Brothers Construction stock and investing the proceeds "in something that produces income," Melvin argued. "Historically, the company has never paid a dividend, nor will it ever do so. All of its resources are required to carry on its business."[60] But Eleanor didn't think Melvin's offer, at $300 per share for McCarthy Brothers Construction stock, was nearly enough. She countered with a price of $500 per share.

Melvin's daughter Fran Fitzgerald remembered how difficult it was for her father to conduct the protracted buyout negotiations. "It was very hard on him," she said. "I mean, we're talking about family."[61]

Yet Melvin persevered. The bonding company's demands, Mike's ambitions for McCarthy, and Melvin's own desire to keep the business whole and alive for future generations fueled his efforts. Negotiations stretched into 1971. A reorganization plan was devised, but since it involved the exchange of stock in three different companies between two corporations, three individuals, one estate, and one trust, the negotiations moved slowly.

Wading through the Workload

Even while Melvin was wrangling for 50 percent control of the company, McCarthy Brothers continued to build: floodwalls and sewage treatment plants, hospitals and university buildings, housing developments, and a high-rise hotel. In January 1970, the company became general contractor for a 14-floor addition to Barnes Hospital in St. Louis. The $23.6 million building, known as the East Pavilion, was to be the first phase of a planned expansion at Barnes Hospital.[62] McCarthy Brothers also continued work on a $21.6 million project for a three-story addition and renovations at the Main Post Office in downtown St. Louis. That year the company worked on more than two dozen separate jobs.[63]

McCarthy had work to do, so it kept building. Indeed, the heavy workload is one of the reasons it took so long for an agreement to be reached between McCarthy Brothers' officers and Eleanor and Hendren.[64]

An Agreement Reached

Finally, on October 12, 1971, the "Reorganization Agreement" was adopted at a special meeting of McCarthy Brothers' directors and stockholders. The board approved the purchase of all McCarthy Supply stock from Melvin, Eleanor, and the trust in exchange for McCarthy Brothers stock, making McCarthy Supply a wholly owned subsidiary of the construction company. Finally, McCarthy Brothers spun off McCarthy Supply to Eleanor and the trust in exchange for all their McCarthy Brothers stock.

The actual closing of the deal, held on November 29, 1971, was a complicated affair involving 18 separate transactions. But when the dust had settled, Melvin controlled slightly more than 50 percent of McCarthy's stock and had reclaimed the construction company for the builders. It was undoubtedly with great satisfaction and relief that Melvin wrote the conclusion to his long quest at the bottom of his 18-point "Memorandum of Closing for Agreement and Plan of Reorganization":

Meeting held in McCarthy Bros Const Co office at 10 AM on 11/29/71 to consummate all transactions listed above. . . . All papers, stock certificates, etc. signed this date."[65]

McCarthy Supply Company Stockholders as of February 5, 1970

Name	Number of Shares
John E. McCarthy family:	
Trustees of John E. McCarthy estate	1,850
Eleanor McCarthy	650
TOTAL	**2,500**
Melvin McCarthy family:	
Melvin McCarthy	2,498
Margaret "Dusty" McCarthy	1
Michael M. McCarthy	1
TOTAL	**2,500**

John E. McCarthy's family and Melvin McCarthy's family owned an equal number of shares in McCarthy Supply Company before Melvin traded his shares to John E. McCarthy's heirs in exchange for their shares of McCarthy Brothers Construction Company.

Back to Business

McCarthy Brothers' directors gathered for their regular annual meeting three weeks later to discuss ongoing business. They also approved an addition to McCarthy's office building; with the builder's booming growth and the need to make room for Mike's parking structure group, McCarthy Brothers had already outgrown its office.[66]

The company was back to business as usual, but vast corporate changes had occurred. McCarthy was now firmly in the hands of the four McCarthys who worked for the company. The only outside interests that remained were the 310 shares owned by Father Bob and Dr. John.

The most important change wrought by the reorganization was Melvin's gaining a crucial majority on the board. Mike, now McCarthy Brothers' chief operating officer, would no longer have to go elsewhere to show what he could do. He was home to stay, and he was brimming with ideas.

McCarthy was able to solve numerous challenges while building Boatmen's Bank Tower. Construction began in 1974 and was completed ahead of schedule in 1976, despite a six-week delay due to a building trades strike. *(Photo courtesy St. Louis Mercantile Library.)*

CHAPTER SEVEN

HARD WORK AND CREATIVE THINKING

1972–1977

We were absolutely the scourge of the industry. Our competitors would kid us, . . . saying things like, "When are you going to let us have some work? You guys gotta have it all?" We were doing well; we were doing very, very well.

—Timothy R. McCarthy, early 1980s

IN THE EARLY 1970s, MCCARTHY entered a period of unprecedented growth, increasing its annual volume from around $35 million in 1972 to $177 million by 1974. Under Melvin's quiet guidance, Mike started new ventures, hired people to run them, and kept constant watch for future opportunities. Not all of his efforts succeeded, but Melvin, Tim, and Paddy knew that each unsuccessful venture, each risk, became a learning experience.

At McCarthy, risk taking is not frowned upon as long as mistakes aren't repeated. The company believes that if employees are allowed to make mistakes, they will be encouraged to make decisions, which in turn opens up opportunities. "If you're not making any mistakes or having some failures, you're not doing anything," observed Andrew Greensfelder, who served as McCarthy's attorney beginning in the late 1960s. "Mike McCarthy is the kind of guy who is willing to do anything that makes sense."[1]

"We as a company are very tolerant of mistakes," said Mike Hurst, who in 1995 became McCarthy's president and chief operating officer. "That's why McCarthy has such loyalty from its people, why it has the guts that it has. Every time people do something, and especially when they make a mistake, they learn from it. If you run them off or fire them, then all you're doing is sending all

that knowledge out the door for the next company."[2]

It was a company philosophy that traced back to the original McCarthy brothers.

Mike's successful ventures were eventually folded back into McCarthy while the less promising ones were discontinued. Still, the unsuccessful ventures were few, and the successes were many in those years as McCarthy Brothers followed Mike into the little known field of construction management.

The Birth of McBro

On January 5, 1972, McCarthy Brothers Construction Company filed registration of the name "McBro" with the state of Missouri. McBro was an abbreviation for the company's name that Melvin often used in his handwritten notes. McBro dated back to the company's time in the Panama Canal

McCarthy's leaders gather for a 1974 photo for the *St. Louis Globe-Democrat* after celebrating another record year: from left, Tim McCarthy, senior vice president; Mike McCarthy, executive vice president; Melvin McCarthy, chairman and president; and Paddy McCarthy, secretary-treasurer. *(Photo courtesy St. Louis Mercantile Library.)*

In 1972 Mike McCarthy founded McBro Planning & Development Company to continue McCarthy's parking structure work. McBro also moved the company into construction management, especially for hospitals.

Zone during World War II, when MCBRO had been the corporation's telex address.[3]

By registering the name, McCarthy signaled the start of a more prominent role for Mike McCarthy, who would transform the obsolete telex address into a hallmark of quality.

When McCarthy parted ways with PPSI, Mike brought the parking structure group's employees to Rock Hill and on January 15, 1972, founded McBro Planning & Development Company.[4] McBro was formed to continue the lucrative parking structure work, but Mike didn't limit the new venture to such a narrow market. Many of PPSI-Midwest's projects had been parking structures at urban hospitals, and Mike saw plenty of opportunity for an experienced hospital builder. Richard Vandegrift and Barry Hayden, who headed PPSI-Midwest's

operations, had told Mike, "It's a shame to do a $1.5 million garage, and here's an $8 million or $9 million hospital addition, and we're not paying any attention."[5]

Maybe PPSI-Midwest didn't pay much attention, but McCarthy certainly did. Mike was confident that he could grow the family company from a St. Louis builder to a national powerhouse, but he needed the family's support. Decades later Mike remained humble, and a little amazed, that Melvin, Paddy, and Tim had enough confidence in him to entrust him with the company's future—and their livelihoods. "It was really remarkable that they let me come charging around like a bull in a china shop to do all these things," he said.[6]

Nobody was better positioned than Melvin, Paddy, and Tim to know McCarthy Brothers' capabilities; their combined years with the family business equaled the company's age. That rich perspective also spotted the risks involved in Mike's plans, but the older and presumably wiser McCarthys must have seen something worth supporting in young Mike's dreams, and they gave him the company's backing.

As it turned out, McCarthy's hospital work gave the company nationwide exposure and allowed it to expand significantly. "The healthcare business was really the vehicle that allowed us to become a national company," said Mike Bolen, who joined McCarthy in 1978 and in 2000 became CEO. "Moving from place to place, we learned a tremendous amount about how business was done in different places, what emerging markets looked like, what dying markets looked like. The healthcare business allowed us to leverage ourselves into a number of long-term sustainable markets as community-based builders."[7]

But that evolution was still in the future. In 1972 McCarthy Brothers invested nearly $75,000 in McBro.[8] In return, McBro paid McCarthy $15,000 in fees for services and overhead during its first year and contributed more than $51,000 in gross profit to the parent company.[9]

Support from the parent company came in other forms as well. Just weeks after forming McBro,

Mike and Melvin hired Roger Burnet, an experienced hospital builder, to help run the new division. Burnet became a McCarthy vice president, as did R. F. Weinberger. They were the first company officers who did not have the last name McCarthy.

"Melvin and Mike McCarthy hired Roger [Burnet] because of his operational experience in building healthcare facilities," said Vandegrift, who worked side by side with Burnet for nearly 15 years and looked to him as a mentor. "He was 100 percent committed, a tireless worker and leader. He and I worked all day, into the evening, and until we went to bed, Monday through Friday. He'd spend time with his family on the weekends, but somehow he'd squeeze out another six hours of work on those days

McBro gave McCarthy more of a national presence, as the U.S. map near McBro's reception desk indicates. The map is dotted with thumbtacks representing McBro projects.

too. There's only 24 hours in a day, and how he jammed everything in there I'll never know."[10]

An experienced construction man when he came to McCarthy, Burnet had graduated from the University of Missouri with a degree in civil engineering and had spent four years in the mili-

tary, which had paid for his engineering degree. He spent two years at Subic Bay Naval Base in the Philippines, where CUBI Naval Air Station was being built. The project was the largest earth-moving endeavor undertaken since construction of the Panama Canal, Burnet said. His experience there convinced him that a career in construction was what he wanted.

After his stint in the military, Burnet worked for a series of construction firms before going to HBE Corporation, a nationwide builder of hospitals, in the late 1960s. Although he gained valuable experience at HBE, Burnet was ready for a change when Mike came calling.[11]

Left: Rich Vandegrift, shown here in 1976, was instrumental in making McBro one of the top three hospital builders in the nation. He also helped create McCarthy's corporate identity.

Below: Mike McCarthy (left) discusses McBro projects with Roger Burnet.

Mike's experiences on the Queeny Tower project had left him with the belief that there had to be a better way to build hospitals than the traditional design-bid-build model. His idea was to have McBro "take over the entire development of medical facilities for clients," he said, noting that his goal had been "a bit presumptuous since we'd never done that before."[12]

Another of McBro's original objectives was to pursue multilevel parking structure projects. Its first two projects, in 1972, were for parking garages in Memphis and St. Louis, valued at about $5 million.[13]

Mike had big dreams for the fledgling division, but McCarthy and McBro had little name recognition outside the St. Louis area. Vandegrift helped devise brochures highlighting McBro's healthcare and parking structure experience. He also helped develop a corporate identity scheme to present a unified, professional image. Previously, construction trailers, trucks, and equipment had been painted a hodge-podge of colors. Some pieces still sported McCarthy's old address. Vandegrift had St. Louis architect Dan Green design a new look for the company, and before long, McCarthy vehicles, signs, equipment, and stationery featured the distinctive orange, tan, and brown stripes of McCarthy's new colors.[14]

Mike, Burnet, and the rest of the McBro team had a grueling work schedule. "Our day job was to run McCarthy's projects, but our night job was to go out and find other work so that we could start this new company that managed hospital projects," Mike said.[15]

McBro was soon doing enough business around the country for McCarthy to buy its first corporate aircraft.

McBro set about prospecting for clients. A copy of the American Hospital Association's hospital directory provided basic information for a cold-calling campaign. Mike, Burnet, and Vandegrift worked their way through the lists of hospitals, analyzing the conversations to learn what was and was not effective in their marketing efforts. They also began attending hospital conventions and building relationships with architects.[16]

Many of McBro's potential clients were in small towns distant from major airports. Because McBro's management team still had their "day jobs," they were often forced to charter flights to get to and from their meetings. This, Mike said, raised some eyebrows back in St. Louis. "I know my father must have wondered what was going on," Mike said. "Some of the planes we chartered were for ungodly amounts of money."[17]

By April 1973, McBro had expanded into nine states, leading McCarthy Brothers' directors to buy a preowned Cessna 421. "Construction management is a service business," the directors explained, "and the success depends upon having our people available for meetings with the owners and architects when needed.[18]

The corporation had expanded enough to need a company plane, and McBro was ready to fly.

ROGER BURNET: A LEGEND IN HIS OWN TIME

ROGER BURNET, KNOWN company-wide for his integrity, high energy, and hard work, had a style all his own. Described by his fellow officers as "extremely focused" and "very intense," Burnet created a legacy that continued to live long after he retired as president in 1995 and as vice chairman in 1996.

"Roger Burnet was a firestorm," said Ken Bonastia, controller of the Midwest division. "He was a mile a minute. If you learned anything with Roger, it was how to talk fast. He was an organizer. He was a detailed, in-your-face kind of guy. But he got it done, and he led by example."[1]

"He was the most impressive individual I think I've ever met in terms of knowledge and experience in the kind of work we were doing," said Lloyd Hansen, who was hired by Burnet in 1981 and rose to become executive vice president.[2]

"Roger always made you feel good about the job you were doing," said Tom Felton, who as a project director did quite a bit of moving from job site to job site. "We used to laugh because whenever he came to your job, he'd always say the same thing: 'This has got to be the toughest job we've ever done.'"[3]

"Roger did everything at 110 miles per hour," said Jim Faust, vice president of Human Resources. Faust remembered the first time he had lunch with Burnet. He was so busy answering Burnet's questions that he didn't have time to take a bite. "All of a sudden, Roger just stopped asking questions and started eating," Faust said. "I think I got two bites of my sandwich before he was done eating and I'm back to answering questions. But that's Roger. He worked hard, and he ate lunch hard. I think he even slept hard."[4]

"He wasn't conscious of time," said Vandegrift. "He'd come up and say, 'I need just a minute of your time.' Well, we'd laugh because that more likely meant an hour."[5]

"Roger always felt the need to be right in your face when he talked to you," said George Scherer, CFO. "The closer he got, the better for him and the worse for you. You finally found yourself backing up to keep your eyes from crossing. He'd back you into a corner, and then you were trapped."[6]

"He literally would be six inches from your face," said Vandegrift. "It wasn't meant to intimidate you; it's just how focused he was."[7]

Mike Hurst remembered some advice Vandegrift gave him about dealing with Burnet. "When Roger gets up in your face, don't back up, because if you do, you'll never be able to stop. You've got to hold your ground."[8]

"He felt the need to have a lot of order in his life," said Scherer. "He had a list for everything, and if he didn't have his list, then he was totally lost."[9]

Rarely did anyone see Burnet at rest. "He had a phenomenal work ethic," said Jim Staskiel, general counsel. "He'd get off a plane, rush into a meeting, and it was just go-go-go-go and never stop until he finally wrote up that list."[10]

Oddly enough, Burnet was a slow driver, but sometimes he became so engrossed in conversation that he was known to drive off the road. "He'd always be talking about business or his family or how our favorite sports teams were doing, and he wasn't thinking about driving at all," said

Roger Burnet, who served as president and vice chairman of McCarthy, was renowned for his work ethic, integrity, and intensity.

Burnet (standing, far right) was an experienced hospital builder when he joined McCarthy as a vice president in 1972. In 1977 he became president of McBro.

Vandegrift. "If the speed limit was 55, he might be doing 35, and he wasn't doing it to be cautious. He had no idea how fast he was going; it wasn't important to him."[11]

While other company officers slept on an overnight flight, Burnet worked. Dubbed a "marvelous operations guy" by Mike McCarthy, Burnet masterminded company-wide systems and procedures that were still being implemented years after he retired.

"He was an exceptional strategist," said Vandegrift. "When we identified an opportunity, he was like a dog going after a bone as he focused on how to convince the prospective client that we had the best service and the best people."[12]

In the late 1970s and early 1980s, McBro's people did a lot of traveling, and in those days they shared hotel rooms to cut down on costs. "Roger was always so absorbed in his work, so focused, that the minute details of life would just pass him by," said Bud Guest, who worked closely with Burnet and Vandegrift before becoming senior vice president of business development for McCarthy's Midwest division. "So when you shared a room with him, you had to be careful that he dressed in his clothes and you dressed in yours because he'd grab a coat off the rack and wear it whether it fit him or not."[13] It wasn't uncommon, in fact, to see Burnet in a green tie, blue shirt, brown jacket, and gray slacks.

Vandegrift remembered driving to a morning meeting after he and Burnet had shared a hotel room the night before. "I went to my closet and couldn't find my clean shirt, so I thought maybe I forgot to pack it and put on the shirt I'd worn the day before. So Roger and I leave the hotel and we're driving down the road, and I look over, and he's kind of fidgeting while we're talking. I said, 'What's wrong?' And he said, 'Boy, this shirt is really tight around my neck.'"[14]

At one time McCarthy was in discussions with an Irish architectural firm about building a state-of-the-art hospital in Ireland. Burnet was at a breakfast meeting with the owner of the firm and was so absorbed in talking about the hospital that he began eating off the owner's plate. Finally, the owner interrupted him. "I have a question," he said politely in his British accent.

Burnet paused, still completely absorbed in the discussion. "Yeah? What is it?"

"Is there some reason why you're eating my breakfast?"

Burnet himself could laugh at his idiosyncrasies and did not mind that other people laughed with him. Everyone who knew him revered his hard work and dedication. They knew him to be an extremely talented builder and regarded him with the utmost respect. So deep was the company's affection that Mike McCarthy named the company's top award after him. Buildings receive the Roger Burnet Award in recognition of their quality.

Pioneering Construction Management

In 1973, McBro signed six new contracts for work valued at $59 million. One of these contracts entailed McBro's first hospital design-build project—a coronary care unit at St. Joseph Mercy Hospital in Mason City, Iowa.

Another contract—a 400-bed replacement hospital for St. Joseph Medical Center in Wichita, Kansas—became its first construction management (CM) job and launched McBro's ride to the top of the booming CM field.

McBro made contact with St. Joseph Medical Center in 1972, when Vandegrift heard the hospital might be in the market for a parking garage. He spoke with its president, Joe Heeb, who remembered McCarthy Brothers from a 1952 project the builders had done for the hospital. Heeb told Vandegrift that the work in question was merely an expansion of surface parking lots, which was of no interest to McBro. But during their conversation, Vandegrift told Heeb about McCarthy's

recent forays into healthcare construction. The call to Heeb was undoubtedly like hundreds of others Vandegrift, Burnet, and Mike made in McBro's early days as they tried to drum up business for the new enterprise. But this call would bear unexpected fruit several months later, when Vandegrift received a call from Heeb.

The hospital was in a jam, Heeb told Vandegrift. The United States Department of Health, Education, and Welfare (HEW) had granted the hospital board some $20 million to build a 400-bed replacement hospital under the Hill-Burton Act, a federally funded program designed to build hospitals in areas where they were needed. The board had followed the usual design-bid-build model for the project, but when the bids came in considerably over budget,

---

McCarthy continued to be a company of hands-on builders even while it delved into the emerging field of construction management. From left: Shade Morris, Don Bourne, and John Flynn.

the board fired the architect and decided to start over. What the board was looking for, Heeb said, was someone to estimate costs during the design process and help keep the project on budget. Although he didn't know the term, what the board was looking for was construction management.

Heeb was not the only person at St. Joseph who remembered McCarthy. The hospital's semiretired administrator was none other than Mother Mary Ann McNamara of the Sisters of St. Joseph, to whom McCarthy had rebated excess profits back in 1948, when its costs for building the sisters' nurses' home had turned out to be lower than expected. It was an act of kindness and integrity Mother Mary Ann never forgot.

Mike McCarthy, Vandegrift, and Tom Dollar met with Heeb and Mother Mary Ann. McBro was interested in building the hospital, but the hospital's board wanted a local builder for the job and already had a list of four potential general contractors. McBro was hired to do estimates during the design process to make sure the project stayed within budget.

Since the hospital was being built with federal dollars, there were plenty of governmental guidelines to be followed. HEW had written a very specific manual on the role and duties of the construction manager. One rule required at least three bids on the job. One of the four approved contractors had dropped out of contention, but enough remained to meet the government's requirement.

When it came time for the contract to be awarded, however, only two contractors were at the table. The HEW representative refused to award the contract with only two bidders, but McBro wasn't about to let Mother Mary Ann and the hospital board down. Mike remembered a provision that allowed the construction manager of a project to also act as general contractor by guaranteeing and bonding the maximum price on the project before the documents were finalized. The construction manager would then monitor the completion of the documents, working with the owner, the architect, and the planners to make sure the project stayed within budget. When the documents were completed, the construction manager would subcontract or self-perform the work and be responsible for finishing the project at or under the guaranteed maximum price (GMP).

If the actual construction cost went above the GMP, the difference came out of the construction manager's pockets.

According to HEW's manual, a GMP contract often included a set fee for profit and overhead. Job costs and subcontracts would be reimbursed up to the GMP amount, and savings might be split between owner and contractor. "This type of contract works best when both the contractor and owner are experienced in this type of contract, are familiar with the type of work, and have had a successful ongoing relationship on prior work," the handbook explained. "The architect must also be sensitive to both owner requirements and contractor costs. A major incentive to both contractor and architect can be the opportunity for future negotiated projects from repeat owners."[19]

Mike remembered the mad scramble that followed his suggestion. "Within about 15 minutes, everybody went crazy, and all of a sudden, we wind up with a $23 million job."[20]

McBro had won the project, but Vandegrift and Burnet were left scratching their heads. They weren't quite sure what services Mike had just sold. "To be honest with you, we barely knew what the term 'construction management' meant," Vandegrift confessed years later.[21]

Mike's McBro associates weren't the only ones who were confused about his off-the-cuff maneuvers, as Mike found out when he returned to Rock Hill. Word of what had transpired reached McCarthy headquarters before Mike did, so he expected to be greeted by jubilation. Instead, he was met by a furious Paddy McCarthy, who thought Mike was about to ruin McCarthy's reputation with architects by taking away their jobs.[22]

Paddy need not have feared; architects and consultants loved the construction management services offered by McBro. In the inflationary 1970s, construction costs were rising at an alarmingly fast rate. Hospitals were becoming more complex and taking longer to build—a deadly combination for owners' bottom lines.

"With the escalating economy, we were scared to death," said Vandegrift. "We wondered what in the world the hospital was going to cost a year from now, when the design was finished. All of a sudden, we were the experts, but to be the experts, we had to be very involved."[23]

Accurate estimating was vital to keeping a project on budget, so rather than relying on subcontractors for estimates, McBro beefed up its estimating staff with electrical and mechanical estimators. "We have to be able to sit across the table from that mechanical designer and ask him questions about the mechanical system: what kind of system he's going to design and why," Vandegrift said. "The clients hear the discussion and understand that if they want a two-pipe system, for example, it's going to cost X. If they want a four-pipe system, it's going to cost Y. Then they can debate the merits of one versus the other and make the decision based on the big picture."[24]

To stand above the competition, McBro promised to keep rapidly rising costs under control and shorten the time needed to complete a project. "We planned to really emphasize the services during the planning and the design processes—known as preconstruction today," said Vandegrift. "Sure, we were going to manage the construction process, but we wanted to focus on that front-end part because that determined whether you were going

to be within the budget. If you weren't within the budget, the project wasn't going to happen."[25]

The preconstruction services were a vital part of the equation, McBro believed. Ideally, the owner would hire McBro at the same time it hired an architect and a planner, creating a partnership that worked towards a common goal. McBro would focus on the estimating, scheduling, and strategy, working closely with the architect and reviewing all documents at every stage of the design process. It would be included in all discussions involving the final design, everything from building exteriors to mechanical systems.

McBro went all out to prove itself in Wichita. McCarthy's best project manager, Tom Dollar, working out of an office for the first time, was put in

Though each of McCarthy's leaders had his own specialty, they often worked together to ensure quality and efficiency of operations. Here Mike McCarthy (left) shares a laugh with Tim McCarthy.

charge of the overall project. Although hitches popped up along the way, McBro ultimately came in under budget and completed the project profitably.

More valuable to McBro than the profit, however, were the relationships established with the architect and hospital consultant. The architectural firm on the Wichita project was the Omaha-based Henningson, Durham and Richardson (HDR), one of the nation's leading healthcare facility designers. Nationally recognized hospital consultant Herman Smith Associates, of Hinsdale, Illinois, was also on the project. Vandegrift said that both firms were involved with other projects that were having difficulties staying on budget and on schedule. After they saw how effectively McBro managed and performed at St. Joseph, they turned to the experts at McBro for help. Over the course of the next decade, McBro would work with Herman Smith Associates on 27 different projects and with HDR on 28.[26]

Rich Vandegrift, shown here in 1976, coheaded PPSI-Midwest before he began working in McBro.

Working Miracles

Only a few months after McBro's triumph in Wichita, Mike McCarthy and Vandegrift were manning a booth at a Chicago hospital convention as part of the educational and marketing campaign the McBro team had undertaken. Allowed time for a presentation, they spoke on construction management. The message was simple, Vandegrift said: "Here's a process that makes sense. And, oh, by the way, we're probably the best guy to do it."[27]

The audience was small, but what the McBro team said that day piqued the interest of Bob Krutz, a hospital administrator from Robinson Memorial Hospital, in Ravenna, Ohio. Krutz invited Mike and Vandegrift to Ohio to meet with his building committee.

Mike and Vandegrift traveled to the little town just east of Akron and made their pitch to the building committee. The project was a 300-bed replacement hospital and had a "seemingly unattainable" budget of about $52 a square foot. The project was in the early conceptual stages, and neither a planner nor an architect had yet been hired. Mike must have been able to convince the building committee that McBro could work miracles, for McBro was hired as construction manager and Krutz even asked for the company's help in choosing the rest of the team.

McBro asked Herman Smith Associates and HDR, its partners from Wichita, to repeat their roles as planner and architect in Ravenna. Initially HDR had some reservations about the design compromises that would be needed to meet the budget. Ultimately, however, both firms joined McBro. Once the preconstruction team was in place, Krutz laid out a timeline for the project. One year was allowed to complete the planning and design, to be followed by a two-month period to bid and award the contracts. In that time, the bonds financing the project would also have to be sold. Then came the two-year construction period, with the hospital dedication set for July 1977.

Burnet, assisted by Vandegrift and a team from McBro, headed up the preconstruction effort. The entire team met 55 times in the 12-month preconstruction period, a schedule that Vandegrift described as "incredibly intense." The architect could hardly keep up. He would return from a meeting in Chicago or Ohio and have to prepare all the documents for the next meeting. This actually worked to the project's advantage because it kept the architect's attention focused on one project.

When McBro made both the budget and Robinson Memorial's dedication date, Krutz became McBro's most enthusiastic reference. His

On-site McBro workers Mike Hurst (left), McCarthy's future president and chief operating officer, and Don Donaldson look over a project's blueprints.

praise was appreciated, but sometimes, Vandegrift said, Krutz carried it a bit too far.

>*Bob [Krutz] had a wired system, and I could listen live to his conversation with our prospective clients, who were asking questions about how we performed. One time Bob told a client, "Now I don't want you to think that I'm on McBro's payroll or something." He'd finish the conversation, then call me back and say, "Well, Rich, how did I do?" I'd tell him, "Bob, you've got to tone it down."[28]*

With such enthusiastic clients as Krutz and Mother Mary Ann, it was small wonder that McBro kept the contracts rolling in. The company went from two projects valued at $5 million in 1972 to 10 projects with a total construction value of $148

million in 1976. Over the next two years, McBro added 23 more projects, worth $405 million.[29]

In 1977, McBro's stockholders exchanged their McBro shares for McCarthy Brothers stock, making McBro a wholly owned subsidiary.[30]

Residential Developments

In 1973, Mike and Bill Godbey teamed up for another business venture. They had both ended their involvement with PPSI but had maintained their friendship, so when Godbey mentioned he would like to partner on another business venture, Mike suggested residential real estate development. Although McCarthy had done almost no residential building in its long history, Godbey had experience building condominiums in California. McBro and Godbey's company, William H. Godbey Enterprises, formed a series of joint ventures. The first, Fallingbrook Town Homes, was to develop 191 condominiums on 40 acres in Springfield, Illinois.[31]

Barry Hayden, who had worked with Godbey in the parking structure venture, represented

McBro's interests in the joint venture. Hayden was a graduate engineer from the University of Missouri at Rolla and had worked his way through an MBA program at Washington University in St. Louis while holding down his job with PPSI-Midwest. He would ultimately found his own successful homebuilding business.[32]

Fallingbrook was a great success, selling quickly and making the partners a good profit. More joint ventures followed. Canyon Company, a construction management project for a 125-unit condominium development, began in 1974. The following year, McCarthy Development Company was formed to develop 101 single-family homes near Fallingbrook Town Homes.[33]

In 1977, after development had begun on yet another residential project, Godbey sold his interest in the joint ventures to Mike and took his boat to the Caribbean and the Bahamas. (The split was amicable—the two remained very good friends, and Godbey later did marketing for McCarthy.[34]) All new residential development was done through the new McCarthy Development Company.

Mike Hurst joined Mike McCarthy in the residential development area. Though Hurst welcomed the opportunity to work closely with Mike, development work wasn't for him. However, Mike McCarthy must have seen Hurst's potential; he later began grooming Hurst to become McCarthy's president.

Corporate Housekeeping

At an April 30, 1973, special meeting (the same one authorizing purchase of a corporate aircraft for the high-flying McBro team), the directors transferred McCarthy's bonding and insurance business from Travelers to Aetna Insurance Company. There were several reasons for the switch. Most importantly, Aetna increased McCarthy's bonding capacity and did not require personal indemnity from the McCarthy stockholders.

As an added benefit, Gerry Murphy, who had worked on the McCarthy account through Aetna, became McCarthy's outside bonding agent. It was a relationship that would result in Murphy joining McCarthy in 1979 and would continue into the next century, when Murphy ended his McCarthy career as president emeritus of the Southwest division, in Phoenix.[35]

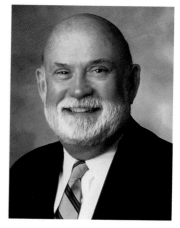

Gerry Murphy joined McCarthy in 1979 and served as president of the Southwest division until his retirement in 2001.

Then in 1974, McCarthy amended its articles of incorporation to expand its board of directors to seven members and mandated that directors need not be shareholders of the corporation.[36] Burnet was among the first nonfamily directors to join Melvin, Paddy, Tim, and Mike on the board.[37]

Big Plans

While Mike and his McBro crew were flying around the country making deals for hospitals, parking structures, and residential housing, Melvin, Tim, and Paddy were keeping busy in St. Louis. The firm continued to pursue and build the types of projects that had been its mainstay. In 1972, a $21 million contract for expanding and remodeling the St. Louis Post Office was joined by others for housing projects, various university buildings, electric tower foundations, several hospitals, and a new corporate headquarters for McDonnell Douglas Corporation (now Boeing).[38] Projects for the next year were much the same, and the number of hospital jobs grew.[39]

In July 1974, Mike gave the board a status report. He had crunched the numbers on various project delivery systems to compare the potential profitability of construction management, design-build, hard-bid, and development projects. He concluded that without the higher profit potential of alternative delivery methods, McCarthy Brothers could hope for little more than to break even in the future. The corporation seemed on the right track with its growing emphasis on construction management. Rapidly rising construction costs were fueling the need for construction management services, and McCarthy was well positioned to take advantage of the rising demand. Mike noted that McCarthy was probably the largest hospital construction manager in the country. It was also the 80th-largest general contractor, thanks in part to the volume of general contracting work McBro generated from its construction management jobs.[40]

Mike then outlined long- and short-term goals for the company. The long-term objectives, to be realized by 1980, included establishing McCarthy as a national construction manager in at least three industries (hospitals, industrial, and commercial were mentioned as possibilities). The firm should also balance its projects between construction management, hard-bid general contracting, and tax-sheltered developments. Mike also wanted to see McCarthy establish a major presence as a construction manager "in at least one major foreign country . . . with tremendous natural resources, comfortable political position, and growth potential as a world power."[41]

The short-term goals were more concrete. Increased profitability topped the list. Mike wanted to expand construction management work by issuing a brochure that highlighted the firm's industrial and commercial capabilities and by "an attack on the entire West Coast and Southwest areas." He also proposed to expand McCarthy's bid market by choosing new areas, preferably in construction management. The development market could also be expanded by seeking areas "of limited competition but critical need."[42]

The second short-term goal was more-unified control of the building and construction management sides. "We need to discipline ourselves in each operating department," Mike explained. "Once the corporate goals are established, each department must channel its activities toward that goal." McCarthy Brothers was no longer the local general contractor it had been a few short years before; instead, it was a rapidly growing, national construction management company. "Controls and vigorous management are imperative for a company of this magnitude," Mike said.[43]

To help facilitate these goals, Ogle "Goldie" Golden was put in charge of shop and yard operations. Golden and Harlan VanderSchaaf set up systems and procedures for the yard. The estimating departments of McBro and McCarthy met twice a month to review bids and schedules. Carter Lewis, McCarthy's new treasurer and chief financial officer, streamlined procedures in the accounting department, and Tim McCarthy compiled a master list of reimbursable items.[44]

Gaining Recognition

Tim McCarthy's 1973 election as president of the Associated General Contractors (AGC) of St. Louis neatly coincided with McCarthy's rise to dominance in the St. Louis construction market. McCarthy's ascendancy must have made the meetings fun for the association's new president. Tim remembered being teased by other contractors about the amount of work McCarthy was winning.

We were absolutely the scourge of the industry. Our competitors would kid us at the AGC meetings, saying things like, "When are you going to let us have some work? You guys gotta have it all?" We were doing well; we were doing very, very well.[45]

McCarthy's St. Louis competitors had reason to be jealous. A 1974 article in the *St. Louis Globe-Democrat* trumpeted the company's phenomenal growth, giving credit to the new cost-control techniques of construction management.[46] Just two months later, McCarthy Brothers figured prominently in another *Globe-Democrat* article on the growing rate of construction in downtown St. Louis. McCarthy was literally rebuilding the downtown skyline with three simultaneous projects "within the shadow of the Gateway Arch."[47] Those three projects were the 22-story, $28 million Boatmen's Bank Tower, the 352-room, $14 million Inn of the Spanish Pavilion, and a new national headquarters building for General American Life Insurance Company.[48]

The McCarthy Brothers name kept cropping up in print more often than was typical of most private companies. In April 1976, *Engineering News-Record* named McCarthy the top construction management firm in the nation. A follow-up profile appeared in August, with Mike, Paddy, and Tim appearing on the magazine's cover.[49]

Reaching the top of the construction management field so quickly must have been a proud moment for McCarthy and especially for Mike,

Opposite: McCarthy gained recognition in *Engineering News-Record* for its innovative problem solving during construction of the 22-story Boatmen's Bank Tower in St. Louis. *(Photo courtesy St. Louis Mercantile Library.)*

During the 1970s, McCarthy worked on the West and East Pavilion additions to Barnes Hospital. McCarthy also built Queeny Tower and the walkway bridge (seen at the left of the main building).

who had pushed the company and assorted relatives well past their previous comfort zones in his zeal to succeed. Sadly, he could not share his joy with the man who had, quietly and away from the limelight, made it all possible.

On February 24, 1976, McCarthy Brothers "suffered a great loss" with the death of J. Melvin McCarthy.[50] He passed away in Barnes Hospital, where McCarthy Brothers had done so much work. The beloved chairman would be missed by family and all those who had known him.

"My dad was an incredible guy," said Mike. He was just a wonderful, sweet, big old bear."[51]

His daughters, Peggy Reynolds and Fran Fitzgerald, remembered their father had worked very hard during their childhood years but always made time for family, whether to check over homework, tell ghost stories, or play softball in the yard. "He always taught us to do our best," said Fran, "and that if we gave something our best and still failed, it was okay because we did our best."[52]

"He emphasized values and integrity," said Peggy. "He always told me that no matter what you do, remember you have to look at yourself in the mirror."[53]

But perhaps Melvin's most lasting eulogy would come from those who were privileged to work for

him and with him. "When I joined McCarthy, Melvin was the boss," said Roger Burnet five years after his own retirement as McCarthy's president. "He was one of the nicest guys, a terrific man. He and I were both big Missouri fans, and every week my wife and I would go with him to the Missouri games."[54]

"I had a great deal of respect for Melvin," said Ken Bonastia, controller of McCarthy's Midwest division. "He was very sincere and would take the time to sit in your office and talk to you about your life and how things were going. You were very, very comfortable with the man."[55]

"He was just a nice, kind person," said Andrew Greensfelder. "He thought people should be treated with respect, and that attitude has prevailed throughout the business."[56]

Four days after Melvin's death, Mike became chairman of the board and president of McCarthy by unanimous vote. Now it was up to the next generation of McCarthys to pass on Melvin's legacy of hard work, integrity, and caring. Father Bob McCarthy was elected to the board to fill the seat left vacant by Melvin's death. Tim became executive vice president, and Paddy was voted senior vice president and secretary. Burnet remained as vice president, and the treasurer's role was transferred to James King.[57]

McCarthy continued to win national attention as its success mounted. An April 29, 1976, *Engineering News-Record* article featured McCarthy's creative approach to challenges on the Boatmen's Tower project. The building's architect, Hellmuth, Obata & Kassabaum (HOK), made some late changes to the plans, adding a new mezzanine level between the top floor and roof. By the time the need for extra internal structural support was discovered, the building was already enclosed and the two derricks that had done the heavy lifting had been dismantled. The remaining small Chicago derrick could have done the job but only slowly and with the risk of marring the tower's exterior. So McCarthy simply opened the roof where a skylight was to be installed and hired a helicopter to lower the needed structural materials into the mezzanine level. The whole process took only a few hours.[58]

The article also described how McCarthy handled the building's challenging excavation, a 200-by-300-foot hole bounded by four downtown streets and an underground telephone cable running just outside the perimeter of the excavation.

Transfer girders (arrows) set into garage walls carry tower frame, as

Sloped columns (arrow) shore the longest one.

Tubular design cuts mid-rise framing weight

By using a tubular frame for a relatively low office building, Jack D. Gillum & Associates saved nearly $600,000 for the Boatmen's National Bank of St. Louis.

The local structural engineer's design trimmed 2.5 lb of steel per sq ft of floor space from the 22-story Boatmen's Tower where the bank will locate its headquarters later this year.

The tube concept, with exterior columns spaced about 10 ft apart taking all lateral loads on the $18-million building, also helped maintain the exterior appearance dictated by architect Hellmuth, Obata & Kassabaum, Inc., (HOK), St. Louis. The tower resembles a 103 x 213-ft aluminum box with openings punched roughly 8 x 10 ft for windows that provide floor-to-ceiling glass inside.

The tower encloses about 480,000 sq ft, rising above a small attached two-story banking structure. A roof garden tops the bank, along with a skylighted tubular-steel frame 90 ft square extending over the entrance foyer between both structures. The buildings stand over a 115,000-sq-ft, two-level garage for 200 cars and occupy an entire block across the street from the city's historic Old Courthouse.

The tower's steel-framed core measures 150 x 20 ft, but appears nonsymmetrical inside because only four of its five 30-ft bays are walled in. They are sufficient to house mechanical rooms, restrooms and other facilities, plus low and high-rise banks of elevators. Two columns at one end of the core are the only ones exposed on any floor. Girders span 40 ft between the core columns

24 ENR April 29, 1976

and those in the longer exterior walls and 20 ft to the end walls.

A conventional rigid frame and a stub-girder layout were among other designs the engineer abandoned as more costly ways of providing the necessary structural rigidity, says Gillum's associate in charge of the project, James Williams. Designers initially considered a standard frame with columns spaced at 10 ft because of the architect's window spacing, but went on to analyze that frame as a tube. That turned out to provide suitable stiffness with only 11.5 lb of steel per sq ft of floor in the tower. This compares with 14 lb for a conventionally framed structure of similar size in the St. Louis area, says Gillum vice president Loren Bartels. A tubular frame is not generally considered economical for structures lower than about 30 stories.

Multiple transfers. The columns of three exterior walls are bolted to deep steel transfer girders set into the garage's concrete walls, which are typically 16 in. thick. Columns in the fourth wall of the tower, one of the longer two, are anchor-bolted 2 ft into the garage wall and have another 2 ft of concrete placed above their footings.

That wall itself serves as a transfer member, though its upper part is pierced by openings roughly 3 x 8 ft for air-handling equipment. Heavy reinforcing between openings helps transfer loads to the lower part of the wall, which has steel columns set into it 30 ft apart.

Similar columns only 20 ft apart under the short walls support the transfer girders. All of the columns stand on

concrete caps over steel H-piles that bear on rock 40 to 50 ft below the lower garage level's 5-in. floor slab.

The longer steel transfer girder had to be shored until the tubular frame took on sufficient rigidity with placement of steel at the 14th floor. McCarthy Brothers Construction Co., the St. Louis general contractor, shored it with cast-in-place columns sloped from each span's one third-points to bear on pile caps until it could remove them with jackhammers.

Two plate girders, 30 ft long and 5.5 ft deep at one end of the core under the second floor, transfer loads from mechanical floors into the core columns. Every two floors are served by a single mechanical room in one end of the core that is two stories high.

Second thoughts. The engineer planned to have the frame erected in prefabricated ladders made of three-story-high column members with cross-members welded between them. Ironworkers were to bolt them into place 10 ft apart, then bolt in beams to connect them. But fabricator and erection subcontractor Mississippi Valley Structural Steel, St. Louis, figured the job would cost less if all members were individually field-welded. The risk of deforming the column assemblies in the shop was eliminated, large transportation equipment and permits were not required, and St. Louis Steel Erection Co., which the fabricator hired for actual erection, could use relatively small cranes. The fabricator estimates the savings at $200,000, which Williams says was easily enough to pay for weld inspection.

This 1976 article from *Engineering News-Record* highlighted McCarthy's creative approach to challenges on the Boatmen's Bank Tower project. *(Image courtesy McGraw-Hill.)*

Cutting that cable would trigger a $5,000-per-hour penalty, a punishment McCarthy was able to avoid by careful shoring.[59] The shoring involved dropping rods anchored with packets of epoxy down cased holes reaching 100 feet below street level and 15 feet into bedrock. The epoxy packets would be ruptured by the rods once they reached bottom. But the packets, designed for fully vertical tubes, wouldn't slide all the way down the inclined tubes, and attempts to ram them into place made the

packets rupture prematurely. A frustrated foreman finally washed the packets to the bottom of the holes with a water hose.[60]

McCarthy continued to garner nationwide attention on other St. Louis projects. The firm once again worked at Barnes Hospital, constructing the $43 million West Pavilion. The project included a four-story addition to the East Pavilion so that both pavilions would stand 17 stories tall, and construction and renovation of the area between the pavilions. There was little working or storage room on site, but McCarthy, with careful delivery management, was able to stay ahead of schedule. All deliveries were carefully timed, as was the hoist time on the construction cranes. Subcontractors scheduled their deliveries around McCarthy's concrete pours and steel deliveries.[61] With the hospital functioning so nearby, the noise, dust, and vibrations inherent in construction work needed to be kept to a minimum, and McCarthy was able to do just that through careful work. In addition, Paddy McCarthy and Whitey Allmeyer, McCarthy's chief estimator, were credited with a modification to the construction methods that saved six months on a project originally scheduled to take 45 months.[62]

A New Parent

In 1977, McCarthy reorganized its corporate structure into a parent company, McCarthy Brothers Company, with three subsidiaries: McCarthy Brothers Construction Company (general contracting), McBro Planning & Development Company (construction management), and McCarthy Development Company (residential development). Mike became president of the parent company and McCarthy Development, Tim was president of McCarthy Brothers, and Burnet presided over McBro. The board also named new officers for the parent company, who would also serve as top-level managers for the three subsidiaries: Tom Dollar, vice president; Ogle Golden, vice president; Thomas "Pat" Waters Jr., director of international operations; and Tom Feldmann, treasurer and chief financial officer.[63]

As president of the corporation, Mike McCarthy was ready to take the next step in McCarthy's growth.

Beginning in the late 1970s, McCarthy significantly expanded its presence in Phoenix. The Commerce Building is one of many office complexes the company built there.

CHAPTER EIGHT

FROM COAST TO COAST

1977–1984

Tim is the engineer, the humanist, the nuts-and-bolts builder, and Mike McCarthy is the entrepreneur. Through interaction with those two guys, I got my download of what this company was about and why it was where I wanted to be.

—Mike Bolen

B Y 1977 IT SEEMED NOTHING could slow the McCarthy juggernaut. Fueled by McBro's construction management work, the company increased its total contract volume 2.5 times to more than $300 million during 1977. Volume for 1978 topped the previous year's mark at $324.3 million, and McCarthy began scouting new geographical areas, including Atlanta and Phoenix, for general contracting prospects.[1] In 1979 volume reached $534.4 million.[2] Only five years later, that number would seem small.

Much of McCarthy's growth during the late 1970s and early 1980s came from McBro, but the company also capitalized on a number of opportunities that helped it diversify and expand into new areas.

Opportunity in Phoenix

In 1978 McCarthy built a $5.7 million parking structure (losing almost $94,000 on the job, a very uncommon occurrence) and completed a $1.5 million contract for St. Joseph Hospital in Phoenix. Though the contracts were large, they were dwarfed by the $53.8 million contract to build an addition to St. Joseph, which McCarthy also took on that year.[3] McCarthy won the contract largely through the efforts of Roger Burnet and Rich Vandegrift.

Then something unexpected happened, and McCarthy's presence in Phoenix grew even larger. A local contractor called TGK Construction Company, under subcontract for McCarthy, had been doing much of the concrete work on the parking structure of St. Joseph Hospital. When TGK founder Theodore G. Knochenhauer died in a grievous automobile accident, the family put the firm up for sale.

Tim McCarthy, who as head of operations spent a lot of time in Phoenix, saw something familiar in TGK's workforce. "I recognized good construction people when I saw them, and they had some excellent construction people," Tim said.[4]

"TGK was one of the top contractors in the valley," said Bob Knochenhauer, nephew to Theodore Knochenhauer. "TGK had built many of the main projects in town, including most of the Motorola projects."[5]

Tim asked McCarthy's independent bonding agent, Gerry Murphy, to help him find the best way

McCarthy's work reshaped the Phoenix skyline with new office buildings, parking structures, hospitals, and other buildings. Pictured is the McCarthy-built office complex One Columbus Plaza.

for McCarthy to purchase the company. Murphy had become acquainted with McCarthy nearly a decade earlier, when he was a bonding agent for Aetna. "I fell in love with the McCarthy people, their attitude, their style," Murphy said.[6]

Tim and Murphy flew to Phoenix several times to learn all they could about TGK. An examination of its financial records was not encouraging; Murphy warned Tim not to buy the company. TGK had problems that would be a financial drain on McCarthy. "There's a lot of good strengths to TGK, but it's a bum deal," he told Tim.[7]

Back in St. Louis, Tim and Mike McCarthy had been debating the best way to establish McCarthy in Phoenix. Mike wanted to open a division office while Tim believed it would be better to gain entrée and a ready-made labor force by purchasing a local firm such as TGK. Murphy's warning about TGK should have nixed the purchase, but Tim, seasoned builder that he was, knew the importance of having a good field force; he didn't give up. It took some time, but McCarthy was able to structure the purchase in a way that sheltered it from any of TGK's unknown liabilities, and in 1980, McCarthy bought all of TGK's shares.[8]

Just before Murphy was to take a Hawaiian vacation with his wife, Mike McCarthy offered him the job of running TGK.[9] Murphy had doubts about his suitability for the job, telling Mike, "I'm a bonding guy and a financial guy and a business guy. I'm not a contractor. I'm not an engineer." But Mike insisted that Murphy would be perfect for the job.[10]

Murphy asked Mike if he could give an answer when he returned from his Hawaiian trip.

Opposite: Government buildings such as prisons made up a profitable sector for McCarthy. Building prisons like this one in Phoenix involved unique challenges because of the security aspects of the design.

Below: During the 1980s, McCarthy built Motorola's office building in Phoenix. It also constructed a number of semiconductor/clean room facilities for Motorola.

Reluctantly, Mike agreed, and Murphy flew back to Kansas City and then to Hawaii with his wife. Two days later, when the telephone rang in the Murphys' Hawaiian hotel room at 6:00 A.M., Murphy turned to his wife and said, "That can only be one guy." Of course it was Mike, wanting to know Murphy's thoughts on taking the job.[11] Clearly Mike wasn't giving up until Murphy agreed. Shortly after he returned from Hawaii, Murphy became TGK's president.[12] Three years later, TGK's name changed to McCarthy Western to more closely reflect its affiliation with McCarthy and its goal to expand into California and throughout the West.[13] When McCarthy restructured in the late 1980s, the division would be renamed the Southwest division.

As Tim had predicted, buying TGK turned out to be a good move. "Getting involved with TGK was key to McCarthy," said Jim Staskiel, who came to McCarthy in 1983 to start its legal department and later became general counsel. "The purchase allowed McCarthy to get another general contractor operation started. Plus, some of McCarthy's great leaders came from there."[14]

Staskiel was talking about Mike Bolen, who in 2000 would become McCarthy's chief executive officer, and Bob Knochenhauer, who became a McCarthy vice president and project director. Bolen remembered his initial concerns when he learned that McCarthy was buying TGK.

I thought McCarthy was the big tough hammer from St. Louis, and we were the local Phoenix guy

that they'd beat up. But very quickly after McCarthy bought TGK, we started seeing a lot of Tim McCarthy. He became my first real sense of what the company was all about. His values are so honorable. He's one of the great human beings. Tim is the engineer, the humanist, the nuts-and-bolts builder, and Mike McCarthy is the entrepreneur. Through interaction with those two guys, I got my download of what this company was about and why it was where I wanted to be.[15]

Building Perryville Prison was one of the new division's first big projects, and it led to other jobs, according to Bob Knochenhauer. "Perryville was a major project for those days," he said. "It was a success, and we had built positive relationships with the Department of Corrections, so years later we also built Lewis Prison, in Arizona, which was a huge project."[16]

McMerit Construction Company

In 1979, before the TGK purchase was finalized, McCarthy had opened a division in Atlanta, Georgia, under the direction of Jack McDonald.[17]

In 1980 McCarthy made a rare acquisition when it purchased J. L. Kelly, a construction firm based in Atlanta. To make it more identifiable with McCarthy, the firm was renamed McMerit Construction Company.

Bo Calbert joined McCarthy in 1982 as a field engineer. Over the years, he held a variety of positions in four different McCarthy divisions, including project manager, project director, vice president of operations, and, most recently, president of the Southwest division.

McDonald had been project director for several McCarthy jobs in the Southeast and had also coordinated the company's marketing efforts in that area.[18] He was elected to the board of directors of McCarthy Brothers Company in February 1979.[19]

Then in 1980, McCarthy acquired Atlanta-based J. L. Kelly Inc. and renamed it McMerit Construction Company. The purchase expanded McCarthy's geographic footprint, for McMerit, described by Mike McCarthy as an "open shop contractor," had performed work in Colorado, Florida, Georgia, and Texas.[20]

To spur short-term growth, in 1981 McMerit opened a second office, in Houston, Texas. The city's "accepting political structure" and positive "community attitude toward the efforts of a newcomer" promised to complement McCarthy's marketing-intensive method of drumming up business. In McCarthy's employee newsletter, Mike McCarthy noted that "the new office would provide opportunities for employees to gain further responsibilities and assist us in maintaining our substantial growth plan." He also pointed out that McMerit's presence in Atlanta and Houston and McCarthy Western's presence in Phoenix had positioned McCarthy "to cover the entire southern United States."[21]

Bo Calbert, who in 2001 became president of McCarthy's Southwest division, began his McCarthy career as a field engineer in the Houston office. He remembered how fast the city was growing. "There was a huge building boom going on," he said. "When I got to Houston, there were probably 65 tower cranes in the air."[22]

Working in a new city, McCarthy soon discovered, had its own set of challenges. Its first Houston project was a 12-story office building. When a bay collapsed while concrete was being poured for the fifth-floor deck, Calbert remembered that "in a matter of minutes, all the news stations were flying over in helicopters, and reports were being made about McCarthy being a St. Louis company, having a young group."[23]

What could have turned into a disaster became a learning experience instead. "We pulled together and did such a good job fixing it that the owner negotiated his next job with us," Calbert said. "We turned a problem into an opportunity."[24]

Construction Management

After a decade in operation, McBro, led by Roger Burnet, Richard Vandegrift, and Mike McCarthy, left little doubt that construction management had become the tail that wagged the dog. "McBro couldn't get out of the way of work," said Tom Dollar, who oversaw all of McBro's construction. "At one time I think I had 10 or 12 jobs scattered across the country. I was traveling all the time."[25]

At Burnet's suggestion, Mike decided in 1977 that McBro would manage its contracts all the way through construction rather than doing only preconstruction management. Previously McBro would bring in a contract, perform preconstruction management, and then turn over the actual construction to McCarthy Brothers.

By 1982 McBro had more than 275 employees at work on projects in 32 states. That year it had better than 60 construction management projects on the books and a contract volume of more than $729 million. In comparison, McCarthy's general contracting segment had just under 60 jobs with a total value of $400 million. McCarthy Western added another $85.5 million in contract volume, mostly from hard-bid work.[26]

By then McBro had grown enough that the St. Louis headquarters had become crowded, and McBro's leaders decided to open additional offices around the country. "We had close to 200 people in the building, and it was cumbersome to manage," said Vandegrift. "We were working coast to coast, and we figured it would be much easier if we were close to where some of

Above: Inside the McBro Rock Hill offices in 1979. McBro grew quickly in personnel, capabilities, and services. By 1982, it had more than 275 employees and projects in 32 states.

Left: Despite its growth, a family atmosphere pervaded McCarthy. McBro employees share a lighthearted moment in 1979.

Opposite: This 1977 advertisement explains that McCarthy Brothers is a general contractor while McBro specializes in construction management. Later, McBro expanded its services to include general contracting, and eventually its services were integrated into McCarthy Brothers.

the work was. Plus, a lot of the young people wanted an opportunity to grow, but their growth was somewhat stifled because we only had one guy at the top."[27]

In March 1981, McBro opened its third regional office, this one in Baltimore,[28] and a fourth regional office, in Seattle, opened in January 1982. The Seattle office was led by Ogle Golden, McBro vice president of construction. The office's primary function was to provide construction-phase support for McBro projects in the West and Pacific Northwest. By that time McBro also had smaller offices in Columbus, Ohio, and Orlando, Florida.[29]

Pursuing hospital jobs was McBro's main focus. "We really had a darn good thing going there," said Bud Guest, who was recruited by Burnet and Vandegrift in 1980. "Our batting average was phenomenal, and I think it was because we were ahead of our time in the hospital business. There weren't too many construction companies in those days that knew anything about hospitals."[30]

In March 1982, *Modern Healthcare* magazine named McBro the number one construction management hospital builder in the United States and called McCarthy Brothers "the undisputed leader among St. Louis construction firms and . . . among the top firms in the country."[31]

"Mike jumped up and down when I showed him the article," said Vandegrift. "We went from having a name that nobody had heard of in 1973 to being number one. We were exploding personnel-wise and working in communities we'd never worked in before."[32]

By the end of 1982, McCarthy was working on dozens of hospitals in some 20 states in every region of the continental United States and in the Virgin Islands.[33] Still McBro continued to grow. In 1983 it announced its first "full-service" regional

office, in Tampa. Prior regional offices had been set up to provide construction-phase support for ongoing projects; this office would offer preconstruction-phase management services as well, which included estimating, scheduling, and contracting services.[34]

General Contracting

While McBro brought in the majority of McCarthy's contract volume, the general contracting segment continued to do well, especially in the St. Louis area. In 1982 *Engineering News-Record* reconfirmed McCarthy's status as St. Louis's leading builder when McCarthy topped the journal's list of the area's most successful general contractors.[35] A look around St. Louis made the ranking obvious; McCarthy Brothers had major projects all over the St. Louis metropolitan area. These included airport terminals at Lambert Airport, bridge and highway overpass work, and several prominent downtown office buildings—the $24.4 million St. Louis Place, the $21 million KSDK-TV (the local NBC affiliate) building, and a $120 million, 44-story headquarters building for Southwestern Bell Telephone Company.[36]

McCarthy's construction management process was a big hit with hospital administrators. In the early 1980s, McCarthy was working on dozens of hospitals in every region of the continental United States, as well as in the Virgin Islands. This is St. Thomas Hospital in the Virgin Islands.

Though McCarthy was expanding across the United States, it continued taking on projects in its home city of St. Louis. Clockwise from left: a twilight view of the Southwestern Bell project under construction; a terminal at Lambert–St. Louis International Airport; and the Vandeventer overpass.

The Southwestern Bell headquarters building was project director John Heidbreder's first job with McCarthy, and it was a true learning experience. "I was the project engineer," he said, "but I was given the opportunity to do a lot of different things." Those things included steel shop drawings and structural changes as well as changes to the architectural finishes on the 41st and 42nd floors. "Getting materials and men up and down

that building was essential to the contractors' work," Heidbreder said. "But the logistics of getting 300 to 400 workers up and down that tower every day were incredibly involved. I think half of [each of] our weekly meetings was consumed by talking about who got hoisting rights and who got to use the crane." As a result of this daily challenge, Heidbreder learned the vital importance of communication and preplanning.[37]

Throughout the early 1980s, jobs in the construction division remained overwhelmingly local in nature. McCarthy's St. Louis clients included such corporate giants as Monsanto, McDonnell Douglas, A. G. Edwards, and Merrill Lynch. Other local clients included the Missouri Botanical Garden, the Lutheran Church, and Jaycees.[38]

Working on the Missouri Botanical Garden in 1980 was one of Steve Jennemann's first projects with McCarthy, and it proved to be a memorable

Opposite: The entrance to the Missouri Botanical Garden in St. Louis was transformed by this magnificent addition, known as the Ridgeway Center.

Below: The angular design of the Lutheran Church—Missouri Synod headquarters in St. Louis. Many of the structures McCarthy has built for religious organizations have unique architecture.

one. (Jennemann later became a project manager.) The emperor of Japan had donated a pagoda tree to the gardens, but the sewer system McCarthy was to install would have run directly into the tree. Project manager John Serafin "was out there digging the tree up, and here come the groundskeepers," Jennemann remembered. "They literally chained themselves to that pagoda tree and told him there was no way he was going to dig it up. So we had to negotiate where we were going to put that sewer line, and of course it went around the tree."[39]

McCarthy continued to win large hard-bid contracts in St. Louis, such as a $49 million clinical sciences building for Washington University. In 1982, of McCarthy's $400 million in construction contract operations, $135 million came from negotiated general construction contracts, all for St. Louis–area clients.[40]

McCarthy Parking Structures

McCarthy Parking Structures had been revived in mid-1977 to build what McCarthy's marketing people called the "Cadillac of parking structures." Though the parking structure division was solely McCarthy owned, the company partnered with Desman Parking Associates of New York, which specialized in parking facility design.[41]

"The garages had kind of disappeared off of McCarthy's radar screen," said Kris Anderson, who joined the parking division in 1980 and later became senior vice president of Compass Services (a McCarthy group that works with the healthcare community on all aspects of building and maintaining healthcare facilities). "We took the parking structures into a more modern era."[42]

McCarthy's modern parking structures were described as "poured-in-place (on site) post tension concrete structural frame" facilities that were

Kristopher N. Anderson (inset), president of McCarthy Parking Structures, oversaw design and construction of more than 100 parking facilities, including this one at St. Joseph Hospital in St. Charles, Missouri.

sturdy, adaptable to all climates, and virtually maintenance free.[43]

Bridge Building

Tommy McCarthy, son of Paddy, was a fourth-generation McCarthy builder, and he liked to build bridges. "He got interested in bridge work and took us into some high-tech stuff," said Tom Dollar, who by the late 1970s had become a senior vice president in operations, working with Tim McCarthy.[44]

Tommy had his father's support, Dollar said, and Mike McCarthy also encouraged Tommy's aspirations. "Tommy was a great engineer, a great theo-

retician," said Mike. "I think it meant a lot to our people to see these really extraordinary bridges go up that were McCarthy structures. They were like nothing anybody else in the country had built."[45]

With Tommy McCarthy as project engineer, in April 1978 McCarthy began to tear down the 64-year-old 12th Street viaduct in St. Louis to replace it with a new bridge. The 1,600-foot span of reinforced concrete had carried motorists across a series of railroad tracks into downtown St. Louis. McCarthy won the $4.7 million contract by bidding almost $300,000 below competitors on the demolition work. Unfortunately, problems cropped up almost immediately, driving up the demolition expenses and endangering the project's potential profits.[46]

The biggest problem involved ruptures to water mains and feeder lines that ran off a 36-inch-diameter cast-iron water main under the construction

St. Luke's West Hospital in St. Louis is one of many hospitals built by McCarthy.

site. The ruptures were caused by falling pieces of the viaduct. McCarthy had to halt work until the pipes could be excavated and repaired at McCarthy's (unbudgeted) expense. To minimize the impact on the underground pipes, McCarthy modified its demolition and rubble stacking procedures and carefully proceeded with the demolition.[47]

Other problems arose because the project was taking place over a series of railroad tracks, a dozen of which were active. All work on the project was subject to railroad schedules and priorities, and McCarthy had to make sure the tracks were undamaged and clear of construction debris. To protect active railroad tracks, McCarthy put crushed limestone between the rails and covered them with cut-up steel storage tank sections. It dismantled little-used tracks and stored the rails and ties, but the buried spikes punctured tires on McCarthy's equipment.[48]

A 58-foot span of the old viaduct that ran over elevated Amtrak tracks needed special handling. The span was made of four fabricated steel beams, each weighing 20,000 pounds. The beams were riveted together, and each beam was covered with 30 tons of concrete. McCarthy had hoped to knock the concrete off while the beams were still in place and then remove the beams. When that plan didn't work, the beams and their supports were stabilized and separated. Then the beams were carefully hoisted and lowered to the ground, where McCarthy's labor crew spent two days breaking off concrete. When

the steel beams were sufficiently free of concrete, McCarthy was able to salvage the steel.[49]

It is a testament to McCarthy's innovation, operations, and perseverance that the demolition problems didn't unduly delay the two-year project. The new 12th Street viaduct opened five months ahead of schedule, and the assistant chief engineer for the city of St. Louis praised the company's work, calling it "excellent."[50]

McCarthy won another bridge contract in November 1979. The $6.4 million Highway 367 Missouri River Bridge project involved building a bridge north of St. Louis over the Missouri River a short distance upstream from the river's confluence with the Mississippi River.[51]

More bridge contracts followed. By 1982 McCarthy was working on a $6.5 million contract for bridges on the St. Louis Innerbelt (Interstate Highway 170), a $4.1 million bridge across the Mississippi River south of St. Louis, and another viaduct overpass in St. Louis valued at almost $6.9 million.[52] McCarthy Western, in Phoenix, was working on a $4.5 million contract for bridges in Williams, Arizona. The subsidiary was also building a water plant, a steam electric station, and a turbine pedestal for a generating station.[53]

Newport Beach

In 1984 McCarthy opened a divisional office in Newport Beach, California, in the southern part of the state. Linda Osborn, who later became the office manager, was one of the first people in the Newport Beach office.

Osborn remembered how large the office was compared to the number of employees. "We wanted the community to know we were here to stay, but we didn't really have a lot of people in the office," she said. "So for our first open house, we had to make it look like we had more people here than we actually did. We decorated the office with papers and plans and nameplates on the wall. We had a great turnout, and from that point on, we just took off."[54]

In 1985 McCarthy's Phoenix office worked on a wide variety of contracts, including heavy civil work like the Mesa Water Treatment Plant, in Mesa, Arizona.

The McCarthy triumvirate in 1977 comprised (from left) Mike, Paddy, and Tim McCarthy.

When the office landed a Holiday Inn project in nearby Irvine, California, Frank Pasztor, project manager, and Greg Perkins, superintendent, were charged with gaining more of a foothold in the Southern California market. Pasztor later became the Southern California division's vice president of operations.

"Greg and I headed to California in a pickup truck, not knowing anyone," Pasztor remembered. "We got started without really having a presence in Southern California at all. We had a marketing element there that was planting seeds for the future, and that marketing effort did a great job in researching the territory, and that gave us opportunities to move forward."[55]

The Midas Touch

Having McCarthy as a last name had never been a prerequisite for advancement in the company, but for many years the majority of McCarthy's leaders bore the family name. Gradually that trend changed. Both old-line McCarthy builders and young go-getters who came into the company through start-up operations were able to rise to the top of McCarthy's ranks. In 1984, Roger Burnet, Tom Dollar, and Rich Vandegrift sat on the board of McCarthy's parent corporation, McCarthy Building Companies.[56] They also sat on

the board of McCarthy Brothers Company, as did Gerry Murphy. Joining Mike, Tim, and Paddy as officers were Burnet as executive vice president and president of McBro; Vandegrift and Dollar as senior vice presidents; and Murphy, Lloyd Hansen, Bud Guest, Will Theerman, and W. E. "Mickey" Morrison as vice presidents.[57]

Mike McCarthy seemed to have the Midas touch. In St. Louis, across the country, and even overseas, McCarthy was expanding faster in its quest to become the best builder ever. McCarthy companies were recognized as leading builders of hospitals and parking structures. Dominant in its home territory of St. Louis, the company was beginning to crack the California market and had seeded offices across the country. McCarthy had tripled the size of its headquarters in Rock Hill and invested in new technologies that would improve operations.[58]

Mike had already proved himself a successful pioneer, but he wasn't about to rest on his laurels. He still had plenty of new ideas to try— ideas involving construction technology, business management, and employee relations.

In 1984 McCarthy began constructing two parking garages in busy downtown Cairo, Egypt. Here, a throng fills a marketplace below one of the construction sites. *(Photo courtesy Chuck Avery.)*

CHAPTER NINE

OVERSEAS ADVENTURES

1977–1987

It was a routine event to threaten to kill someone's family. It was terrifying.

—Mike Bolen

THROUGH MCBRO, McCarthy had extended its footprint across the nation, and that success spurred the company to seek international business. It would have some success in Saudi Arabia, but after a nightmare project in Cairo, Egypt, the company's leaders decided not to actively pursue jobs away from American soil.

A Rich Project

Pat Waters had worked for McCarthy as a teenager in 1941 and had been a project superintendent in the early 1950s before leaving to run his own construction firm. He returned to McCarthy in 1977 as director of international operations, and he and his old friend Tim McCarthy began traveling to the United Arab Emirates, Kuwait, Saudi Arabia, and Nigeria in search of building projects to establish McCarthy on the international scene.[1] In June 1978, McCarthy won its first major overseas contract, a $93 million Armed Forces Hospital in Jeddah, Saudi Arabia.

McCarthy had plenty of competition for the petrodollars of the Arabian Peninsula, for Saudi Arabia was in the midst of a $142 billion development program.[2] Builders from around the world were looking to catch part of the action, but contracts were often won in Saudi Arabia through personal contacts rather than by open bidding—

and that's how McCarthy finally found its way into the lucrative Saudi market.[3]

"We finally hooked up with a Saudi prince who lived in Riyadh, a young man who went to school in St. Louis," Waters remembered. "He had married a St. Louis girl and had a brother who was quite influential. They hooked us up with a German construction company, and we joint ventured the military hospital in Jeddah."[4]

The German construction company was Held & Francke, a civil contractor and road builder with experience working in Saudi Arabia. Held & Francke's experience in that country and McCarthy's hospital expertise promised to make a good team. Although a minority partner (McCarthy owned 35 percent of the joint venture), the company would play a very public role.

"As far as the name and the government were concerned, we were the lead," said Mike Krueger, a McCarthy project director who spent three years working in Jeddah. "But financially, Held & Francke took the lead. They had a larger financial risk than

---

McCarthy was confident it could build parking structures for the Governorate of Cairo, but the company did not anticipate the drastically different socioeconomics and culture of Egypt. *(Photo courtesy Chuck Avery.)*

we did. As it turned out, we made a lot of money on the job."[5]

The Armed Forces Hospital was an elaborate facility, for the oil-rich Saudis spared no expense. Some patient rooms had imported marble coffee tables and Barcelona leather chairs. "The lobby was more like a Hilton Hotel than a hospital," Krueger said. "It had a three-story lobby, and all of the patient floors had balconies overlooking the lobby."[6]

The hospital in Jeddah was a turnkey project. When the builders turned it over to the client, it was fully equipped and ready to go. "When we finished, there were 100 cases of Pampers and 100 cases of rubber gloves in stock," said Krueger. "Surgical cabinets were filled with instruments. Everything was there: caps, gowns, sheets, towels, blankets. Except for the people and drugs, everything was there."[7]

Lessons Learned

The logistics of building a hospital in a country so far from home were challenging, but McCarthy rose to the occasion. "Everything had to be imported," said Krueger. "I think they even imported some of the aggregates [to make the concrete]—the sand wasn't the right coarseness."[8]

Even the labor had to be brought in. The contract specified that all necessary labor would be imported for the duration of the project and then removed from the country. McCarthy also had to build housing for its workers. Twenty-four housing units were built on the shores of the Red Sea, and

McCarthy built the Armed Forces Hospital in Jeddah, Saudi Arabia, and learned valuable lessons about building in a foreign country.

snorkeling near the sea's world-class reefs became a popular pastime for the McCarthy team.[9]

In addition to the hospital and housing units, McCarthy built a nearby water tower, underground water storage tanks, a warehouse, and a large commercial laundry facility.

Living and working in Saudi Arabia's strict Muslim society required some adjustments for the McCarthy crew. Alcoholic beverages were forbidden, and women were not allowed to work. But with the influx of outsiders looking to share in the Saudis' oil wealth, McCarthy was not the only western presence in Jeddah. Krueger remembered the diversity of his neighbors.

I lived in an apartment complex that had been built by a British company and was managed by a Japanese man who worked for a very wealthy Saudi—who was investing his money in this apartment complex. And everybody who lived there was European or Japanese or American. They were all educated foreigners who had management-type or technical jobs.[10]

Although Krueger didn't worry about crime while in Jeddah, he was never able to forget that he was in one of the most volatile regions on earth.

"All the people at McCarthy had most of their paycheck deposited in the United States so that if we had to leave, there wouldn't be a problem trying to remove savings," Krueger said.[11]

Krueger and the other McCarthy workers were in Jeddah on November 4, 1979, when militants stormed the United States embassy in Tehran, touching off the 444-day Iranian hostage crisis. Muslim fundamentalists also occupied the Great Mosque in the holy city of Mecca, just 30 miles from Jeddah, and held that holy site for two weeks. More than 100 were killed when the mosque was finally retaken.[12] During the siege, the state-owned Saudi press blacked out coverage of the politically volatile occupation. In Jeddah, rumors abounded. The BBC became the preferred news source for Krueger and the other westerners there.[13]

Great Expectations

In May 1984, Pat Waters, from McCarthy International, led a team to Cairo, Egypt, to take on McCarthy's next international project. Given the success and relative ease of the hospital project McCarthy had finished in Saudi Arabia, building a couple of parking garages in Egypt didn't set off any alarms.

"We were all kids," said Mike Bolen. "I mean Roger [Burnet] was the adult. And we'd had enough success that we convinced ourselves that this was all pretty easy and that we could do anything."[14]

McCarthy, aided by designs from its old partner Desman Parking Associates, won contracts from the Governorate of Cairo to build the Ataba Square garage and the Opera Square garage. McCarthy was also aided, or so it seemed, by the arrangements it had made with El-Refai Company (ERC). ERC was a limited partnership made up of members of the El-Refai family, including Osman El-Refai, who was also president of Phoenix Management and Systems Engineering, a U.S. firm specializing in technical services and training. Osman was joined by Gamal El-Refai, the general manager of a New Jersey corporation, who had a master's degree in engineering and eight years of U.S. field experience. Dr. El-Sayed El-Refai was a Cairo businessman who managed apartment buildings, and Dr. Abdul Monem El-Refai had spent the preceding five years supervising the construction of some 200 Cairo apartment units.[15]

On their résumés, the Egyptians appeared reputable and experienced. More than 15 years later, Kris Anderson summed up the reason McCarthy had so many problems in Cairo. "Our Egyptian partners sold us a bill of goods on what their capabilities were, and unfortunately, we didn't check them out well enough."[16]

In February 1984, McCarthy International and Dr. El-Sayed El-Refai signed an agreement: McCarthy, "one of the most reputable American

Above: An artist's rendering of the Ataba parking garage, built under contract to the Governorate of Cairo by McCarthy Brothers Construction and designed by Desman Parking Associates.

Right: The parking structure construction site in Cairo as seen from a hotel balcony *(Photo courtesy Chuck Avery.)*

The sign for McCarthy's office in downtown Cairo was printed in both English and Arabic. *(Photo courtesy Chuck Avery.)*

Corporations," according to Dr. El-Refai, would be responsible "for all technical and financial aspects of the project." ERC would provide "local management services."[17] ERC was also required to provide a 10 percent performance letter of credit.[18]

In May, after McCarthy had signed its contracts with the Governorate, it signed a 30-page Labor and Material Services Agreement with ERC that included eight pages of associated exhibits.[19] But what had originated as a simple project for two parking garages had become suddenly much more complicated, explained Chuck Avery, who spent several years in Cairo and later became vice president of quality and training.

We were the low bidder in an international design competition to build two parking structures in downtown Cairo, and the Egyptians managed to finagle that money out of the World Bank. Then, as soon as they got that money, they redesigned the plans to include two office buildings that adjoined the parking structures. The office buildings became a major part of the project. We ended up building two stand-alone parking structure/office building complexes in downtown Cairo.[20]

Although the scope of the project had grown, McCarthy was confident it could get the job done. Its strategy was smart; teaming with a local partner on a new job in a strange land should help ease the outsider's entrée into a foreign city. Unfortunately, McCarthy had chosen the wrong local partner.

Instant Trouble

It didn't take long for problems between ERC and McCarthy to surface. At first they were minor ones: questions about ERC's insurance policy or a letter from the bank requesting a change to ERC's letter of credit. Perhaps McCarthy should have been warned when the bank said it "would deem it preferable . . . that you request your subcontractors to secure irrevocable bonds confirmed by any New York money center bank."[21]

The problems quickly grew in scope. Two months into the project, ERC was already six weeks behind.[22] But that wasn't all. According to the agreement signed in May, McCarthy was to "furnish for the supplier's use" a new 45-cubic-meter

concrete batch plant, a fork truck at each job site, and a front end loader at the batch plant. McCarthy would deduct 25 percent of the equipment's value from the advance payment to ERC with further deductions from ERC's monthly payments. When the work was done, ERC was to pay McCarthy "the unrecovered portion of the cost of the concrete batch plant," which would then be turned over to ERC.[23]

In September ERC asked McCarthy project manager Mike Krueger for immediate funds to buy

A prominent sign in English and Arabic tells residents that the parking garages are being built for the Cairo Governorate. *(Photo courtesy Chuck Avery.)*

As subcontractor, ERC hired local workers to help build the parking garages. *(Photo courtesy Chuck Avery.)*

concrete equipment for the job: a concrete batch plant, concrete pump, and three trucks.[24] Instead McCarthy bought the equipment and tried to work out a lease purchase agreement with ERC. The subcontractor was not happy with that arrangement.

Legal counsel from the United States and Egypt advised that McCarthy's plan of a lease with option to buy was the best way to go, considering the circumstances. "We must control the equipment throughout the life of the project if we are responsible for purchasing and supplying the guarantees for the financing of the equipment," George Scherer told Osman El-Refai. "This position on our part is not negotiable."[25]

Scherer then brought up a second issue: the 10 percent performance guarantee required by the contract. He reminded Osman that McCarthy had agreed to accept a 5 percent performance guarantee with the understanding that ERC would "resolve

[its] financial situation in 6 to 8 weeks and be in a position to supply the balance." Despite frequent requests from Waters, the additional guarantee had not been produced. Scherer told Osman that McCarthy would stop consulting payments "until we have withheld a value equivalent to the 5% performance guarantee, or until you can deliver an acceptable performance L/C [letter of credit] as required by your Agreement." McCarthy said it would welcome alternative solutions.[26]

At ERC, Osman was reading the situation differently, as he made clear in a telex to Roger Burnet, who by then was McCarthy's chief operating officer. "I am astonished that you concur with [Scherer's] demands," he wrote. Doing so showed that "McCarthy does not abide by our contract. . . . McCarthy is determined to create unnecessary problems."[27]

On October 31, 1984, Osman answered Scherer's earlier letter, which he said asked him "to accept your nonnegotiable decision to make us pay you about £E470,000 as a gift to McCarthy or at best as additional guarantees to be put under your control until the last day of the project." He said he was "shocked and amazed at how you and your people in St. Louis think of us. Are we so naive?" McCarthy's "nonnegotiable position is absolutely unacceptable," and he found it "insulting and . . . an indication of what to expect from McCarthy."[28]

Nor was Osman pleased that McCarthy was withholding the consulting payments. ERC's "prices and effort were essential" in McCarthy's winning the Cairo jobs, Osman said, and "any profit resulting from this project is simply a sacrifice on my part and an unappreciated gift" to McCarthy.[29]

Osman agreed that he had promised the letter of guarantee within six weeks but argued that the promise "was based on everything moving as it should," including ERC's payments. He expressed his anger and offense at McCarthy's attempt to "discipline" him by withholding his consulting fees.[30]

McCarthy was willing to negotiate with ERC on those items it considered negotiable. Scherer sent ERC a revised lease-purchase agreement for consideration. He reiterated that McCarthy would pay the consulting fees in exchange for the required letter of credit.[31]

Tensions between ERC and McCarthy mounted. Osman sent a telex to Roger Burnet, appealing for his "personal intervention." He said Scherer's "demands" were unreasonable and that "the overall behaviour" of McCarthy's Egyptian team was "most disturbing and ungrateful to whatever modest assistance I rendered your company." McCarthy's attitude and demands were "an open request" for ERC to quit, Osman continued. Nonetheless, "[We] are willing and obliged, due to our moral values, to keep all our commitments to McCarthy which includes price sacrifices translated into the profit your company will receive from this project."

The dispute rolled into 1985. In mid-January, ERC replied to Scherer's earlier lease-purchase proposal with a marked-up copy of desired changes. ERC also began to threaten, in a veiled and polite way, job delays and resulting penalties from the Governorate.[32]

A few days later, Scherer sent a telex to Waters discussing ERC's latest demands. ERC wanted more money: a 25 percent discount on equipment and cash for "remobilization and job schedule condensation costs." Moreover, ERC wanted the right to use McCarthy's concrete equipment on other jobs. "This means we would be financing his other work for him if we let him do this," Scherer wrote.

Workers hoist materials using McCarthy equipment. ERC wanted to be able to use McCarthy's equipment on its other projects without having leased or paid for it.

"You'd have no guarantee the equipment would be there when you needed it."[33]

Waters wanted to try negotiating once more. In mid-February, he and Burnet met with Osman, but the meeting was a failure.[34]

Bolen explained how disconcerting the Egyptians could be. "There were a lot of threats going on, but we ended up finding out that such threats were a part of normal, everyday business. It was a routine event to threaten to kill someone's family. It was terrifying."[35]

A letter from Waters to Osman outlined his major concerns and his expectations for ERC. Job-site supervision was inadequate. McCarthy's "investigation and experience" suggested that none of ERC's supervisors had anywhere near the minimum 15 years' experience possessed by each of the McCarthy staffers in Cairo.[36] He also worried about the whereabouts of materials that would soon be needed for concrete pours, and he worried that the lack of proper tools and equipment was affecting the quality of the work."[37]

Waters then informed Osman that since the two parties had been unable to arrive at a lease-purchase agreement for the concrete equipment, he was withdrawing McCarthy's previous offer. Instead, McCarthy would "determine equitable long-term rental rates for your use of this equipment provided there is no change in our contractual relationship." ERC was told to turn over the equipment's registrations and duplicate keys.[38]

Letters and telexes continued to fly. Osman complained about McCarthy's attitude and said ERC was committed to doing the work it had contracted to do. He promised cooperation on all accounts and asked Waters's help in salvaging the companies' relationship.[39]

McCarthy was working hard to make the partnership with ERC work. In a handwritten cover memo to one of ERC's letters, Burnet scribbled, "Obviously our Egypt friend is going to take a much more reasonable approach. Let's try to continue to meet him 'half-way.'"[40]

The Proverbial Straw

Whatever cooperation sprang up between ERC and McCarthy was short lived. By the end of June, Waters had notified the Governorate of Cairo that McCarthy intended to terminate relations with ERC. The governor, Fathi Abou El-Ghar, responded that McCarthy "was fully responsible for all teams, works, workmanship and quality. . . . [T]he Governorate has no intervention in this respect."[41]

ERC, meanwhile, wasn't about to be fired without a fight. Osman sent McCarthy a "second and final notice" demanding immediate payment for work completed in March and April and threatening a work stoppage a week hence if not paid. He copied the governor and the Governorate's consulting engineers on the note.[42]

On July 2, 1985, McCarthy, ERC, and the consulting engineers met. McCarthy reiterated its position that ERC had fallen woefully behind schedule but agreed to postpone termination pending another meeting to review job progress. ERC claimed McCarthy had delayed its deliveries of rebar, failed to notify ERC about "quality problems," and withheld its payments in violation of the contract.[43]

That same day, Osman sent McCarthy a letter saying it was McCarthy's responsibility to get the Governorate's approval of all subcontracts and that if McCarthy had not done so, "our mutual contract is invalid and McCarthy did not have the legal power to sign it." McCarthy would be liable "for all financial and intangible damages caused to our company," Osman said, claiming that McCarthy had repeatedly directed ERC's work at the site "apparently without having the approval to do so by the owner."[44]

At a July 15 meeting between the Governorate's engineering consultant, McCarthy, and ERC, the consultant agreed to give McCarthy an extension for completing the work but warned it would be the last one he recommended. McCarthy told ERC it could earn a £E30,000 bonus by completing work on time.[45]

By August, however, the situation was only getting worse. Telexes flew between Cairo and St. Louis. As the international war of words raged, Burnet and

Opposite: As tensions between McCarthy and ERC mounted, work fell behind, and McCarthy's Pat Waters told ERC that the job site "lacked qualified supervision." *(Photo courtesy Chuck Avery.)*

Scherer met in St. Louis to find a way to extricate the company from a situation that was becoming surreal. An internal memo from Scherer to Burnet tried to quantify the extent of the damage. A breakdown comparing "payments made to and on behalf of" ERC showed ERC ahead by about £E925,000, or more than $761,000.[46]

Meltdown

Burnet had learned that ERC had privately contacted the Governorate and given "a distortion of fact." Trying to negotiate by telex was not working, Burnet told Osman. He suggested a meeting in Cairo in early September.

The proposed meeting was rebuffed, and the telex communication continued. "There seems to be considerable difference between your statements regarding current delays on the job and the record that Mike [Krueger] has maintained," Burnet wrote. "Further McCarthy is continuing to supplement your contract by financing the purchase of materials for your work."[47]

ERC was apparently getting desperate. Osman's next telex had an angry tone. "Work is progressing, proving to all involved that I am serious and capable of finishing the job." ERC accused McCarthy of "intransigence and foot dragging" in response to its "sensible plea for cooperation." McCarthy had seven days to meet ERC's demands or face unspecified response.[48]

Burnet continued to be polite but firm.

I do not understand the positions you are taking relative to the performance of El-Refai Company's agreement for the project. We believe McCarthy's position was clearly communicated to you in previous telexes. . . . [Y]ou have now delivered an ultimatum to McCarthy concerning items which McCarthy will not agree to.[49]

Although Burnet maintained a cordial, or at least polite, tone in his written correspondence with Osman, Burnet's and Osman's dislike of each other sparked a confrontation during one of Burnet's many Cairo visits.

I was staying over there in a hotel, and one day Osman and I got into the biggest fistfight you've ever seen—two old guys just banging away. Well, fortunately we had people on both sides that held us back or we both would have killed each other. I hadn't gotten into a fistfight since I was 14 years old. I just couldn't stand this guy, and I lost it.[50]

McCarthy continued to prepare for ERC's termination and on September 12, 1985, told the Governorate that the firing would take effect in a week. Mike McCarthy personally informed the governor of McCarthy's decision and affirmed McCarthy's ability and commitment to the project.[51]

On the day of ERC's termination, McCarthy applied to the Cairo Bank for payment of ERC performance bonds totaling £E741,416, or $610,185.[52]

Relations between ERC and McCarthy were already quite tattered, and they fell apart entirely when ERC was fired. ERC occupied the job sites and shut down the work. McCarthy had its people ready to work, but the threats and "incidents of violence" directed at Waters and others on the site had them fearing for their safety.[53]

Issuing threats seemed a normal part of doing business for the Egyptian contractors, so when Mike McCarthy sent a telex to Osman telling him that if any of McCarthy's people came to harm "it will be your last day of rest on the face of this earth," Osman took the letter as a death threat.

"The Egyptians had been making all these death threats, but Mike's letter turned everything around," said Avery. "All of a sudden these guys were like, 'These Americans are crazy.' Mike meant that he'd legally pursue Osman to the ends of this earth, but Osman interpreted the words as a death threat. That was the turning point."[54]

Though Mike's words were misinterpreted, ERC's threats were all too real. As Mike McCarthy remembered, the day after McCarthy fired ERC, Osman sent in a gang of "thugs with guns," who shot up the job site. When the authorities were slow to respond, McCarthy hired a few dozen professional wrestlers, who apparently were "idolized" in Egypt, to serve as security. When the two forces met, "all hell broke loose," said Mike.[55]

The thugs with guns won. Mike McCarthy repeatedly appealed to the governor for help for McCarthy's people and for the benefit of the project. Finally, on October 11, 1985, Mike received a telex from the Governorate. "The site has been cleared for McCarthy to resume work," it blandly advised. No one, including ERC, would be allowed to delay the project.[56]

Just like that, the war was over. "We showed up one morning at 7 o'clock, and all these guys were gone," said Waters.[57]

To the Rescue

Once ERC was off the site, McCarthy scoured the country in search of workers and brought in reinforcements. "I spent about six months running around the States, recruiting people to send to Cairo to do the work," said Bolen.[58]

Right: McCarthy brought in a number of American workers to finish the job.

Below: After McCarthy fired ERC, it had to visit the marketplace every day to hire local workers. *(Photo courtesy Chuck Avery.)*

McCarthy took over as general contractor, but the role wasn't quite like being general contractor on a job in downtown St. Louis. Although McCarthy imported over two dozen of its own people, it still needed to hire laborers on a daily basis at the local market—an incredible feat in a foreign land, Avery said, but one McCarthy was determined to accomplish. With ERC out of the way, "the rate of the project, everything, just turned right around, and we started pouring concrete every night."[59]

In the minds of McCarthy's people, there was never any doubt the job would be finished, though as Bolen observed, "It would have been very easy to quit. It would have probably even been the bright business decision. But we found a way to solve all the problems. We taught ourselves how to work internationally."[60]

"I really didn't know much about McCarthy at all," Avery said. "They were just another construction company that I'd hooked up with. I'm looking at this and thinking, 'Boy, this might be a good one to pull out on.' But that was just unheard of. For the hardcore McCarthy guys who had come over from St. Louis, it was just not an option."[61]

It Ain't Over . . .

Although the situation in Cairo had drastically improved and McCarthy was making good progress on the two projects, the company's woes were far from over. By January 1986 McCarthy was still mired in legal disputes with ERC. It had been unable to collect on the letter of credit, and worst of all, the Governorate hadn't paid McCarthy for work done since the previous July. McCarthy had been financing the work out of its own pocket to the tune of $2 million.[62]

ERC had requested that the Governorate hold back $3.5 million of McCarthy's contract against a potential arbitration award in its favor. Because ERC's total contract had been for only £E3.3 million (about $2.7 million), McCarthy felt ERC's request was ridiculously high. McCarthy had been striving mightily for a compromise that would satisfy the Egyptian firm. It had agreed to arbitration in Cairo rather than a neutral location. It had offered to drop its demands for payment on ERC's performance letters. But nothing it offered was enough.[63]

McCarthy looked for help wherever it could. In Cairo, the company appealed to the Governorate, saying it had become "apparent to all concerned that [ERC's] sole purpose was to stall negotiations and bring about a stoppage of the project."[64] Burnet even sought a meeting with Egypt's president, Hosni Mubarak. Back in the United States, the company asked Missouri Congressman Richard Gephardt to use his influence to help.[65]

McCarthy was struggling against the entrenched bureaucracy of a country it didn't understand. "There were a lot of issues, and Cairo is not Shreveport, Louisiana; it's not St. Louis, Missouri," said Scherer.[66]

The United States, Bolen explained, is a business-friendly place, but many other countries had a different philosophy. "You get outside the United States, and you expect to be able to rely on laws and rules and procedures. You find out that you can't, that it isn't about that. It's about today and who has the power and what it takes to get them to exercise it on your behalf. It's a very corrupt process, and we were kids. We were naïve. We had no clue."[67]

In February 1986, Burnet informed the Governorate that the courts in Cairo had ruled in McCarthy's favor on some of the ERC-generated lawsuits, which meant the Governorate could pay McCarthy the full amount owed to date. Payment requests for work from July 1985 to December 1985 were ready to submit, lacking only the paperwork for an approved time extension.[68]

In a letter, Burnet explained to the governor that the project had been on an accelerated schedule since October. McCarthy couldn't keep operating at the current rate without getting paid, and Burnet asked that the governor use his "good offices to expedite" approval of the time extension so McCarthy could continue financing the work.[69]

A few days later, the Governorate's engineering consultants informed McCarthy they were prepared to sign and forward the time extension documents but wanted McCarthy to sign a statement waiving its rights to additional extensions or additional money for delays.[70]

The statement did not jibe with what McCarthy understood to be the agreement of previous meetings with the governor. At an earlier meeting McCarthy had agreed, at the governor's request, to continue working even though the company was under "extreme financial hardship" for lack of payment. The governor had promised then that an extension would be forthcoming. McCarthy agreed to keep working, at an accelerated pace when possible, "to show McCarthy's faith to your excellency and the Cairo Governorate of McCarthy's commitment to abide by its contractual obligations." McCarthy believed it had justifiable claims in excess of £E750,000. To force the company to waive its right to pursue those claims in exchange for approval of the undisputed claims was "unreasonable and unfair," McCarthy argued.[71]

After a few more weeks of negotiations, the two sides reached an agreement. McCarthy would waive claims for further time extensions on work done to date and would waive claims for additional monetary compensation. In exchange, the Governorate would issue a certificate of substantial completion even if certain parking equipment and elevators, which had been sitting in the Port of Alexandria for nearly a year waiting to clear customs, hadn't yet been installed. Interim completion was set for March 25 and the

handover date for July 20. If McCarthy met those dates, its contractual obligations for "timely and complete performance" would be considered fulfilled.[72]

Within a few weeks, however, Burnet was once again appealing to the governor, for McCarthy had not received any of the things it had been promised.[73] Nearly five months later, in late August, Burnet visited Cairo and got some good news. All work performed and approved by the consultants would be paid within 10 days.[74] Part of the money owed McCarthy actually was paid, but not all. Burnet once again wrote the governor for help.[75]

In October 1986, at long last, certificates of substantial completion were granted on both the

---

In October 1986, after a long battle with ERC and officials in Egypt, McCarthy was able to complete the Ataba Square and Opera Square parking structures. The garages could hold a combined total of 2,000 cars. *(Photos courtesy Kris Anderson.)*

Ataba and Opera projects. McCarthy submitted its final billings to the Governorate and once again waited for its money. The project was finished and the Governorate had its garages, Burnet wrote to the governor, "so there should be no reason why McCarthy should continue to bear the burden of financing the project for the Governorate."[76]

As the year drew to a close, Scherer tried to quantify the extent of McCarthy's losses from the Cairo project. He made his calculations assuming no recovery for sales of remaining assets and equipment, a total write-off of ERC's claims and any outstanding subcontractor back charges, and full payment from the Governorate. The total was a staggering $4.2 million.[77]

The nightmare of lawsuits and nonpayment would not let up. Waters met with the Governorate regularly in hopes of speeding up McCarthy's payment even though he believed it a futile gesture. "I don't have any hopes at all; no contractors working for the state or federal governments have been paid lately and many jobs are shut down," he wrote at one point.[78] By February 1987, it had been nearly

Representatives of McCarthy and Egypt at the dedication of the parking garages. Standing at far left is Fathi Abou El-Ghar, governor of Cairo. Standing third from left in the row immediately behind the men kneeling is Egyptian President Hosni Mubarak. To Mubarak's left is Bob Waters, superintendent (and brother of Pat Waters). To Waters's left, in red tie, is Mike Krueger, project manager, and to his left, Ajaj Andary, a Lebanese American hired by Pat Waters who returned to the United States to do several other jobs for McCarthy. *(Photo courtesy Pat Waters.)*

a year since McCarthy had received a payment from the Governorate, but the payments were still being delayed for lack of the signed documentation for the time extension that had been granted more than a year earlier.

At least there was a glimmer of good news; in February McCarthy reached an agreement with ERC.[79] The details of the agreement were not disclosed, but by that time McCarthy must have been happy that it would never have to hear from ERC again.

Epilogue

A 1989 profile of Mike McCarthy reported Mike saying he had recently received a letter from the Governorate of Cairo inviting McCarthy to do another project there. Apparently McCarthy was the only construction firm that had managed to finish a project on time.[80]

Though McCarthy's disastrous experience in Cairo certainly deterred the company from actively seeking overseas contracts, McCarthy did complete a few other international projects. At around the same time as the parking structures were being built in Cairo, McCarthy was designing and building Subanj Jaya Hospital, in Kuala Lumpur, Malaysia. Later, McCarthy served as construction manager for St. Thomas Hospital, on the island of St. Thomas in the Virgin Islands, and was general contractor for Blue Water Bridge, in Ontario, Canada. In the early 1990s, McCarthy would partner with IDC, a design firm in Portland, Oregon, and Ishimoto, a Japanese architect, to manage construction of a computer chip fabrication plant in Serdai, Japan, for a Toshiba-Motorola joint venture.

McCarthy worked on a number of airports, including the Sky Harbor Airport, in Phoenix, Arizona. Its construction was completed in 1990.

CHAPTER TEN

DIGGING ITS WAY OUT

1985–1993

*All growth comes through pain and suffering. If you want to grow,
you'd better get ready to suffer.*

—Mike McCarthy, 2001

BACK IN 1971, WHEN MIKE McCarthy became chief operating officer, the company had billed almost $25 million.[1] Over the next 14 years, McCarthy exploded out of St. Louis, sprouting branches across the country and overseas. In 1985 McCarthy's gross revenue was 25 times what it had been in 1971.[2]

But the cost of doing business finally overwhelmed the rapid growth, and even robust income couldn't stem the rising tide of red ink. McCarthy lost money in 1985, 1986, and 1987.

A number of factors contributed to McCarthy's financial woes. Many companies were suffering during the recessionary 1980s, and McCarthy faced increased competition in its core businesses as other construction firms sought to emulate its success. The company had begun expanding beyond the healthcare market and into real estate development and had opened offices around the country to take advantage of that market. Then the real estate market tanked. Internationally, a promising start in Saudi Arabia had been soured by an expensive nightmare in Cairo. The financial losses from Cairo were not insignificant, but perhaps as damaging to McCarthy were the other company resources poured into that insatiable project: the attention, time, and energies of McCarthy's top management and the sudden stateside depletion of experienced field forces.

The Phoenician

In 1986, in the midst of the company's troubles in Cairo, the Phoenix office began work on a luxury, five-star resort near Scottsdale, Arizona, called the Phoenician Resort Hotel. The difficult project was managed by onsite project director Bob Knochenhauer, who had come to McCarthy in 1980 with the TGK acquisition. The initial contract was for $55 million, but that figure grew to nearly $150 million due to numerous change orders from the owner, Charles Keating Jr.

Keating, known for his conservative values and risky business ventures, owned American Continental Corporation, which in the early 1980s had become the largest residential homebuilder in Arizona. In the mid-1980s he bought Lincoln Savings and Loan, based in Irvine, California, and began expanding the business, at the same time deftly avoiding federal regulation. (In 1979 Keating had settled with the Securities and Exchange Commission, which charged him with issuing fraudulent bank loans through his Ohio-based

Chairman Mike McCarthy led the company through its downsizing and restructuring in the late 1980s, a period in the company's history that he referred to as "very rough."

insurance and bank holding company.) When he began the Phoenician project, Keating was the country's number one donor of "soft" campaign funds and was well known in Arizona as "the deepest pockets in Phoenix."[3]

The Phoenician was dubbed by analysts a "stunning monument to Keating's ego." So it was little wonder that Mike Hurst remembered the project as one of the most challenging he'd ever worked:

> Charlie [Keating] and his wife Mary Elaine were deeply, personally involved in the design and would walk the project every weekend and start changing things. This was a project where literally we would have people up placing concrete, and the Keatings would come out and say, "Stop." We'd say, "We're already pouring. The concrete is in the forms," but they'd say, "Stop. Take the form apart and get rid of it." And so we'd get out water hoses and wash out the concrete and wait until they decided what they wanted to do.[4]

Though the project was taxing, Hurst acknowledged that Charlie and Mary Elaine had created a wonderful facility. They were more than glad to pay for the changes they demanded, and they paid on time—at least at first. "We had received 33 consecutive monthly payments on the 10th of the month just like clockwork," Hurst said.[5]

The Phoenician opened its doors on October 1, 1988, but on the 10th of the month, McCarthy had yet to receive its expected payment of some $18 million, a huge sum of money for the then struggling company.

"So we started talking with them, and they gave all these reasons why they couldn't pay it," Hurst said. A month later, with tensions between McCarthy and the owner escalating, "The feds came in and indicted Charlie, and his whole world started collapsing," Hurst said.[6]

Federal regulators had had enough of Keating's questionable practices. In April 1989, American Continental filed for bankruptcy, and federal agents

Right: An artist's rendering of the Phoenician. Little did McCarthy know when it took the contract how complicated the project would become.

Below: During construction of the Phoenician, Charles Keating (the owner) and his wife submitted numerous change orders.

seized Lincoln Savings and Loan. Keating's business practices had set off the savings-and-loan crisis of the 1980s.[7]

Unable to wrangle its $18 million from Keating, McCarthy began talking to the Office of Investment for Kuwait, which co-owned the hotel with Keating's savings-and-loan company. The talks dragged on for many months, and then in 1990 McCarthy finally arrived at an agreement with the Kuwaitis. "They were going to issue us a check and get us paid off," Hurst said.

But nothing seemed to be easy for McCarthy during this time. In August Kuwait was invaded by Iraq, under Saddam Hussein. As if that weren't enough, the U.S. government's Resolution Trust Corporation (RTC) began questioning McCarthy in connection with Keating.

In 1987 McCarthy had taken a $1.4 million contract to build a guesthouse at the Keating residence. When the government investigated Keating's business dealings, "They started looking at McCarthy because they were absolutely sure that we had taken money from the hotel to build the house and that Keating had moved the money," Hurst said.[8]

When the RTC mentioned racketeering charges, Mike McCarthy called Gerry Murphy, who was president of the Southwest division in Phoenix.

"Be honest with me, Gerry," Mike said. "We've talked about this from the beginning. Don't kid me. Is there any dirt on our skirts here? Because I don't think there is."

Murphy replied with no hesitation. "Absolutely none."[9]

In the spring of 1992, Hurst accompanied Murphy to a meeting with the RTC. "They were going through this whole theory of how we improperly

McCarthy finished building the massive and gorgeous Phoenician Resort Hotel in October 1988, but it had to wait until 1992 for the final payment.

allowed Keating to build this house on money from the hotel," said Hurst. After an hour-long presentation on McCarthy's theoretical malfeasance, the RTC lawyer asked for Murphy's response to the allegations.

Murphy, no longer able to tolerate the baseless accusations and bullying, stood up and cried, "F— you, f— you, f— you!"

"He said that at least 50 times as he's walking out of the room," Hurst remembered.

After Murphy had left, the lawyer calmly turned to Hurst and asked what he had to say.

"I think he said it all," Hurst said.

That was the last time McCarthy met with the RTC. "We got our money in about 30 days," said Hurst.[10]

Ironically, it was the federal government that paid McCarthy what it was owed, from escrow funds that had been set aside before the project began. McCarthy received a cash settlement, and the RTC assumed McCarthy's subcontractors' liabilities on the project.[11]

"It was bad. That was a really tough time," said Mike McCarthy. "But tough times are what make you. The easy times don't make you. All growth comes through pain and suffering. If you want to grow, you'd better get ready to suffer."[12]

Though the situation was certainly nothing to chuckle at while it was unfolding, Project Manager Steve Jennemann was able to joke about it years later.

When I talk about the Phoenician [with prospective clients], I'm always asked if I can get a recommendation from the previous owner. I have to tell them, "Well, I can—but he's in prison right now."[13]

Dartmouth-Hitchcock

Around the time the Phoenician was being built, McCarthy was hired by Mary Hitchcock Memorial Hospital, in Hanover, New Hampshire, to manage a $30 million hospital addition. It was a sizable contract, but it was about to get a whole lot bigger.

The hospital was "already the biggest thing in town," said Bud Guest, and the new hospital would have dwarfed ivy-league Dartmouth College's campus, which was built around downtown Hanover's

The $165 million Dartmouth-Hitchcock Medical Center, in Lebanon, New Hampshire, was a crucial project for McCarthy. Construction began in the summer of 1988 and was completed on time and on budget in October 1991.

quaint town square. The area's troublesome traffic flow would only be worsened by a larger hospital. For these reasons, Mary Hitchcock Memorial decided to build an entirely new hospital on undeveloped land in nearby Lebanon, New Hampshire.[14]

What had started as a $30 million hospital addition grew to become the $165 million, 1-million-square-foot Dartmouth-Hitchcock Medical Center, comprising Mary Hitchcock Memorial Hospital, the Dartmouth Medical School, and the Hitchcock Clinic. "It was probably the biggest change order we ever had in the history of the company," said Guest.[15]

McCarthy was originally hired as construction manager for the Dartmouth-Hitchcock job, but when the bid from the general contractor came in too high, McCarthy requested a rebid. "We knew there weren't any contractors up in that area big enough to do the job," said Roger Burnet, then McCarthy's president.[16]

Though the general contractor knew McCarthy would also be bidding, its numbers were unchanged for the second bid. Burnet had anticipated this and had set McCarthy's bid at about $1 million lower than the general contractor's original bid. "It was a small amount," said Burnet, "but we had the job—and it was one of our best jobs."[17]

Dartmouth-Hitchcock Medical Center was a watershed project for McCarthy. As construction began in the summer of 1988, the company was reeling from three years of losses and was in the midst of restructuring. It was McCarthy's largest contract to date, a demanding job with unique requirements. It was also being built on a remote mountaintop in faraway New Hampshire.

"It was a huge project," said Mike McCarthy, "and Roger put a very young man on the job."[18]

That "very young man" was Bo Calbert, who at age 29 was viewed by some as too young and inexperienced to handle such a large, important job. "There were a lot of guys who were a lot more qualified," Calbert remembered, "but Roger really stood behind me, and Mike did too."[19]

Calbert had worked in Houston under Jack McDonald and had managed jobs for McCarthy in Texas and Florida, where he spent a year working closely with Burnet to finish the company's projects after McCarthy closed its Tampa office. Calbert had impressed Burnet enough that he was willing to put the company's future in Calbert's

hands. Calbert was well aware of what was at stake. "Roger told me I was the right guy for the job," Calbert said. "But he said, 'By the way, if it doesn't go well, we'll probably lose the company.'"[20]

Burnet had chosen his man wisely. Dartmouth-Hitchcock became one of McCarthy's most successful projects. Calbert credited the amazing teamwork of all those involved, from the owners to the tradesmen in the field. McCarthy's meticulous construction management also deserved credit. Its careful planning allowed for harsh winter weather that could shut down unprotected work. Subcontractors were screened and prequalified based on their abilities, financial stability, and willingness to negotiate special pricing.

The preconstruction stage took about three years, and once construction began, the benefits of all those well-laid plans became evident. The project progressed on schedule, aided by regular scheduling meetings and careful follow-up by McCarthy. Any problems were quickly addressed, which kept delays and cost increases to a minimum.

Dartmouth-Hitchcock Medical Center was finished in October 1991, on time and on budget. McCarthy made "a good fee" on the project, but more importantly, the struggling company had gained credibility. "We did it, and nobody believed it could be done," said Mike McCarthy. "The owner/client became our best reference. I think most hospital owners felt that if we could build a hospital of this quality away from any recognizable labor force, then we could probably build anything any place. That's why Dartmouth-Hitchcock was so important."[21]

The Problem with Bridges

By 1986 McCarthy had created a separate division to pursue highway work, bridges, and heavy civil projects such as wastewater treatment plants. Unfortunately, the Heavy/Highway division, as it was called, lost money in 1987 and 1998.[22] Most of the losses were incurred on bridge projects.

Just as Mike McCarthy had been allowed to pursue parking structures and hospital construction management, Tom McCarthy had been allowed to pursue bridges. Unfortunately, the inherent aspects of bridge building—the complexity of the design and the uncertainty of extenuating circumstances such as flooding—made bridge building exceptionally prone to problems.

Bridge building, explained Tom Dollar, who was appointed president of the Heavy/Highway division, was very high-tech, very high-risk, and very unlike McCarthy's other work.

Your temporary facilities are so much more complex, and your engineering is so much more complex. There's so much that's not on a drawing that you have to do, and you have to understand the process to get the work. We got into something we didn't know anything about. It was not only new to this company; it was new to this country. We just weren't very well versed in it.[23]

McCarthy lost money on both the Robert E. Lee Bridge, in Richmond, Virginia, and the Bayview Bridge, which spanned the Mississippi River at Quincy, Illinois. Working on both bridges at the same time was one reason McCarthy lost money. Both bridges were very high risk projects, and each gobbled up a nice chunk of the company's

The Robert E. Lee Bridge, in Richmond, Virginia, was a highly complex construction project and required a lot of McCarthy's resources. Both the Robert E. Lee Bridge (above and below) and the Bayview Bridge (next page) were high-risk projects for McCarthy, and the company lost money on both.

The Bayview Bridge, which spans the Mississippi River at Quincy, Illinois, entailed a complicated twin-tower design and was a difficult project for McCarthy.

resources. When unforeseen circumstances occurred (the cofferdam at the Richmond site washed out due to floodwater, for example), they ate up even more resources.

By the time McCarthy realized it was losing money on the projects, there was little to be done but finish them. "We had the job to do, and there was nothing we could do about the numbers," Dollar said. "We just had to go there and hack it out."[24]

Years later, Mike McCarthy credited people like Dollar and Tom McCarthy for their tenacity. "The fact that they endured said a lot to our people about what we could accomplish," he said. "And I think it meant a lot to our people to see these really

extraordinary structures go up that were McCarthy-built and that nobody else in this country had ever built. . . . I think the division was real important. Every one of the projects won an award."[25]

The Clark Bridge

In July 1990, McCarthy began work on a bridge that would span the Mississippi River at Alton, Illinois, a few miles upriver from St. Louis. The new Clark Bridge, named for explorer William Clark of the Lewis and Clark Expedition, used a cable-stayed design that was selected for its beauty and ability to allow wide, unobstructed spans for the river traffic passing below.[26] (The nearby Lewis Bridge spans the Missouri River and was also built by McCarthy.) The Clark Bridge had some pioneering features, including the saddle-styled pylon that held the supporting cables high above the bridge.[27]

McCarthy, as part of a joint venture, won the contract for the three-span, 1,360-foot, cable-stayed section of the bridge. The more conventionally designed approaches were bid and built separately.[28]

Below and opposite: The Clark Bridge, spanning the Mississippi River between Alton, Illinois, and St. Louis, was a major undertaking for McCarthy. Construction began in July 1990 and was completed well before the January 1994 opening. All of the bridges McCarthy built in the early 1990s won awards, but the Clark Bridge was truly a star, winning numerous awards for engineering and construction.

The design and construction of the Clark Bridge were carefully documented by architect-turned-filmmaker Neil Goodwin, of Peace River Films in Cambridge, Massachusetts. "To Build a Bridge," his documentary on the Clark Bridge and the people who built it, aired on PBS's *Nova* series in 1997. Goodwin praised the bridge builders for the job they had done under difficult and dangerous conditions, noting, "They built it as a team and solved every problem that came their way."[29]

He also documented the problems the builders encountered. One of the worst was some bad concrete at the top of one of the towers, which had hardened before it was discovered. Workers with jackhammers labored 24 hours a day for 14 days straight to chip off the concrete so it could be replaced. Another problem occurred when the cabling failed a strength test after a batch of steel had corroded before receiving protective coating.[30]

There were also triumphs, or at least small victories. The bridge's steel superstructure was built from the two approaches to meet in the middle, high above the water. The trick was to make sure the two sides met. On a warm spring day in 1993, the two ends of the bridge deck were joined when a 15-foot steel beam was "deftly hoisted" into place for a fit as nearly perfect as could be.[31]

A week later an engineer from another contractor reported that the project would be completed on budget and that they had "run into very few surprises."[32] But the workers were about to get a major surprise, compliments of Mother Nature. The Great Flood of 1993, although thwarted in St. Louis by the floodwalls McCarthy had built in the 1960s, still devastated areas along the Mississippi and Missouri Rivers. The incomplete Clark Bridge was undamaged, but all work halted for two months after the Army Corps of Engineers shut down barge traffic on the river. Without barges to deliver workers and materials to the bridge, McCarthy was paralyzed.

"The water was high, and the current was very strong," said Tom Dollar. "Docking facilities were a problem, and then the river traffic, what little there was of it, was dangerous."[33]

By late August, the flood relented enough for work to continue, but now labor disputes and logistics plagued the project. A local union threatened strikes, and traffic bottlenecks hampered concrete deliveries. Delivering concrete to the bridge was a complicated undertaking. Trucks had to cross the river on the old bridge to reach the barge that would carry the concrete out to the construction site. There, it was pumped into other trucks that earlier had been hoisted to the bridge deck. Those trucks then drove the concrete where it was needed.[34]

As the months passed, McCarthy raced against the clock, trying to make up for lost time. "We were working long hours to begin with," said Dollar. "But we did use some overtime techniques to save ourselves some time in the overall schedule."[35]

The company performed admirably well considering the circumstances. The bridge opened on January 5, 1994, and except for some "cosmetic" work that couldn't be done until spring's warmer temperatures, the bridge job was complete.[36]

The Clark Bridge quickly became a star. In 1994 it won awards from the American Society of Civil Engineers-St. Louis Chapter (Project of the Year), the Structural Engineers Association of Illinois (Most Innovative Structure), the Consulting Engineers Council of Illinois (Eminent Conceptor Award), and the American Consulting Engineers' Honor Award. In later years, the bridge garnered awards from the Concrete Council, the American Institute of Steel Construction, and the *St. Louis Construction News and Review* (Readers' Choice Award). In 1995, as tribute to its soaring beauty and sturdy functionality, the Clark Bridge was named one of the 12 best bridges in America by the American Consulting Engineers Council.[37]

Too Many Branches

In the mid- and late 1980s, McCarthy had offices across the country and overseas. In addition to the home office in St. Louis, McCarthy offices could be found in Kansas City, Missouri; Houston, Texas; Phoenix, Arizona; Tampa, Florida; Newport Beach, California; Boston, Massachusetts; Arlington, Virginia; London, England; and Cairo, Egypt.

The rapid expansion had been costly for McCarthy, especially after the economy took a sharp slide in 1987. It took deep pockets to come into a local construction market as an outsider. "We actually thought that we could do all these things," said Roger Burnet. "We found out the hard way that when you're the low bidder going against the local people, you've got a problem. You don't know where the problem is, but you got a problem."[38]

Jim Faust, a director in human resources, joined McCarthy's accounting department in 1983. A year later, he transferred to Houston as part of McCarthy's efforts to decentralize accounting procedures and became the company's first division controller. According to Faust, "When we started our growth pattern in the early to mid-1980s, we had this misconception that being big meant having a lot of offices and volume. We were spread way too thin."[39]

Bo Calbert, who joined the Houston office in 1982 as a field engineer, acknowledged that Houston in the early 1980s was a builder's dream but admitted that McCarthy's people there "were very inexperienced. Many of them were brand new," he said.[40]

All those rookies faced a steep learning curve and tough competition in new markets. "We had way too many new people in positions that they weren't qualified for or trained to be in, and we paid the price," said Faust.[41]

In 1986, the only business segments that did not lose money were the building division, the office in Phoenix, and the office in Newport Beach.[42] In 1987, however, the Newport Beach office slipped into the red, and the building division barely kept in the black.[43]

Clearly something had to be done, and Mike McCarthy took it upon himself to do it.

A Tough Job

Early in 1987, McCarthy closed both the Houston and the Kansas City offices. But still McCarthy's economic woes continued. "It was a rough period," Mike McCarthy said. "The bank shut us down, the bonding company shut us down, and most everybody was running around scared. I decided if we were going to go through this, I wanted to come out of it as the best construction company in America."[44]

"A lot of it was timing," said Mike Bolen. "We hit Texas just before the oil market crashed, and when that happened no one could stand up under it. Our business is a sine wave. You can start as far back as the pyramids and just watch it go. You have to be in the right place with the right circumstances and have the right people. And in the mid-1980s we experienced bad timing and had the wrong people in the wrong place. And in some cases, we had the wrong people in the right place."[45]

McCarthy continued to close branch offices until only St. Louis, Phoenix, and Newport Beach, California, remained.

"We were digging our way out of this black hole we were in," said Karl Kloster, who became president of the Midwest division in 1987.[46]

Mike McCarthy knew layoffs were necessary, but he wasn't about to send pink slips.

I personally drove around the country with my wife and two children and laid off every single management person so that I would be able to thank them and ask their forgiveness because all this happened on my watch. I had run the company to this point, and I knew I would never do it again.

It was a wonderful trip in a lot of ways. Many of those people came back to us. Nobody was mad. They understood what had happened. I met with their families and their kids. The experience was seminal to my being able to build the kind of company that I wanted to build.[47]

Mike returned from the trip and began to reassign jobs. Salaries were cut by 25 percent across the board. Not everyone was happy with the changes, Mike said. "A lot of the people who had gotten into high management positions had to take a step or two back, and I said, 'We're going to put you back where we know you can do what you're assigned to do, and your choice is either to accept that or not, but that's what we're going to do.'"[48]

Next McCarthy's management began redefining the company's identity and mission by asking a series of questions:

Do we want to be real builders, or do we want to be managers?

"Everybody said they wanted to be real builders," Mike said.

Should the company continue to pursue growth and perhaps go public or remain privately held?

The consensus was to keep the company in private hands and keep it fairly small, to a "size where we knew one another, so it could be fun, and it would be fun because we were all in one family," said Mike. "So that's how we set it up."[49]

Tim McCarthy (top) and Paddy McCarthy (middle) both held the title of vice chairman in 1993, and Mike McCarthy was fast becoming the company's driving force.

By the summer of 1990, CFO George Scherer (bottom) was able to report that McCarthy had successfully completed its reorganization and that it was in a much stronger financial position than it had been a few years earlier.

Mike, the ultimate big-picture guy, turned his attention to oversight rather than looking for the next exciting opportunity. He charted out each of McCarthy's administrative positions and the qualifications of those who filled them. He carefully scrutinized each job McCarthy bid to be sure no detail was overlooked and to "make sure that we could have a pretty decent chance of achieving our margin."[50]

In hindsight, Mike was able to see the good that came out of the company's slump, and he was energized by the challenge. "It was a wonderful time," Mike remembered. "I loved being in that position, where the bank said we couldn't do it. Everybody said we couldn't do it, and we did it. We never borrowed a nickel."[51]

McCarthy's healthy cash balance was a big help in getting back on track. The company added to that healthy balance in October 1986 when it sold its 938 shares of Rock Hill Quarries back to Rock Hill Quarries Company.[52] For 40 years, McCarthy had held on to the quarry stock. Its sale must have been a bittersweet moment for Paddy and Tim McCarthy, for it was their father, Merryl, who had bought Rock Hill Quarries. But the sale helped boost the company's cash position.

For McCarthy, 1987, with its $12.7 million loss, was the nadir. After that, the company began rebounding. As unprofitable jobs were finished, McCarthy's financial picture stayed healthy.

Back in Business

In June 1990, CFO George Scherer reported "a successful conclusion to management's restructuring and downsizing of the company." McCarthy now focused its core operating divisions on its traditional markets. Scherer noted the company's "outstanding" performance over the past three years, especially considering the obstacles it had faced at the close of 1987.[53]

More than a decade later, Scherer marveled at how quickly McCarthy had been able to turn itself around.

When we realized we'd overgrown, we were able to take the steps immediately to reorganize the company, and Mike McCarthy was the driving force behind that. He often talked about the dragons he had to slay, his personal dragons. He made difficult, difficult decisions, and as a result we became more astute in how to run our business, which then allowed us to grow without having to take some of the risks we had taken early on.[54]

In 1987 McCarthy had 10 regional divisions, plus McCarthy Brothers International, McCarthy Properties, and McCarthy Company.[55] By 1990 most of those divisions had been eliminated. McCarthy's reconfigured operations comprised Parking Structures and Heavy/Highway, plus regional offices for the Midwest (in St. Louis), the Southwest (in Phoenix), and the Pacific (in Newport Beach).[56]

"We hit the California market just right," said Mike Bolen, who at that time was president of the Pacific division. "We got there with the right capabilities at the right time, and there was enough left in the boom to where we could take our healthcare 'foot-in-the-door' and leverage that into a number of long-term, sustainable markets as community-based builders."[57]

Breaking ground in a new location was difficult, but in California McCarthy managed to make all the right moves. "We were new to the area, so our strategy was to establish our presence by working on projects that weren't attractive to other contractors," said Carter Chappell, who later became president of the Southern California division. "We established our credibility and our presence. Gradually, over the years, we got the opportunity to be exposed to those owners and architects and other contacts in the industry that had previously been locked up by other contractors."[58]

The Pacific division, aided by its success at subcontracting work to itself at a fixed price, maintained strong margins in 1990 and a diversified mix of work that included hospitals, office buildings, parking garages, and a retirement facility. The Southwest division was hampered by a depressed economy and slow job starts in 1990, but several major projects were scheduled to start soon, and a backlog of $165 million in contracts gave the division plenty of opportunity for future success.[59] Unfortunately the Parking Structures division was affected by poor performance on several projects and inability to get new projects started, but the Heavy/Highway division had a good year in 1990. Scherer credited lower-than-expected costs on several nearly completed projects and "outstanding performance" at the Bissell Point Water Treatment Plant. Despite recent success, Heavy/Highway's future depended on its ability to find enough profitable new work. "To date they have had only minor success," Scherer reported. The Midwest division also had a good year in 1990.[60]

McCarthy was doing so well by 1991 that the *St. Louis Business Journal* ran a story headlined "McCarthy Everywhere You Look," which observed that "If you're driving eastbound on the Daniel Boone Bridge over the Missouri River into Chesterfield, you'll see a sign that says 'St. Louis County.' It might as well say 'McCarthy County.' Because if you're going east, you'll see the handiwork of St. Louis' largest construction firm all around you."[61]

The article went on to note that McCarthy had built the Daniel Boone Bridge and was working on a compan-ion bridge a few hundred feet to the east. It also built the Doubletree Hotel and Conference Center, Maryville Centre, Baur Properties' office park, a Marriott Hotel, St. Luke's Hospital, the Highway 40/Interstate 270 interchange, and St. John's Mercy Medical Center. "McCarthy built it all, either alone or in joint ventures," the article said. "And you're only halfway downtown."[62]

The story continued, listing other McCarthy projects in St. Louis, and observed that the company had worked on projects in 41 states. "Even so, the firm is about 25 percent smaller than it was a few years ago," the newspaper reported. "The new watchwords are 'moderate growth.'"[63]

The Dude

Once McCarthy had successfully restructured, in early 1991 Mike McCarthy felt it was time to develop a new company logo, one that described "who we are," said Mike. "We're not about paper shuffling; we're about the visceral process of building."[64]

Mike laid out the guidelines to the design team.

I didn't want it to be male or female. I didn't want it to be Anglo-Saxon or Hispanic or black. I wanted it to be androgynous and meaningful for all people. I wanted it to be high impact. I didn't want a lot of verbiage on it. I wanted it to be simple and read easily from a distance, and I wanted it to be dramatic and memorable. I wanted it to represent to our clients who we were and what we did, but more importantly, I wanted it to represent to our people how we saw ourselves—not as black or white or male or female but inclusive of everyone.[65]

Once the design team came up with a prototype logo, Mike spent three months working with the team to refine it. The original figure wore a hard hat but didn't carry a hammer. "So we added a hammer," Mike said, "and then we had to raise the hammer up. We went back and forth trying to achieve the

The McCarthy logo extols the company's roots as a hardworking, hands-on construction company.

perfect colors, which weren't on the typical color chart. Then we had to get the shadings correct so that you couldn't really tell if it was male or female, black or white. We truly made an exhaustive effort because we knew we'd have it for a long time."[66]

The finished logo was very well received and even "won a bunch of awards," according to Mike. "A shoe company in New York actually copied it and put it on their boots," he said. "They'd sold thousands of boots before we caught it. We didn't want any money out of them; we just wanted them to stop."[67]

When Hannah Roth, who worked closely with Mike throughout the logo's development, referred to it as "the Dude" (a popular moniker among California surfers at that time), the name stuck, much to Mike's chagrin. "It was an irresistible force," he said. "I tried to stop it, and it was hopeless."[68]

A Northwest Hold

In April 1991, McCarthy formed a new regional office in Seattle called the Northwest division after it bought 50 percent of Seattle-based general contractor SDL Corporation.[69]

Seattle's location on the West Coast and its strong economy made it an attractive area. Bolen had been checking out the Seattle market for some time when "the opportunity to buy SDL came to us," he said. "We liked the culture. We liked the company, so we bought it."[70]

Buying an existing company to carve a niche in the local construction market was a change in strategy for McCarthy. SDL had "what we term a special projects capability," said Kris Anderson, senior vice

president. In other words, SDL had the ability to take smaller contracts (defined as less than $5 million) and still turn a profit. "McCarthy had always fought the label of being too big to handle small work," he explained. "There are a lot more companies that can do a $5 million job than can do a $50 million or $100 million job. The cost structures are different, and the quality and speed and efficiency capabilities are different for smaller contractors on smaller jobs. But we always knew that a lot of our big clients like us to stick around and do their smaller stuff. That was one of the key things SDL offered."[71]

The Sacramento Convention Center

In 1992 the Pacific division opened an office in Sacramento. Management believed it needed a presence in the state's capital to gain a foothold in California's Central Valley and to grow in the northern part of the state. California promised to remain a strong market.[72]

Winning a bid to build the Sacramento Convention Center had given McCarthy the volume it needed to open the Sacramento office. The company lost money on the project, and petition drives by locals who didn't want the center's traffic made it difficult to get the project off the ground, but as always, McCarthy learned some valuable lessons from the trials and tribulations, especially about building for government agencies.

Although government agencies were mandated by law to accept the lowest bid, the rules had become somewhat flexible. Lydia Dawson, office manager for the Sacramento office, who was also in charge of trying to stop the petition drive against the convention center, explained that "because they're mandated by law to take the low bid, they put in alternates. Then they can accept or reject those alternates and have some discretion on what contractor they work with."[73]

McCarthy didn't submit the lowest base bid on the convention center, but it bid extremely low (by mistake) on one of the alternates, the stainless

McCarthy's work on the Sacramento Convention Center included the 80,000-square-foot exhibit hall (pictured), a ballroom, a rooftop terrace, meeting rooms, and a central plant.

steel roof. "So the city council took the base bid plus the alternate that we were so low on and made us the low bidder," said Dawson.[74]

Bolen was at the city council meeting when the vote went to McCarthy. Though it was almost midnight, he signed the contract that night to prevent a protest from the base bidder. The McCarthy team went out to celebrate, and that's when Bolen met his future wife, Debi, who had worked at McCarthy for several years.

Building the convention center gave a number of McCarthy people the opportunity to advance their careers because, as project director Gary Akin pointed out, it was so difficult that the people who worked on it "had to grow and mature in a very short period of time."[75]

In Control

McCarthy's restructuring had succeeded. The company reported a record year in 1993, earning $5.1 million despite the ongoing recession, a general decline in the construction industry, and disappointing results from some divisions. With stable finances, McCarthy could now concentrate on long-term objectives for growth by developing new geographic markets and identifying new technologies and emerging markets. But management had learned its lesson. No longer would McCarthy grow for the sake of getting bigger. Now the company would focus on controlled growth, or as Scherer put it, "being the best building company through sustained profitability and improved operations."[76]

McCarthy built the $615 million Hollywood & Highland® entertainment development in Hollywood. The complex has a Babylonian motif and is framed by a pair of 30-foot-high concrete and fiberglass elephants.

CHAPTER ELEVEN

STRIVING TO BE THE BEST BUILDER

1994–2003

Our Mission is to be the "Best Builder" in America. . . .

—McCarthy's mission statement, 1999

A MORE MATURE McCarthy had emerged from the restructuring of the late 1980s, and strategic planning for the company's future became an ongoing process. Early in 1996, the company's leaders charted a five-year strategic plan, setting specific goals to increase market diversity, develop employees, and cut costs.[1] In November 1998, McCarthy's board approved another strategic plan, in which national marketing became "the top priority." The plan also emphasized expansion in education, real estate, and technology markets, along with employee retention and training.[2]

As 1999 came to an end, McCarthy unveiled a new mission statement that reaffirmed its intent to utilize the latest technologies and to provide "ever-improving diversified services to regional and national customers." McCarthy also pledged to foster a healthy employee environment, one that encouraged innovation and provided advanced resources and training. Overall, the company was committed to integrity and to bringing value to its customers "through creative, intelligent solutions" to challenges. The mission statement ended with a summary of its vision:

Our Mission is to be the "Best Builder" in America by providing:

FOR OUR CUSTOMERS, intense and creative focus on their needs. FOR OUR PEOPLE, the best resources and training with exceptional financial rewards. FOR OUR COMMUNITIES, support and improvement through our participation.[3]

"We came up with the idea that being 'the best builder in America' would be how our clients would think of us," explained Mike McCarthy. "There are many qualities and values that make you the best builder, but in the end, it's your client who says whether you do the best job."[4]

Size Doesn't Matter

For McCarthy, being the best builder was not something that could be measured in revenue or number of projects, offices, or employees. It did not mean being the biggest builder. Rather, it meant quality, reliability, integrity, trust—even sensitivity toward people and involvement in the community.

McCarthy is dedicated to worker safety through proven safety procedures and training. Its safety rates are significantly better than the industry average.

"We came up with that mission statement at a time when a lot of our competitors were deciding that bigger was better," said Mike Bolen. "At McCarthy, we certainly wanted to grow but not just for the sake of growth. Rather than bigger is better, we think better is better, and the bar is constantly rising. We strive to provide better people faster, and we focus on the complex and difficult rather than the commodity kind of stuff."[5]

"Initially I thought that being the best builder meant you made the most money," said Bo Calbert. "But over the years I've learned that being the best builder means you're a builder with high integrity and high standards, and you deliver those to your clients, and you build some wonderful projects in the process."[6]

"We're never satisfied with what we did the last time," said Carter Chappell. "We're always looking ahead and continually evaluating what we've done to see how we can improve it. We have extensive training programs for our people at all levels. We have approached several key market areas with expertise, and we continually focus on improving upon that expertise."[7]

Geographic Diversity

Though McCarthy did not equate size with being the best builder, it did value geographic diversity and variety in the types and styles of projects it undertook. Since 1864, when family patriarch Timothy McCarthy began his lumber business in Ann Arbor, Michigan, the company has continually expanded into new geographic areas and taken on more types of projects. Timothy McCarthy specialized in building barns and residential structures, but after 1907, the year Timothy McCarthy's three sons (John W., Charles, and Mr. Tim) incorporated the company, McCarthy branched into the greater commercial market and soon gained specialties in building government buildings, churches, and other large structures. After moving its headquarters to St. Louis in 1917, McCarthy continued to expand its footprint during the Great Depression and World War II, building in such faraway places as Anchorage, Alaska, and the Panama Canal Zone. By the 1950s, McCarthy was building across the entire Midwest, and in the 1970s, the company became even more geographically diversified when

it entered two new markets: healthcare and parking structures. Around the same time, McCarthy launched into construction management, becoming even more diverse. During the 1980s, McCarthy got its feet wet in bridge building and heavy construction and took on a few international projects as well.

By the 1990s, McCarthy's work could be seen all over the nation, and its specialties covered a wide range: healthcare, commercial, industrial/manufacturing, public works, heavy/civil, parking, education, and research and development (R&D). At the same time, McCarthy had expanded its technical expertise and could help clients handle such activities as coordinating equipment procurement and managing design teams. Moreover, many of McCarthy's clients were repeat customers—a testament to its ongoing commitment to being the best builder in America.

A Retiring Generation

Even the best vision is worth little without the people to carry it out. One of Mike McCarthy's main goals in the late 1990s was to select and shape the people who would lead McCarthy into the future.

The leaders who had grown McCarthy far beyond its deep St. Louis roots were turning the corporation over to new management. In 1994 Francis F. "Paddy" McCarthy retired, followed two years later by his brother Timothy R. McCarthy.[8] Paddy had led the company's estimating department for 45 years, from the era of sharp pencils and slide rules into the world of computers and dedicated software. Tim, who earned his first McCarthy paycheck when he was 11 years old, had become the corporation's vice chairman and informal ambassador of trustworthiness. "Above all, Tim has given McCarthy and its clients integrity. People knew they could trust Tim," said lifelong friend Larry Glynn upon Tim's retirement.[9]

In 1999 Rich Vandegrift, one of the initial McBro team and vice president of business development, retired. Vandegrift once calculated that he had been involved in more than 500 interviews on McCarthy's behalf and that more than a third of those interviews had led to McCarthy jobs.[10]

But if any single man were to be credited with building Mike's vision, that person would have to be Roger Burnet. His retirement in 1995 left some

Left: Roger Burnet retired as president in 1995 and as vice chairman in 1996. He had joined the company in 1972 as a vice president.

Below: Mike McCarthy's innovation and leadership became hallmarks of McCarthy's growth. By the time he stepped down as chairman in the spring of 2002, the company was well positioned to handle whatever challenges came its way.

big shoes to fill. "Roger was a team player internally as well as externally," said Vandegrift, who presided as master of ceremonies at Burnet's retirement party. "He treated everyone equally, and he was very generous with everybody. He was concerned that people enjoyed what they were doing, that they had the amount of responsibility they desired, and that they were adequately compensated. For me, he was like a second father. I could never have had a better mentor."[11]

The Triumvirate of Mikes

Roger Burnet had been the perfect balance to Mike McCarthy's "ready-fire-aim" personality. Mike's wife, Kathy, provided the sensitivity and continually reinforced the importance of even the lowest salaried person on the team. The company had long depended on Burnet's discipline, organizational abilities, attention to detail, and impeccable integrity, so Mike looked long and hard for someone with similar traits. Mike Hurst, an up-and-comer in the Southwest division, soon caught his attention. According to Mike, Hurst equaled Burnet in organizational talent and integrity and had the kind of "disciplined, driven," and hardworking nature that was Burnet's trademark. Hurst could "make the engine run on a day-to-day basis" and "pick it apart and make it run better and better."[12] In 1995 Hurst became McCarthy's president and chief operating officer. Burnet was elevated to vice chairman, joining Tim McCarthy in that capacity.

Hurst's first duties were to revamp McCarthy's systems and procedures; expand quality, training, and safety programs; oversee research and evaluation of potential acquisitions; and provide the operating divisions with the "well thought out resources and management" needed to develop new markets.[13]

Next Mike McCarthy began looking for someone who would fill his shoes once he had retired. He wanted "a people person who is a visionary, who would gather everybody together to keep us headed in the right direction on values."[14]

That someone was Mike Bolen, president of the Pacific division. Although Bolen "had some stretching to go through," he was a natural, according to Mike McCarthy. A former athlete and always a team player, Bolen was "very nurturing" to the people in his division.[15] In 2000 he became McCarthy's

first CEO from outside the McCarthy family.[16] Mike McCarthy remained chairman.

Building a Family

Mike McCarthy's other big challenge of the late 1990s was to transform the McCarthy company into a new McCarthy family. "I have to face the fact that I am not going to live forever," Mike said in 2001. "So I had to figure out what kind of company I wanted to leave as a legacy, and I want to leave a kind of family company."[17]

When Timothy McCarthy founded the company in 1864, he treated nonfamily employees as members of the family, and the tradition continued through subsequent generations: from John W., Charles, and Mr. Tim to Melvin, Merryl, and John E.; then to Paddy, Timothy R., and Mike.

"We carried the tradition forward because that's the way we wanted to do things," said Mike. "We wanted to have personal relationships with our employees, and that, in turn, helps us reach a common goal. Everybody has been focused together, and the McCarthy people know their jobs and families and problems are really important to us."[18]

Rich Henry, president of the Northern Pacific division and the leader of McCarthy's K–12 education initiative

Small wonder, then, that many of McCarthy's people considered their coworkers as a sort of extended family and stayed with the company for all of their working lives. In fact, more than one generation of many families worked for McCarthy: Tom Dollar and his sons Ken and Rick, for example. Ken, who had been with McCarthy for some 15 years, was a project manager in the Midwest office, and Rick, a trade carpenter, had been associated with McCarthy for more than 10 years.

"McCarthy afforded the opportunity for success regardless of family, and I think that's what has kept a lot of people here," said Tom Dollar. "As long as you do a good job, you progress. In many family companies, you're not promoted unless you're family, and that's not the way it is at McCarthy."[19]

Rich Henry, who was hired full time in 1980 as a project engineer and later became vice president of education services and most recently president of the company's Northern Pacific operations, gravitated toward McCarthy after seeing his father, Glenn, work for the company for almost a decade. (Rich's brother Ron also worked for McCarthy for a number of years.) "I liked the family atmosphere," Rich said. "I was part of a big family business even though I wasn't a McCarthy. Mike McCarthy has been a mentor to me my entire career. He's made me feel like one of his own. Mike Bolen has always mentored me and been a great advisor. And Mike Hurst has always been a great friend and a supporter of everything I do."[20]

Glenn Henry had worked for another local general contractor before McCarthy, and Rich remembered his father saying that switching employers had been "one of the scariest things he had ever done but that ultimately it turned out to be the best thing that had ever happened to him. My father really enjoyed working for McCarthy," Rich said. "Years after his retirement, he still stays in touch with a number of people in St. Louis."[21]

Dan Petry joined McCarthy in 1986 and later became a project manager. His father, also named Dan, worked for McCarthy for more than 25 years. "I remember when I was a boy, talking with my father about working for McCarthy," said Petry. "The family atmosphere at the company was very appealing, especially because we moved around a lot. We'd go to a new place and not know anyone, but we'd still see people we knew from

TRAVELING MANAGERS

MCCARTHY EMPLOYEES ARE A DEDIcated lot, and few are more dedicated than the mobile field people, also called traveling managers. Every one to three years, these men and women willingly pack up their belongings and move themselves and their families to wherever McCarthy needs their skills. Their devotion has allowed McCarthy to maintain its national presence by always having skilled people on hand. They also allow the company to pursue a wide variety of markets. In turn, being diverse and dispersed has helped McCarthy avoid downturns in specific markets and locations.

Being a traveling manager can be disruptive, but it also has its benefits. Those who are willing to move around the country have more opportunities and tend to accrue more wide-ranging experience than stationary managers. "Work has its hills and valleys," said Greg Montgomery, a project manager who joined McCarthy in 1981 and has since relocated 11 times. "But when you have the option to move around, you don't have to think about what might happen if work dries up in your area." In addition, Montgomery, like other traveling managers, has had the opportunity to work on a variety of different projects, including healthcare, parking structures, industrial, concrete restoration, and laboratories.[1]

"Every area of the country is different, from the soil on up," said Bill Schuttler, a project manager who began his McCarthy career in 1981. "The soil is different in different areas, and some of the buildings may be steel and others may be concrete. We just get a variety of experience."[2]

Traveling managers also have the rare opportunity to see and live in different areas of the country. "The wife and I have enjoyed it," said Project Manager Harl Buckallew, whose wife, Barbara, worked as his secretary during much of his 35-year McCarthy career. "You meet so many nice people, and you get to see a lot of interesting locations. We were in Steamboat Springs for a year and a half and got to play in the snow, and then from there we went to Galveston, Texas, and got to play on the beach."[3]

Of course, McCarthy remained sensitive to employees' needs and desires. As part of their yearly evaluation, employees filled out questionnaires to express their personal goals and desires, and McCarthy listened.

"If we were looking to be promoted or looking to work on a certain type of project, we put that down on the questionnaire," said Schuttler. "They want to hear from you, and it helps them when they staff projects. They don't want to send a person to work on a specialty office project who has no interest in working on that. When they send you out to a project and send you your staff, they do a very good job of matching you up personality-wise, and it works. It makes a better team."[4]

Project Manager Dan Petry didn't mind moving his family around when his sons were younger, but once they got into high school, he wanted to keep them rooted. "McCarthy understands that your kids don't necessarily want to be changing schools when they're in high school," Petry said. "In grade school they're more adaptable."[5]

McCarthy has striven to show its appreciation for these mobile field people by offering a top-notch relocation program, which helps employees find and secure housing and even helps other family members with their job search. In addition, traveling managers are given a relocation incentive bonus.

"The salary is great. There's no doubt about it," said Schuttler. "But it's not the material things necessarily that make me stick around. It's more of an attitude."[6]

"McCarthy makes it as easy on you as they can for relocating," said Buckallew. "They try to meet family needs too. They've taken care of us."[7]

McCarthy's St. Louis office, and that made it feel more like home."[22]

The younger Dan Petry's wife, Mary, worked at McCarthy for more than 10 years, first as project secretary and later as office manager in Dallas. His brother Damian also worked at McCarthy for about 10 years before leaving to start his own business.

Other McCarthy employees who spanned multiple generations or family members included Whitey Allmeyer and his son Jim; Neil, William, John, Lauren, and Jennifer Bauer; Harl and Barbara Buckallew (husband and wife), their daughter Brenda Hubbard, and Harl's twin brother Darl; Lloyd Knochenhauer and his son Bob; Rob and Ron Langhoff (brothers); August Mayberry and his son Leslie; Jim, John, and Dana Metoyer; Curt and Carol Olson (husband and wife); Chris and Candy Schwarz (husband and wife); Nelson Snelling and his son Bob; and Tom Waters, his son Pat, and Pat's mother, Mildred.

To ensure that the family tradition continued after his eventual departure, Mike traveled the country, meeting with construction crews and sharing his vision of the new McCarthy family. "I was trying to convince these guys that if they work together as brothers in the bond, they'll be able to achieve something they'll never achieve on their own," he said. Intellectually they understood, but natural competitiveness often stood in the way. Mike found ways to harness that competitive spirit, and having fun was a large part of the equation. One notable get-together included "some competitive, if not war-like, fun on the side" as Mike and McCarthy's "merry crew of tribal chieftains" (also known as project directors) spent an afternoon in the Missouri Ozarks on the paintball field.[23] Such events were common; McCarthy worked hard, but it played hard too.

Of course it wasn't all fun and games. The chairman had a serious mission. He was still the family patriarch, and he had lessons to teach. "We have to share our problems," Mike explained. "We have to respect one another. We can't have personality problems where we're accusing each other of being the bad guy. We respect each other's talents, and we support each other's weaknesses, and we head on."[24]

As Mike saw it, the cardinal family sin was to try to handle problems alone.

If you have a big problem—or if you have a small problem and it looks like it could grow—and you don't declare it to the brotherhood, you're out on that limb all by yourself. If you declare it, we'll get out there with you, and we'll help you any way we can, and now it's our problem, not yours. But if you get out there all by yourself, and you hide it from us, that limb is going to be sawed off, and you're going to be on it.[25]

Similarly, sharing and fellowship were rewarded through bonuses and stock options "for staying true to the course we've set to share problems and share resources," Mike explained.[26]

Mike set the bar high, but he was fair. Family members did not merit a place in the company simply because their last name was McCarthy. Positions had to be earned. "We want to be the best builder in America," he explained, "and if you're unwilling to make the sacrifices that are necessary to get us there, then this is not the place for you."[27]

It took Mike nearly a decade, but by 2001 he had nurtured a new McCarthy family by grooming employees, managers, and leadership into a team of people who were well prepared to take the company into the 21st century. "They're very client-centered. They're very people-centered," Mike said, adding that the company's finances and cash flow were strong.

Still, Mike wasn't taking any chances. "We should be just fine, but I'm still watching over things," he said. "If anybody falls off the horse over the next couple of years, I'm still there. I made my life doing this. I don't intend for the ship to sink."[28]

Relationships Are Key

McCarthy's relationships, both within and outside the company, were viewed as vital to the company's success, so it was imperative that those relationships be valued and nurtured. "That doesn't mean hiding when there are areas of weakness, but addressing those weaknesses within the confines of a healthy family," Mike explained.

At many corporations, especially ones as large as McCarthy, a wall divides top management from rank-and-file employees. But because many of McCarthy's top executives started in the field, their rise to management positions strengthened

McCarthy's roots as a hands-on builder and its credibility with its workers. Moreover, McCarthy created team relationships with suppliers and subcontractors rather than treating them as "lackeys who just supply a service," Mike said. McCarthy respected their important roles and saw that they were paid on time and recognized for exceptional performance.[29]

Customer Relations

McCarthy was proud of the relationships it had forged with its customers over the years. Some clients refused to use any builder but McCarthy, "not because there aren't other competent people out there," Mike said, but because of the trust they had in McCarthy. "Whatever problem they have, even if it isn't in the confines of the contract, they trust that we'll use every resource we have to fix it. We won't run from a problem. When we do something wrong, we lay it on the table and say, 'Here's where we screwed up. Now let's see what we can do to solve the problem.' A lot of our competitors will try to brush mistakes under the rug. We don't do that. We're about relationships. Relationships are key to what we are doing."[30]

One of Hurst's experiences exemplified McCarthy's attitude toward mistakes and relationships. Hurst was vice president of operations for the Southwest division when it was constructing a clean room facility for Motorola in Austin, Texas. The project was plagued with problems.

Mistakes were being made, and the budget was way off track. "It turned into a real mess," Hurst said, "but we ended up getting it fixed."[31]

"Getting it fixed" was no easy task. It required a very focused effort from McCarthy and the owner's representatives to manage the cost overruns and changes that were being driven by the users of the facility. "It took a huge effort to pull together all the subcontractors on the project to get it under control and understand truly where we were cost-wise and what we could do to impact those costs going forward," said Hurst.[32]

In March 1995, when Mike McCarthy was considering who should fill Burnet's shoes as president, Hurst thought he didn't have "a chance in hell" because of what had happened in Austin. That's why he was so surprised when Mike invited him to become president.

Hurst asked his boss, "What finally made you decide that I was the right guy?"

"Well," Mike said, "you had a really nasty problem in Austin. It was your fault. It was on your watch. But you took care of it."[33]

And Hurst had taken care of it, thus furthering McCarthy's reputation for satisfying its clients. "It was probably the fastest-track project that you'd ever want to be involved in," remembered Dennis Tucker, vice president of operations for the Southwest division. "We were literally building just as fast as they could design. We went from groundbreaking to manufacture of the first line of chips in 18 months, which was pretty phenomenal."[34]

In 1995, when McCarthy was building an addition to the Salk Institute in La Jolla, California, Dr. Jonas Salk, the polio vaccine developer for whom the Institute was named, became a regular visitor. The workers were thrilled when Salk would join them for a burger and a chat during their job site

Through activities such as company picnics and charitable events, McCarthy has created a family atmosphere that employees value and appreciate.

cookouts. "By the time we finished the project, these guys were higher than kites," Mike remembered. "They knew they were building for Jonas."[35]

The crew was so enthused about working with Salk that some of the superintendents "traded their titles for tool belts just to work on the project," said Dennis Katovsich, senior vice president of business development for the Southern California division. They even got Salk a very special birthday present for his 80th birthday. The design of the original building included chalkboards outside so that research scientists could make notes while enjoying nature. But the original design did not provide chalk trays for the boards, which meant the scientists had to bring their chalk and erasers outside with them. The crew had heard Salk comment that if he had to do something over again with the original design, he would provide chalk trays for the scientists. So the crew built Dr. Salk his chalk trays.

Having good relationships with clients also meant showing respect. Steve Jennemann, project manager, began every new project by reminding his field forces of the dynamics of McCarthy's relationship to its client. "I tell them we are guests in this facility," he said, "that this is not our facility. It's not going to be ours when we leave. I tell them we have a client that requires our expertise, but we are guests, and we should treat the people here as if they are the boss."[36]

McCarthy even assigned a team, headed by Superintendent Dan Cummings, to maintain good relations with the union tradespeople it worked with. "We try to make sure they have the tools and equipment they need to do their jobs correctly," said Cummings. "That's good for morale, and it's something that's near and dear to me because I know what morale can do for a job."[37]

Neil Bauer, a project manager at McCarthy's St. John's Hospital job site in St. Louis, could attest to McCarthy's good client relations. "We might have done four, five, six projects with the same head nurse," said Bauer. "I think that's because McCarthy carries one of the best reputations around as far as the quality of work and how it trains its people."[38]

Such repeat business exemplified McCarthy's Close the Loop (CTL) program, launched in 1999 to change "the traditional transaction orientation to a relationship-based mode of thought and action." CTL's goal was twofold: to improve relationships with clients by seeking feedback on their satisfaction with McCarthy and to garner possible job leads or referrals ahead of the competition. More than half the company's new jobs came from old clients.[39] The Trend Spotter Program (TSP), launched in 2000, was similar in that it helped identify potential new markets as well as good workers. Everyone at McCarthy was urged to alert the company to emerging trends and to stay on the lookout for McCarthy's next generation of doers and thinkers.[40]

Devoted to Safety

Project directors and supervisors also saw to it that the field forces worked in a safe environment. McCarthy's hands-on safety program, led by Gary Amsinger, vice president of corporate safety, provided supervisors with continually updated safety guidelines. "I call it a tool for the field staff to understand how McCarthy does safety," Amsinger said. "People sometimes call safety requirements 'rules,' but they're really guidelines so that everybody is planning ahead for safety, and that makes it a lot easier."[41]

Each operating division had a divisional safety director, and Amsinger managed the loss control program on the corporate level through them. Work hazards were eliminated through careful preplanning, and every McCarthy team member was trained to perform his or her work in a safe manner. Foremen analyzed potential hazards with their crew before each work activity, and McCarthy inspectors made scheduled and unscheduled visits to pounce on and correct potentially unsafe conditions.

"Every time they come on a project, all of our people are indoctrinated to the safety program," said Jennemann. "Not only our safety program but whatever safety requirements are on the specific project we're doing."[42]

"We have incentive programs for jobs that perform safely and utilize the teamwork concept for those trade workers in the field," said Amsinger. "We utilize safety as a value of equal measure with

Opposite: Dr. Jonas Salk was a regular visitor at the site where McCarthy was building the Salk Institute in La Jolla, California.

all the other things that you measure success by. If you measure success by how much money you make on the job or how early you can complete a project or how well it's constructed, we add safety as an equal measure to all that."[43]

McCarthy's dedication to safety paid off each day when its workers returned safe and sound to their loved ones. "If you've ever seen the impact that a fatality or a serious injury has on a coworker's family, you would try to make sure that everybody understands they need to take responsibility for doing their part to promote a safe work environment," said Amsinger.[44]

In March 2002, McCarthy was a finalist in the Associated General Contractors of America (AGC) 2001 Construction Safety Excellence Awards. AGC is the largest industry construction group in the country. For 2001, the average accident rate for the construction industry was 8.3 accidents per 100 full-time employees whereas McCarthy's accident rate was 2.3. McCarthy's safety performance record was so good, in fact, that its workers' compensation insuror had given McCarthy a credit on its premium for every year since 1994.[45]

McCarthy realized other benefits as well. Some owners looked at safety history to prequalify contractors, not allowing unsafe contractors to bid. Employee morale tended to be higher too, which helped McCarthy maintain a qualified workforce.

"Safety is an operational necessity," said Amsinger in late 2002. "Our safety has improved over the past three years, and so have our profits, so no one can tell you that being safe costs you money; it actually makes you money."[46]

Employee and Client Relations

All over the corporation, employees were able to take the initiative and try new things. If valued employees were dissatisfied, they might be reassigned to something more suitable to their skills and ambition.

"As the company has grown, a lot of employees were given opportunities to venture out and do new things," said Kris Anderson, who was made vice

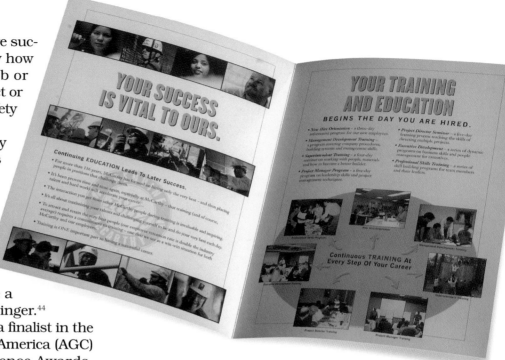

McCarthy offers continuous professional development training that begins on an employee's first day of work.

president of St. Louis business development in 2002. Most of the company's current leaders, in fact, had created or discovered some special component of their business and been allowed the chance to build it. That entrepreneurial spirit was one reason McCarthy was able to grow and diversify. "One thing you won't do around here if you're a keeper is get bored," Anderson said. "There are always new opportunities and challenges."[47]

"There have been times in my career—and I daresay in a bunch of McCarthy people's careers—when, if I hadn't been able to pursue a different kind of challenge, I would have gone somewhere else," said Russ Wenzel, who began his McCarthy career in 1983 and by 2001 was presiding over Compass Services, a business unit that he had helped create. "We all sort of joke about it: Be careful what you suggest or raise your hand for because tomorrow you'll be doing it."[48]

Of course, trying new things posed its own set of risks, and that's where another of McCarthy's philosophies proved invaluable. "We know we're going to make mistakes," said Mike McCarthy. "So we're forgiving of a mistake once or twice."[49]

As a 30-year veteran with McCarthy, Ken Bonastia was able to witness again and again the care McCarthy had given its people. "McCarthy has always appreciated its people," he said. "It was true 30 years ago, and it's true today. I would never want to see this company lose that respect for people. If you're going to say you're family, then you need to be a family, and that means people."[50]

The family atmosphere extended well beyond the upper reaches of management. It was just as important that the field forces, which included a fair number of second- and third-generation McCarthy employees, become part of the McCarthy family. "Management doesn't pound any nails, we don't tie any wire, and we don't pour any concrete," Mike McCarthy said. "The ones who can make us or break us, the ones who really set the tone of this company, are the ones who are physically doing the craft."[51]

Above: Randy Rotolante (left) poses with Carter Chappell, president of the Southern California division, after receiving a 15-year service award. Rotolante was one of McCarthy's first superintendents in California.

Left: Mike McCarthy has been the driving force behind the company, and his belief in offering employees perks, such as voyages on the company boat, only adds to McCarthy's success.

"This company has so many talented and dedicated people," said Bo Calbert. "As a leader, I'm supposed to provide inspiration, but inspiration comes to me from our people in the field who devote so much of themselves to what they do."[52]

The family feeling wasn't limited to McCarthy employees either. Spouses and children were included in the larger McCarthy family. In January 1994, *McCurrents*, the McCarthy newsletter, was redesigned and mailed directly to employees' homes. "Our goal is to provide employees and families, McCarthy's most valuable assets, the most interesting and timely information available," the readers were informed.[53] Since the 1990s, *McCurrents* has been studded with family tidbits—milestones, achievements, and tragedies—along with profiles of workers and special jobs, company news, and other information.

Aside from a company culture that made McCarthy a secure, comfortable, and fun place to work, McCarthy offered a number of perks designed to reward employees for jobs well done. Mike McCarthy and his wife, Kathy, owned vacation homes at the Lake of the Ozarks and in Snowmass, Colorado, where employees, based on seniority, were invited to spend a week's vacation with their families—at no cost, of course.

Continuing the tradition of Eleanor and Dusty McCarthy in the 1940s and 1950s, Peggy Burnet and Kathy McCarthy were instrumental in fostering the family atmosphere. Their beauty, style, and warmth helped attract many new employees and clients. Their parties, the athletic competitions they organized, and most especially the boat trips they organized were highly conducive to team building.[54]

Career advancement based on ability was another McCarthy tradition. Tom Dollar, who never completed high school, was president of the Heavy/Highway division for many years. "If you are a good performer, if you're a solid performer, then you get rewarded in this organization," said Henry. "I'm [only] 44 and am a division president."[55]

In 1999 McCarthy Brothers Company, "an old and proud name," was changed to McCarthy Building Companies in recognition of the chang-

McCarthy employees at the St. Louis headquarters enjoy some Halloween fun.

ing nature of the company's ownership. "In the past, the name reflected the participation by and ownership of the company by the McCarthy family," reported *McCurrents*. "Today, the ownership of our company includes the McCarthy family as well as management and employees."[56]

McCarthy people protected their family culture, explained Kevin Kuntz, senior vice president of operations for the Midwest division. "If something happens that goes against our culture, one of us will throw up our hands and say, 'Guys, we don't want to do that. This is contrary to what makes people want to stay here.'"[57]

McCarthy's family culture is viewed as essential to the company's success. The construction industry was inherently stressful, Bolen explained. Workers were sent all over the country, often to isolated places. Work teams constantly changed, and someone's next assignment could be among unfamiliar people. "The pressures created by that reality make the family culture so valuable," said Bolen. Even unfamiliar people were not considered strangers because they, too, were a part of the McCarthy family and thus shared the same work values.[58]

Peggy Burnet (left), wife of retired president Roger Burnet, and Kathy McCarthy (shown with husband Mike) helped foster McCarthy's family-like atmosphere.

Such consistency was important in the construction industry. "Consistency in your people breeds confidence in the subcontractor community," said Henry. "And that leads to good, positive numbers from the subcontractors. Consistency in your operations breeds confidence in your owners and in the clients you pursue, because they see the same people, and they know you've got a good, solid track record. It's all about relationships."[59]

Community Relations

McCarthy made a concerted effort to improve and support the communities where it worked, including its corporate offices and individual job sites. Specifically, it offered support to charitable organizations in which McCarthy employees were involved. "All of the money we give has people attached to it," said Mike McCarthy. "We never give money without following it with people who get involved."[60] Such donations included a variety of efforts from all of McCarthy's divisions to benefit underprivileged and at-risk children.

Karl Kloster, president of the Midwest division, became a board member of the Make-A-Wish Foundation's St. Louis chapter. His interest in Make-A-Wish® led the McCarthy family to donate a new office to the foundation by remodeling an unusual building on its St. Louis campus.

The Midwest division built the Barnes-Jewish Hospital in St. Louis, Missouri.

The McCarthy family donated a newly
renovated building (right) to the St. Louis
chapter of the Make-A-Wish Foundation®,
and many employees gave their time and
money to support the charity (below).

Even some of McCarthy's subcontractors donated labor and materials. Every year, McCarthy hosted a charity golf tournament in which a Make-A-Wish child got to play. Barb Saey remembered what a great feeling it was to recruit famed St. Louis Cardinals baseball player Ozzie Smith to play golf with a Make-A-Wish child.[61]

Lloyd Hansen, vice president and project director, is chairman of the board for Lighthouse Community Outreach Center, a faith-based ministry in inner-city St. Louis that works with young people to expand their horizons into the arts, sports, and other activities that enhance their self-worth. "We're really trying to save some of the inner-city children from the terrible fates that we see in the news," said Hansen. "We are remodeling an existing building in the neighborhood to make it into an arts center, and with the encouragement of McCarthy and my boss Karl Kloster, we've been able to get some of our subcontractors to help out on the project."[62]

McCarthy was also involved in Rebuilding Together, a national organization that preserves and revitalizes houses and communities to assure that low-income homeowners, particularly those who are elderly or disabled, live in warmth, safety, and independence. In 2001, dozens of McCarthy employees, including Mike McCarthy, lent their hands (and in many cases, their expertise) to repair and renovate homes on National Rebuilding Day, held on the last Saturday in April.

The offices in California also performed extensive charitable work and sponsorship. In Sacramento, for example, McCarthy supported Safetyville USA, which works to reduce deaths and injuries among children through safety training in "a typical American town built at $\frac{1}{3}$ scale [where] children learn safety awareness in a realistic environment of miniature buildings." As a sponsor, McCarthy built and leased one of the miniature buildings.[63]

In 1998, McCarthy won an award from the Associated General Contractors (AGC) of California for renovating and remodeling, free of charge, a sports complex in Sacramento and turning it into

Left: Many McCarthy employees participate hands-on in Rebuilding Together, an organization that helps low-income homeowners live in warmth, safety, and independence.

Below: Deputy Donald Northcross (right), O.K. Kids founder, pays McCarthy Vice President of Operations Tom Sims $1 for a bus to be used to transport underprivileged children to O.K. Kids programs. McCarthy renovated and remodeled, free of charge, a sports complex in Sacramento to turn it into the national headquarters for O.K. Kids.

the national headquarters for O.K. Kids. O.K. Kids provides after-school study groups and activities for at-risk kids. O.K. teachers and mentors received training at the new national headquarters to start other O.K. Kids programs all over the country.[64]

Beginning in 2000, the Sacramento office began an annual tradition of supporting the Children's Receiving Home of Sacramento, which provides temporary, emergency shelter to abused, neglected, or abandoned children. That year alone, McCarthy and 57 area subcontracting firms raised $7,000 during the First Annual McCarthy Golf Tournament. McCarthy also ran annual toy drives to donate to the Children's Receiving Home.[65]

McCarthy supported many other charities and not-for-profit organizations. Employees donated their time year after year to help athletes in the Special Olympics, for example. McCarthy employees also became involved in LEAP, which helps empower Asian Pacific Americans and promotes interethnic collaboration. As testament to McCarthy's dedication to the community, in 1996 the Pacific division created the Big Scoop award, bestowed annually to the "office, department, or job site" that exceeded its public relations duties. One measure for the award was the level of participation in local community and charitable events.[66]

Pride of Ownership

Kris Anderson remembered that when he joined McCarthy, very few people outside the McCarthy family owned stock in the company. "I was always very envious of those people, and that was long before I knew what the company made," he said. Then in 1991 Anderson got his chance to be one of the people he envied when McCarthy allowed a select group of key employees to buy into the company; 4,636 shares, or 15 percent of the company's total stock, were sold to this group.[67] By 2001 McCarthy's core leadership group of about 65 people owned roughly 20 percent of the company's stock.[68]

Then in 1996 McCarthy established an employee stock ownership program (ESOP) that gave most employees the chance "to become true partners and participants in the future of McCarthy."[69] Mike McCarthy's goal was to transition the company from a closely held family business into an employee-owned business. He wanted to leave McCarthy with the people he had worked with over the last 30 years, the people who had helped make the company a success. By 2002 employees owned nearly 50 percent of McCarthy stock, and the percentage was growing every year.[70]

McCarthy also set up a stock option program for the directors in order "to encourage a small core of management to make dramatic changes towards an end goal of enhanced mutual participation in addressing difficult issues." Options were earned by achieving short- and long-term increases in profit.[71]

Employees who shared ownership of McCarthy tended to work harder for the company's success. "I'd jump through hoops for this place to figure out ways to clean the floors better if it meant something for the bottom line because it affects my bottom line also," said Anderson. "Everyone is much more aware of what it takes to make a buck, how easy it is to lose a buck, and the value of that buck—meaning we all think about ways to do our jobs more efficiently."[72]

The sentiment worked both ways. "Now that we've made the employees shareholders in the company, we have a responsibility to those shareholders, just as a public company does," said Jim Faust.[73]

Training for Today and Tomorrow

One of McCarthy's biggest challenges for the future was recruiting people who met the company's high standards, for as Mike Bolen said, "The neck in the hourglass of our growth is in finding the kind of people we need to expand our business. The average tenure of our people is probably triple what the industry average is, and that's how our

business model works, but we still need to get rid of that bottleneck."[74]

To better qualify its people, McCarthy developed company-wide training programs that would give employees the tools they needed to advance the business and become self-fulfilled. Formal training programs were not new to McCarthy; Jim Ulkus had been appointed both director of training and director of human resources in the early 1980s. But Mike McCarthy felt it was time to step up the company's efforts.

Thus McCarthy adopted the Total Quality Management (TQM) philosophy. TQM posits that attaining quality is a process that can be managed. It is a philosophy based on ferreting out and removing obstacles to customer quality and involves all activities and everyone in the company.

In the early 1990s, Kevin Kuntz was appointed McCarthy's first director of TQM and began a company-wide program to adopt the TQM principles that involved education and training. These were first adopted by McCarthy's front-line managers in each division. These men and women were given extensive training before passing the training on to other employees.

When Kuntz was appointed vice president of operations, Chuck Avery, vice president of quality and training, became the new TQM director. Avery had already proven in Cairo that he knew how to manage employees using TQM concepts. Burnet had chosen Avery to be director of TQM because he "wanted someone who used to wear tools," said Avery. "He wanted someone the carpenters and the laborers would respect and listen to."[75]

Getting employees to accept the principles of TQM was not difficult, according to Avery, for the culture of the company had always followed the basic tenets of TQM: do the job right the first time, always try to satisfy customers, and think of ways to improve quality and process. Another TQM principle involved respecting employees, taking time to listen to them, and understanding that in many ways, they know best how to do their individual tasks.

"TQM is centered around improving quality by working closely with the people who are doing the actual tasks," Avery explained. "The philosophy promotes a much better relationship between management and employees to where they pull together."[76]

McCarthy's respect for its tradespeople led it to create a new goal: "to have everyone in the company receive training that not only makes them more competent and capable to do their jobs but also enriches them so they can perhaps be promoted," said Avery.[77]

Engineers, for example, gathered every quarter for special training that would help nurture them into management positions. The sessions hosted speakers from both inside and outside McCarthy and sometimes involved job site tours. The sessions also included a fun, team-building event.[78] "There are two things that you're going through here when you come in for the training," Kevin Kuntz would tell the engineers: learning the intricacies of the job and bonding with fellow engineers. "As you grow and develop in the company, that helps us keep our culture."[79]

To introduce new employees to the company's family culture, McCarthy held multiday training sessions in which the three Mikes (McCarthy, Bolen, and Hurst) and other top executives gave presentations.

As McCarthy captured more of the booming high-tech market, it created divisional MEP (mechanical, electrical, and piping) directors to oversee MEP work in all projects. These directors prevented problems, developed educational programs on MEP systems, and mentored on-site engineers, thus "broadening the base of McCarthy people able to effectively direct MEP subcontractors."[80]

McCarthy was led by a "triumvirate of Mikes," which included (from left) Mike Hurst, president and chief operating officer, who joined the company in 1974; Mike M. McCarthy, chairman of the board, nicknamed "MMM" (pronounced "Triple M") to distinguish him from the other Mikes; and Mike Bolen, chief executive officer, who had been with McCarthy since 1978.

The MEP directors were part of a larger strategy to transform McCarthy from a collection of "stand-alone divisions into a coordinated national construction network using interdivisional teams." The executive network (divisional presidents and top corporate executives) formed policies and planned McCarthy's future. Marketing heads shared information on prospective customers and project delivery methods. The National Estimating Steering Committee, the Information Services Committee, the Vice Presidents of Operations Committee, divisional safety directors, and TQM directors were some of the other interdivisional groups that met regularly to share information, expertise, and good times.[81]

Avery emphasized that McCarthy's training was results oriented. "We determine what the desired outcome is, and the training accomplishes that," he said. "As long as we do that, I keep finding a lot of very receptive people around the company. They want to talk in those terms."[82]

Information Technology

Training was only one tool McCarthy used to help employees better perform their jobs. Providing cutting-edge information technology (IT) was another. "We really are pushing the envelope when it comes to information technology," said Michael McSorley, who was hired into the information technologies department in 1985 as the "personal computer person" and who later became information technologies manager. McSorley noted that throughout his McCarthy career, the company had been very supportive of investing in the information technology that would make employees more productive and efficient.[83]

But it wasn't until 1998 that McCarthy really got serious about utilizing the vast benefits of IT. According to Mike Oster, who came on board in 1998 as vice president of information technology, that's when McCarthy's leaders decided the company was behind the competition in terms of technology. "At that time, McCarthy made a commitment to invest a significant amount of money in its infrastructure," Oster said. "Then in April 1999 we turned on the 'McCarthy McNet.'"[84]

The "McNet" was the much-needed successor to "McBrain," an IBM 400 mainframe computer (with several upgrades) that for many years had powered the company's operations all over the country. McNet gave the company a networked e-mail system, an intranet, and provided computer and Internet access to all employees. In addition, everyone in the field could dial in and connect to the network.

Moreover, McCarthy implemented weekly Web-based training sessions to better serve the field forces. And it was one of the first construction companies to use a project Web site. Mike Oster explained how a project Web site worked.

The owner of the project may be in New York City, the architect may be in Washington state, and the project might be in Texas, but McCarthy can use Web technology to collaborate and coordinate the job in real time. We can post pictures of the job going up, so the owner can watch as it's being built, and we can document meeting minutes using the Web.[85]

McCarthy's IT developments were so groundbreaking that in September 2002 *Information Week* magazine featured McCarthy as one of the most innovative information technology developers in the country.

As Oster pointed out, the IT department's mission was to help McCarthy reach its goal of becoming the best builder in America. "We believe that communication, both voice and data, is critical," he said. "We're seeing more high-speed Internet lines from the job site back to St. Louis. We're looking at technologies such as voice-over IT, which would allow us to eliminate long-distance calling. And we're looking into imaging systems that will let us reduce the amount of paper that moves back and forth between jobs and the division offices."[86]

Special Projects, Compass Services, Industrial

When McCarthy bought SDL, in Seattle, part of SDL's appeal had been its special projects capability—that is, the ability to run smaller projects (less than $5 million) profitably. McCarthy took what it learned from SDL and in 1995 began developing Special Projects teams, or teams that dealt specifically in smaller projects, in other divisions. Specialists from the Seattle office helped the Southwest and Pacific divisions create their own Special Projects segments.[87]

The Special Projects teams shared their knowledge with all McCarthy's operating divisions. "All of our divisions now are doing small projects," said Kris Anderson. The divisions learned how to do the work competitively, but more importantly, the small projects provided the "ongoing, sustaining work and service that a lot of these clients want." That kind of relationship-based service kept McCarthy highly visible, so when those clients had larger contracts, the first builder they looked to was McCarthy.[88]

Rob Langhoff, vice president of the Southwest division and head of the division's Special Projects group, described how McCarthy came up with the name "Special Projects":

Everybody knew McCarthy here in the Southwest as a very large contractor. We had to distinguish ourselves from that. Obviously we wanted them to know we were McCarthy and

had the core strength and knowledge of this great company, but we wanted them to know we could be competitive in the smaller arenas too. So we toyed with what we were going to do, and we finally just decided it was our special project.[89]

The eight-story Paragon Center One office tower in Houston includes a four-level parking structure and integrated retail center. It is a fine example of the Texas division's skill at building office complexes.

In 2001 McCarthy combined its expertise in Special Projects with its mastery of healthcare construction to form the Compass Services group with the goal of providing "ongoing, on-site facilities planning and implementation" for the healthcare industry.[90]

Compass Services as a department had been formed a few years earlier and was the brainchild of Russ Wenzel, who became the group's executive vice president. Wenzel, noting that the healthcare market had transformed McCarthy into a truly national builder and accounted for up to half of the company's business, recognized an untapped market in hospitals' regularly budgeted repairs, remodeling, and other small-scale work.[91]

Compass Services was designed to give healthcare facilities a convenient, one-stop source for everything from budgets, scheduling, infection control, and construction management to strategic planning and programming. "Everything that we know about healthcare is pointing to a lot of growth down the road," Anderson said. "This is a way to keep us involved in these institutions. And when the larger jobs roll around, we will be positioned to do those also."[92]

"Changes in technology and changes in healthcare are driving changes in hospitals. They're building new facilities, refurbishing, remodeling," said Karl Kloster. "We want to be an extension of the owner. We want to be the facilities component that helps them figure out how to get the new stuff fast and inexpensively so they can be successful, so when the big projects come down the pipeline, we're the first guys they look to. They trust us, and they know we have superior knowledge."[93]

Successful Diversification

Seeking new markets through Special Projects and Compass Services was part of McCarthy's diversification strategy. McCarthy had learned its lesson in the 1980s. Healthcare construction had fueled the company's growth, "but we were so focused on it that we forgot about everything else," said Kevin Kuntz. "We probably have five or six sectors now that help us if one market slows down."[94]

In particular, McCarthy chose to develop expertise in certain key markets: industrial, education, and research and development. "We're trying to walk the fence of being diverse enough to know the ups and downs and ins and outs of the marketplace while remaining focused on individual expertise so that we're selling ourselves as a differentiator," said Bolen.[95]

To become an expert in something, Bolen said, "takes a long time, and the average tenure of our people is double the industry average. And then the company has to be willing to support them so they can deliver the product, and McCarthy is a company that gives employees the resources they need to grow."[96]

In 1998, Rich Henry, who had been with McCarthy since 1980, was tapped to head up the company's education initiative. As vice president of education, Henry was in charge of exploring, pursuing, and developing McCarthy's interests in the education market, primarily the K–12 sector.

"We were looking for something to augment the healthcare market to bring balance to our portfolio," Henry said. "The education market appeared to be huge, but our findings showed us that it was much bigger than we had realized."[97]

At first, Henry and his team thought McCarthy should establish a core group of market specialists to operate over divisional boundaries, as it had with healthcare. "Not everybody can build a hospital, and that's the reason it worked for healthcare," explained Henry. "But we ultimately found that the

K–12 market work is highly political, and education jobs are very locally procured. You have to have a local presence to tap into the market. So we looked in the areas that we currently existed in—Phoenix, Southern California, and the Northern Pacific—and created opportunities that we could hand off to the different divisional operations folks."[98]

By 2001, the education initiative had come to a successful conclusion, thanks to McCarthy's willingness to be flexible. "Mike Bolen and I were convinced that we needed to be flexible because we didn't know how this industry operated," said Henry. "We ultimately brought the initiative to a conclusion by showing our divisions that were interested in doing K–12 work whether the market was viable in their area and how deep it was. If it was significant in their area, we assisted them in getting a foothold and then let them take it from there."[99]

Proof positive of Henry's efforts, in the fall of 2002, the Southern California division had a backlog of more than $300 million in K–12 work.[100]

Bolen named a project that represented McCarthy's excellence in each of the three areas targeted for diversification: the renovated and upgraded Tums plant in St. Louis (industrial); the Donald Danforth Plant Sciences Center in St. Louis (R&D); and the Newport Mesa School District eight- to ten-year project in Southern California (education), which involved upgrading existing facilities and building new ones.

In addition, McCarthy tried to maintain a balance between public and private work, even pursuing public and hard-bid work while turning away safer, more profitable, private-sector negotiated work. As Bolen explained, economic downturns could wipe out private clients in a flash. "It's already starting," he said in the spring of 2001. "The work is going to be in education, in healthcare, in the public sector, and if we're not able and trained and up to speed, if we're not in shape to pursue it, we'll get nailed."[101]

Developing new businesses in the swiftly changing markets of the 21st century could be risky, but the risk was necessary for McCarthy to remain competitive. Sometimes a market was so new that estimates of building costs were way off. That had been the case in the 1980s when McCarthy took on its first microelectronics, or clean room, jobs. "We can lose money if we don't accurately estimate," said Mike McCarthy, "but if we didn't try to build in these new fields, we wouldn't have a business."[102]

McCarthy had achieved success in a variety of industries. In 2002, commercial work, which included entertainment, hospitality venues, office and retail, tenant improvements, and residential/ retirement building, made up 33 percent of the company's total volume. Healthcare represented 22 percent, and industrial markets accounted for 15 percent. Completing the mix were education (9 percent), parking (8 percent), institutional (7 percent), and heavy/civil (6 percent).[103]

The Midwest Division

Karl Kloster—described by his colleagues as the "energy behind the machine," the "strategic mind behind the development of the company," and "our most visionary guy"—continued to preside over the Midwest division's operations in St. Louis. Like the other divisions, the Midwest division was expanding into new areas, especially biopharmaceutical, heavy industrial, and microelectronics, or clean room manufacturing.

In Kloster's opinion, such expansion was essential to the company's future. He, in fact, left the small, general contracting company he co-owned, Kloster Company, because "they wanted to stay small, not take any risks, and I was interested in trying new things."[104]

Kloster joined McCarthy in 1987, at the peak of the company's financial troubles. "I liked the people," he said. "I liked their attitude, the way they handled risk, the way they solved problems. I chose McCarthy because

Left: Karl Kloster, president of the Midwest division, was already a 17-year construction veteran when he joined McCarthy in 1987.

Right: Derek Glanvill, who joined McCarthy in 1996, is executive vice president of the Midwest division and spearheaded that group's launch into industrial and lab work.

it was either going to be gone or it was going to come back, and if the company made it, I thought there would be lots of opportunities."[105]

He was right. McCarthy had learned that being in a niche market could be good or bad, depending on how the market was doing. "When the market is strong and you're on the front end of that curve, it can make you hugely successful," Kloster explained. "But when the market matures and slows down and more competitors get into it, if you don't get out of there, you're going to become a dinosaur."[106]

McCarthy clearly needed to grow beyond that boom-and-bust cycle. It needed to diversify. The Midwest division began focusing more aggressively on the St. Louis market and the relationships the division had forged with subcontractors and people in the public sector markets. It initiated better communication with its clients, an effort that turned into the Compass Services group, and it began pushing its way into industrial markets.

Initially only two project directors, Don Wright and Dale Robertson, were involved in industrial projects, but that soon changed. The industrial workload increased so phenomenally, in fact, that the Midwest division created the Industrial group, led by Derek Glanvill. "Glanvill's background in industrial has really boosted our success in that area," said Dennis Bryan, scheduling director for the Midwest division.[107]

The industrial jobs led McCarthy into building clean room manufacturing and microelectronics facilities. Under Glanvill's direction, these markets enhanced the Midwest division's technical and self-perform capabilities.[108]

Rich Corey, a project director in the division's Industrial group who started with the company in 1979, remembered how challenging it was to be job superintendent on McCarthy's first clean room facility, built for Digital Equipment in Boston in the late 1980s. "It was one of the first Class 10 clean rooms, which means it had very strict

requirements," said Corey. "It was a definite learning experience, and it allowed us to do more work in microelectronic and clean room environments."[109]

Slowly, McCarthy built up its portfolio of clean room projects. But even by the mid-1990s, the Midwest division was still on a learning curve. Tom Felton, another project director in the Industrial group, remembered the challenges of a job for MEMC Electronics in St. Peters, Missouri. McCarthy signed on in 1995 as general contractor to build a microelectronics facility. "We didn't really know what we were getting into," said Felton, who was project manager for the MEMC job. "It was a huge project that had to be done in about 14 months."

To complete the job, the Midwest division pulled from McCarthy's other divisions a team of people with experience in clean room construction.

"It was neat to see the full nationwide depth of the company," said Felton. "The job was a huge administrative nightmare, but we ended up with a great family atmosphere with all the people from the different divisions. We did a lot of things together, and that helps us get through those kinds of jobs."[110]

Next the Midwest division broadened its scope to target research and biopharmaceutical facili-

Above: The Southwest division built a 465,000-square-foot wafer fabrication facility, which includes this clean room, for Motorola's Semiconductor Products sector.

Below: The Midwest division built the two-story Gateway Elementary School, the three-story Gateway Middle School, and the one-story Michael School. The Gateway schools share a common library, gymnasium, greenhouse, weather station, and math and science "Hall of Fame." Gateway is a recipient of the coveted Roger Burnet Award, which McCarthy gives out once a year to the project that embodies "the finest integrity, personal service, and commitment to quality."

ties, many of which were associated with hospitals. "Hospitals have long been our clients," said Kloster. "And often the hospitals would need a research component as part of their project. So we started carving that out and looking at it, and all of a sudden, we said, 'Holy cow! Maybe there's something going on here.'"[111]

Bud Guest, senior vice president of business development for the Midwest division, noted that McCarthy was "way ahead of the curve" in building research laboratory facilities.[112] The Donald Danforth Plant Sciences Center and the Sigma-Aldrich Life Science Technology Center, in particular, allowed McCarthy to prove its abilities in building laboratories.[113]

In addition, the Midwest division worked on a number of renovation projects. In 2002, for example, the company finished transforming a 102-year-old French revival mansion into the St. Louis University Museum of Art. The historical nature of the building brought unique challenges. For starters, McCarthy had to perform significant upgrades to meet current code requirements, which included coordinating asbestos and lead abatement and installing a new front entrance and other fixtures to make it comply with the Americans with Disabilities Act (ADA). In addition, McCarthy preserved the original design of the building by matching its new construction materials to its original millwork. And to solve the space constraint caused by adjacent buildings, equipment was hoisted inside or on top of the building with cranes. Because of the Midwest division's excellent work, the project was a finalist for an Associated General Contractors of St. Louis Construction Keystone Award, which recognizes outstanding performance in construction.[114]

The Midwest division's recent projects included biopharmaceutical projects for Dial, Genetics Institute, Sigma Chemical, and Washington University, all in St. Louis; industrial projects for Enterprise Rent-A-Car in Clayton, Missouri, McDonnell Douglas/Boeing in St. Louis, and Mallinckrodt in St. Louis; microelectronics projects for MEMC Electronic Materials in St. Peters,

Missouri, and Motorola/Toshiba JV in Sendai, Japan; heavy industrial work for General Motors in Wentzville, Missouri, Toyota-Bodine Aluminum in Troy, Missouri, and AmerenUE in St. Louis; education projects for the Gateway School Campus in St. Louis, the Mehlville School District in St. Louis, the St. Louis Public Schools Renovation Program, the Mayo Clinic in Rochester, Minnesota, and a number of projects for Washington University; healthcare projects for the University of Colorado Hospital, Children's Hospital in New Orleans, St. Luke's Hospital in Chesterfield, Missouri, University Hospital of Cleveland, and Dartmouth-Hitchcock Medical Center in Lebanon, New Hampshire; institutional projects for Lambert–St. Louis International Airport, the Eastern Reception Diagnostic & Correctional Center in Bonne Terre, Missouri, the St. Louis Justice Center and the St. Louis County Justice Center, America's Center Convention Center in St. Louis, and the Centers for Disease Control and Prevention in Atlanta; and commercial

Left: Walter R. "Bud" Guest joined McCarthy in 1980 and is senior vice president of business development for the Midwest division.

Below: The Midwest division has built a number of laboratories, including the Donald Danforth Plant Sciences Center in St. Louis.

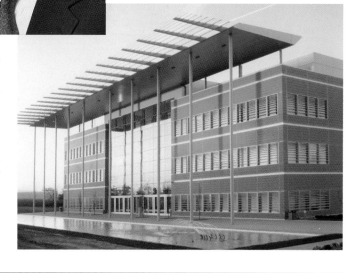

projects for Stouffer's Airport Hotel in St. Louis and St. Louis Marriott West.

The Texas Division

Because Texas highway work was a large part of the Heavy/Highway division's contract volume, in 1995 the division moved from Houston to Austin, where the Texas Department of Transportation kept its offices.[115] Unfortunately, winning profitable contracts continued to be a challenge for the division. In 1998 Heavy/Highway was absorbed by the new Texas division, in Dallas, a full-service division offering heavy/highway services in addition to healthcare and other services.[116]

The decision made business sense. Although Heavy/Highway had been profitable since digging its way out of the disastrous losses of the 1980s, it tied up an inordinate amount of McCarthy's resources. "We had more equipment in my division than in the rest of the company," Tom Dollar observed.[117]

Moreover, the division's work was risky and the competition very tough. "The people who are successful in that business are totally focused on that kind of work," explained Bolen. "While we could build the jobs, we couldn't do it profitably. It was too different from the other things we were doing and too competitive."[118]

By 2002 the Texas division, led by division president Mike McWay, had become a $100 million contractor with a 50-50 mix of commercial and civil work and a similar ratio of hard-bid to negotiated jobs. "We have a very diverse group in terms of the type of projects we're doing," said McWay. "The healthcare and civil work especially help keep the valleys in our business a lot more shallow."[119]

The division's water and waste treatment jobs included four design-build projects for Texas Instruments in Dallas; the DOS Rios Waste Treatment Plant in San Antonio; and the Northwest Waste Treatment Plant in El Paso. Some of its largest jobs in the bridges and marine market included Lamar Street at Loop 360 in Austin, interchange reconstruction on US 290 at Loop 360 in Austin, and the US 290 interchange bridge deck in Houston. In the industrial market, it built the Kroger Meadow

Lake Creamery in Conroe and did work for Cisco Systems in Austin. In the education market, it completed projects for the University of Texas-Austin Psychology & Child Development building. Healthcare projects included the Department of Veterans Affairs Medical Center in Houston, Knapp Medical Center in Weslaco, Memorial Hospital Southwest in Harlingen, Shriners Hospitals for Crippled Children in Galveston, and Valley Baptist Medical Center in Harlingen. Commercial jobs included offices and parking for Paragon Center One in Houston, Signature Place in Dallas, and Nortel Networks in Dallas. The Texas division also built a number of residential buildings.

Of course, every job is demanding, but Gary Akin, vice president and project director for the Texas division, found that work at the Dallas/Fort Worth (DFW) International Airport had some unique

Above: The St. Louis County Justice Center in Clayton, Missouri, was built by the Midwest division and includes 960 jail cells, two courtrooms, one grand jury room, police evidence processing facilities, a complete medical area, and a skybridge to the existing courthouse.

Below: Among the Texas division's many projects is the Knapp Medical Center in Weslaco.

Opposite: The Texas division built a portion of the people mover systems for the Dallas/Fort Worth International Airport.

challenges. In 2002 McCarthy was building an automated people-mover system for the new international terminal. "Airport security and airport construction have been heavily scrutinized since the September 11 attacks," he said. "So everything that's been designed to date has undergone blast analysis. Numerous changes and provisions are occurring, so we have to stay on our toes in order to keep up with all of those various design provisions."[120]

Despite the flat construction market in Texas, Akin was confident that when the economy picked up again, the division would be "right there shoulder-to-shoulder with some of our great competitors. We'll be able to play like the local boys in getting a larger portion of work."[121]

The Southern California Division

The Southern California division, headquartered in Newport Beach, was led by division president Carter Chappell. Like so many of his colleagues, Chappell had worked his way up the McCarthy ladder; he had been hired in 1981 as a carpenter.

Healthcare, which included research laboratories, represented about 50 percent of the division's business each year. The Newport Beach office got its first healthcare contract in 1987: construction

of Huntington Memorial Hospital. The project was hugely successful, and the division subsequently did four other projects for the owner. "Huntington really established our credentials in the healthcare business here," said Chappell.[122]

Because of the high risk of earthquakes in California, hospital structures had to meet certain seismic requirements set by the Office of Statewide Health Planning and Development. That same office mandated that all acute care hospitals in Southern California meet a minimum level of seismic safety by 2030. "They have to comply or else shut down," said Steve Mynsberge, senior vice president of healthcare services for the Southern California division (and a member of the California Hospital Building Safety Board). "Right now there's a tremendous volume of work, and it will only get busier as we get closer to 2030." Mynsberge noted that most of the existing hospitals, because they were older buildings, were choosing to replace their facilities rather than upgrade, "especially since they're trying to meet a date that's 30 years down the road," he explained.[123] And building from the ground up rather than restructuring meant more opportunity for McCarthy.

Constructing the addition to the Salk Institute in 1995 was one of the Southern California division's most ground-breaking projects. "The original building was, in architectural circles, one of the highest-profile architectural concrete buildings in the country, and we essentially doubled its size," said Mike Bolen. "We were trying to match an existing architectural monument on Salk, which was an original

Louis Kahn design, by a young architect named Jack McAllister. Jonas Salk had a very clear idea of what he wanted the building to look like. He said we needed to make the concrete look like liquid stone."[124]

"The Salk building was cast in architectural concrete that is 100 percent exposed," said Chappell. "Also, it was architectural concrete as well as structural concrete, so the structure is the finish of the building." In addition, Chappell said, "We self-performed our own concrete work, and that's another layer of expertise that a lot of our competitors and contractors don't perform."[125]

Aside from the novelty of having Jonas Salk act as "armchair superintendent" on the project, Chappell noted that the "very high-end architectural concrete building led to some other high-end architectural concrete projects."[126]

Another key project for the Southern California division was Arrowhead Regional Hospital, the largest project McCarthy had yet undertaken. As with the Salk Institute, McCarthy self-performed all the concrete work. "Arrowhead was mainly structural concrete, but the hospital is a base-isolated building, and that made it unique," said Chappell. "It's a seismic system that's used throughout the world, but it was the first time we had ever done it."[127]

Chappell noted that laboratories and hospitals required a different level of technical expertise than other types of buildings. "They're more complex in their inner workings," he said.[128]

Both the Salk Institute and Arrowhead Medical Hospital enhanced the Southern California division's reputation. "Dealing with the technical complexities associated with Salk, a very prestigious research lab on the West Coast, and Arrowhead, a base-isolated hospital and one of the largest hospitals on the West Coast, was pivotal in that climb for recognition," said Chappell.[129]

"Arrowhead really moved us toward being the contractor of choice in Southern California because it was a complex and difficult and very large project," added Bolen.[130]

Parking structures were the Southern California division's second core market. "McCarthy has been doing parking structures since the 1960s, so it's been natural for us to embellish on that," Chappell said. "In California there's a huge need for places to park cars, and we've developed a specialty in that niche market. It's also a market that takes advantage of our self-performing concrete capabilities," he explained. "We actually perform the work with our own labor forces." Chappell noted with some pride that from 1984 to 2001, McCarthy had built more than 55,000 structured parking spaces in California.[131]

The division made education, especially K–12, its third core market. "We brought a builder's mentality to a traditional management approach that was more administratively oriented," said Chappell. "As a result, we've been able to establish ourselves in the education marketplace very rapidly."[132] By

the end of 2001, the Southern California division was working with nine school districts and had about $400 million worth of school construction projects under contract.

Dennis Katovsich, the division's vice president of business development, said that the Newport

Above left and right: The Southern California division faced unique challenges when it constructed an addition to the famous Salk Institute. McCarthy had to match the new construction to the existing unique architecture.

Below: Arrowhead Regional Hospital was another challenging project for the Southern California division. It was the largest project the division had yet undertaken, and it was the first base-isolated structure the division had built. It received the Roger Burnet Award.

The auditorium of the Kodak Theatre (above right and opposite) seats 3,500, and the architecture (above left), designed by New York architect David Rockwell, is stunning to behold. McCarthy spent three years constructing the project, which is adjacent to the famous Mann's Chinese Theater.

Beach office had made a commitment to bid about 25 percent of its work. "It keeps our numbers sharp and keeps our people sharp," he said. "That way when we have negotiation opportunities and we're sitting across a table from clients, we know what things cost. We can speak from a base of real knowledge because we've had to know what things cost in the tough, competitive, hard-bid environment."[133]

The division built the $615 million Hollywood & Highland® retail and entertainment destination, home to the new Kodak Theatre, where the 2002 Academy Awards® were held. Located in the heart of Hollywood and surrounded by the historic Hollywood Walk of Fame and Mann's Chinese Theater, the development is expected to be visited by more than 13 million people annually. "The Hollywood project was the most challenging project I've been involved in," said Frank Pasztor, vice president of operations for the division. "It was a multiphase project and includes a six-level, below-ground parking structure which goes down into the earth about 70 feet. On top of that sits about

650,000 square feet of mixed-use retail space. The value of the theater alone is on the scale of $65 million."[134]

By 2002 the division had completed a wide array of projects, including a number of parking structures for offices, hotels, airports, shopping centers, hospitals, and universities; education contracts with California State University in Fullerton, Laguna Beach Unified School District in Laguna Beach, Juan Rodriguez Cabrillo High School in Long Beach, the Braille Institute in Los Angeles, and several jobs for the University of California in Irvine and La Jolla; healthcare contracts for Cedars-Sinai Medical Center in Los Angeles and Daniel Freeman Hospitals in Inglewood; several

McCarthy did work for Kaiser Permanente all over California. The Southern California division built the Kaiser Permanente Medical Center and parking structure in Baldwin Park. The project was a winner of the Roger Burnet Award.

airport and correctional facility jobs; scientific projects for the Loma Linda University Medical Center Cancer Research Institute and Proton Beam Therapy Facility in Loma Linda and the Salk Institute for Biological Studies in La Jolla; and hotel work, including the Lodge at Torrey Pines in La Jolla and the Irvine Conference Center Hotel.

Chappell saw continued growth for his division, both geographically and in new markets. "The growth is limited only by the economy," he said. "We've got plenty of experience. We welcome any challenge ahead."[135]

The Northern Pacific Division

Landing a contract with Bank of America in early 1995 gave McCarthy a sturdy foothold in the Northern California market and allowed it to open an office in San Francisco, where the bank's headquarters were located. The contract also gave the company an opportunity to shine.

"Bank of America came to us and said it had 1,600 branches in 10 different states that needed to be renovated for ADA compliance," said Mike Lipton, a project director who had been with McCarthy since 1984. "McCarthy hadn't done anything like that before. We had four years to do 1,600 branches."[136]

To accomplish such a feat, Lipton, who was in charge of "developing the game plan," worked with other McCarthy divisions. Lipton and his team developed a special procedure that let them finish the ADA compliance upgrade of a branch in only one night. "We ended up with a very happy client and the satisfaction of undertaking and develop-

ing something the company had never done before," Lipton said.[137]

As Mike Bolen was transitioning out of his leadership role in the Pacific division to become McCarthy's CEO, he wanted each of the three California offices—Newport Beach, Sacramento, and San Francisco—to be self-sufficient. In late 2001, McCarthy closed its offices in Seattle and Portland, Oregon, and split the Pacific division into Northern Pacific and Southern California to concentrate on the growing markets in the Central Valley and the northern part of the state.[138]

"That was a horribly tough decision." said Bolen. "When we purchased SDL in Seattle, that was the only time this division purchased another company to grow. SDL was a fine, small company, but it worked on smaller, more commodity-based projects, and we spent 10 years trying to figure out that market and trying to integrate that group into the rest of the company. At the same time, that Pacific Northwest market is very susceptible to boom and bust. The construction market has been very depressed up there."[139]

Like the other McCarthy divisions, the Northern Pacific division continued to pursue the healthcare market, for as Henry pointed out, the company had been doing healthcare work in Northern California through McBro for close to 20 years even though it didn't establish an office in Sacramento until 1992. Since the early 1990s, McCarthy had done numerous projects for Kaiser Permanente all over California, including hospitals, hospital upgrades, parking structures, and medical office buildings. The Northern Pacific division continued that long-standing relationship—a relationship built on mutual respect and trust—building Kaiser Permanente Medical Center in Stockton, California, among other projects.

Other key markets for the division included parking structures, microelectronics, biopharmaceutical manufacturing, education, and real estate. "We're diverse in that we do bid work and negotiated work, and we are involved in different markets," said Henry. "That way, when one market is in a downturn, we won't get hammered."[140]

By 2001 the division was, in the words of Rod Thayer, vice president of business development for the Sacramento office, "reaping the rewards of the seeds we planted five years ago. We have a ton of

The Northern Pacific division has built a number of biopharmaceutical facilities, including the Genentech W.A.F.E.R. building on Genentech's Vacaville, California, campus. The project includes a two-story office building, a two-story warehouse, and adjacent site improvements. Existing office space was also remodeled.

opportunity in front of us. We have very talented people here, and it's exciting to see how we've matured over the last three or four years—myself and other people who were placed in similar positions of authority who didn't necessarily have a lot of gray hair."[141]

In 2002 the Northern Pacific division was focusing its marketing efforts on education and had even developed a special business unit for K–12. California voters had approved a bond issue of more than $100 million to improve schools and build new ones, and McCarthy was well positioned to catch a good share of this lucrative market. The division was also expanding into the competitive Bay Area.

"We're definitely a young division," said Frances Choun, vice president of business development for the San Francisco office. "We're trying to become as successful as some of our brethren divisions that have been situated for quite some time. But I really feel that the potential is here, and I'm going to be here to help make us a success."[142]

Lipton agreed. "We're developing an excellent reputation," he said. "Working with the people here in San Francisco is very exciting right now, and helping to make the Northern Pacific division a success is very satisfying."[143]

By 2002 the Northern Pacific division had completed a diverse array of projects, including a biopharmaceutical project for Amgen Building 25 in Thousand Oaks, California; design-build facilities for Foster Farms in Oregon City, Oregon, and

McCarthy's Northern Pacific division renovated the architecturally unique Space Needle in Seattle, Washington.

Top: The Sutter Roseville Medical Center in Roseville, California, built by the Northern Pacific division, includes a three-story medical center and single-floor trauma facility, plus a separate Central Plant.

Left: The Northern Pacific division built Harbor Steps West, a luxury apartment complex in Seattle. The project included 200,000 square feet of apartments, 40,000 square feet of enclosed parking, and 30,000 square feet of retail/recreation facilities.

Kelso, Washington; projects for Boeing in Auburn and Everett, Washington, Hewlett-Packard in Corvallis, Oregon, and Hyundai in San Jose, California; various schools and facilities throughout the region; Valley Children's Hospital in Madera, California; airport work in SeaTac, Washington, and Sacramento; several correctional facilities; research and development projects for Genentech in San Francisco, the University of Washington in Seattle, and the University of California in Berkeley; renovations for the Space Needle in Seattle; and several hotels, including Westin Hotel in Seattle and Radisson Hotel-Fisherman's Wharf in San Francisco.

The Southwest Division

By the late 1990s, with a five-year average volume of around $150 million per year, the Southwest division had become firmly established as one of the premier builders in Arizona. Contract volume for 2002 was expected to reach $240 million, according to division president Bo Calbert, who wanted to expand into Nevada and New Mexico.

The Southwest division had already opened an office in Las Vegas and finished two major projects in New Mexico. "We're kind of stretching our wings here," Calbert said. "My job is to make sure we capture as much market as we can and make a profit doing it."[144]

When Arizona changed its state procurement law in August 2001 and introduced

Right: Niketown at Caesars Forum Shops, in Las Vegas, Nevada, is among the Southwest division's many entertainment projects. It is a 45,000-square-foot high-tech retail shop and includes interactive displays for the public.

Below: Lewis Prison was one of several correctional facilities built by the Southwest division.

the use of alternative project delivery methods (APDM), the Southwest division was in a prime position to benefit. With APDM, contractors could be hired based on qualifications rather than low bid. McCarthy had such a strong reputation and had maintained such good relations with the hard-bid clients that when APDM was introduced, the company qualified for every job it competed for.

Project Director Bob Knochenhauer mentioned McCarthy's relationship with the Arizona Department of Corrections as

Left: In 1998, Mike McCarthy (front row, left) congratulates Southwest division president Gerry Murphy as Southwest employees celebrate the division's 20th anniversary.

Below: The Southwest division won the Roger Burnet Award for building the Pueblo of Sandia Casino in Albuquerque, New Mexico.

an example. Back in 1981, the Southwest division had built Perryville Prison for the state. That was followed by Lewis Prison in 1996. Then in 2001, the division won the contract to design and build the Arizona Psychiatric Hospital, Arizona's first APDM project. "Our relationships helped us get the state's first APDM project," Knochenhauer said.[145]

Diversification within the division has been an important factor in its growth. "We're probably the most diversified contractor in the Southwest," said Calbert, who noted that the division did everything from "very tough, hard-bid, water and waste treatment plants to luxury resorts and hotels."[146]

The Southwest division had completed industrial contracts for the Water Campus Lab for the City of Scottsdale and the Motorola Treatment Facility in Scottsdale; biopharmaceutical work for Abbott Laboratories in Casa Grande, Arizona; microelectronics facilities for Hexcel Corporation in Chandler, Arizona, Honeywell Avionics in Glendale, Arizona, and Motorola in Tempe, Arizona; education work for Arizona State University in Tempe, the University of Arizona in Tucson, the Glendale Library in Glendale, Arizona, and Sunnyside School

Two winners of the Roger Burnet Award, given each year to McCarthy's best-of-the-best projects: Motorola MOS 13 (above) in Austin, Texas (built by the Texas division), and the Anaheim Entertainment parking structure (right), in Anaheim, California (built by the Southern California division).

in Tucson; healthcare projects for the Arizona State Civil and Behavioral Health Hospital in Phoenix and the Yuma Regional Medical Center in Yuma, Arizona; various institutional projects such as airport work, correctional facilities, and research and development facilities; and commercial projects for Niketown at Caesar's Palace in Las Vegas, Gold River Hotel & Casino in Laughlin, Nevada, the Sandia Casino in Pueblo of Sandia, New Mexico, the Blue Water Resort & Casino in Parker, Arizona, the Hyatt Regency Tamaya Resort

Corporate chefs Gerry Murphy (left), president emeritus of the Southwest division, and Bo Calbert, who took over as president of the Southwest division after Murphy's retirement.

in Bernalillo, New Mexico, and the Scottsdale Hilton and Scottsdale Princess Hotels in Scottsdale, Arizona.

Gerry Murphy, who had been president of the Southwest division since McCarthy opened the office in Phoenix, retired in April 2001 but stayed on as president emeritus for two more years. "I've struggled for years trying to establish McCarthy," Murphy said a few months after his retirement. "I'm proud of what I was able to do about getting us very solidly established as a top contractor in Arizona."[147]

Laurie Happ, marketing coordinator for the Southwest division, started in 1988 as Murphy's assistant. She expressed how deeply Murphy would be missed. "He was like a father figure to me. He is just a great guy. It seems everybody knows McCarthy through Gerry Murphy, and now that he's retiring, it's like we're moving into a new era."[148]

Chris Schwarz, vice president for the Southwest division, was a young project engineer when Murphy hired him in 1979. Schwarz remembered how Murphy had fostered his development within McCarthy and how he also showed an interest in Schwarz's family. "He took care of us along the way," said Schwarz. "There were bumps and bruises and tough times and such, but he never made me feel like a commodity."[149]

Continuing Traditions

In 1993 Mike McCarthy had created an award to honor one project each year from each division, calling it the Melvin Award in honor of his father. "I wanted an award that would challenge our people to excellence," he said. "I named it after my father because he was a high-quality guy."[150]

A second award, the Roger Burnet Award, or "Rog" as it was called, was the best-of-the-best prize, chosen from among the winners of the Melvin Award. The winning project embodied "the finest integrity, personal service, and commitment to quality." Mike named it after the man "who helped me build this company in all the arenas we went into.... No one else has advanced this company more in its values than the man whose name this very special trophy bears."[151]

"The projects are evaluated on fairly broad-based criteria," explained Bolen. "Performing to budget, to schedule, to quality; owner and sub-

Mike McCarthy takes pride in the family-like company he helped create, just as he takes pride in his own family. From left: Mike's wife, Kathy McCarthy; sister Fran Fitzgerald; Mike; sister Peggy Reynolds; and Peggy's husband, Jim Reynolds.

contractor satisfaction; and the net impact of the project against a hypothetical perfect standard.

These criteria are subjective enough so that the different projects can compete. It's not about which of them is the prettiest."[152]

A management committee from each division nominated jobs for the Melvin Award, and three finalists from each division made written and oral presentations before their peers during the holiday seminar at the end of the year.

"It's a great honor," said Bolen, "and the competition is very tough, but the trick is to make it a little tougher each year so we have more projects operating at a higher standard."[153]

The Melvin and Roger Burnet awards honored much more than buildings. They also paid tribute to the entire project team: the skilled workers, supervisors, engineers, secretaries, estimators, schedulers, and all those who labored for the cause. The integrity, client-centered service, and commitment to excellence honored by the awards have remained constants in McCarthy's ever evolving equation.

"We're hands-on builders," said Mike. "If you can dream it, we can build it, and this company can do that because it's made up of people with exceptional integrity. These are hard-working, talented people, people who respect each other and stick together when times get tough."[154]

In April 2002, McCarthy Building Companies completed the transition that turned it from a family-owned company to one that was 100 percent owned by the dedicated employees who worked so hard to make McCarthy the company it is today.

AN EMPLOYEE-OWNED COMPANY

This company is my life's work. I wanted to build a great company. I wanted to set it up so it had every opportunity to be everything I hoped it would be.

—Mike McCarthy, 2002

IN APRIL 2002, MIKE McCarthy took the final step in turning over the corporation to non-McCarthy-family control when he sold his remaining ownership of McCarthy to its employees. After that, 70 percent of the company was owned by the employee stock ownership plan (ESOP); the remaining 30 percent was owned by members of top management. As chairman emeritus, Mike McCarthy would continue his oversight of the company and his relationships with clients, and Mike Bolen assumed the role of chairman in addition to CEO.[1]

McCarthy's transition from a family-owned company to an employee-owned one began in 1990. As Paddy and Tim McCarthy prepared to retire from the family business, leaving Mike McCarthy as the last family-member leader, Mike started selling and awarding his stock to employees. The stock was greatly discounted for those who chose to buy, and it was awarded based on such factors as performance and safety.

Meanwhile, Mike was gradually buying stock from the remaining McCarthy-family shareholders. "I told them what I was doing," Mike said, "that I was taking the stock that I bought from them and getting it to those people who would run the company after we were all gone. I told them how this would raise the standard of the company and make it a company of which they would always be proud. And that's really why they sold—because they wanted to see the company that their great-grandfather had started reach its highest potential."[2]

Then in June 1996, Mike recapitalized and created the employee stock ownership plan, which made every salaried employee an owner in the company. The ESOP initially bought approximately 20 percent of the company's outstanding stock from the McCarthy family trust and acted as the controlling shareholder. Gradually, the ESOP bought more stock so that by 2002 it owned about 70 percent of the company.

Each salaried employee owned a piece of the ESOP, with the size of the piece depending on how long they had been employed with McCarthy and what their responsibilities entailed. The higher up on the management ladder, the larger the piece. The balance of the stock was owned by 65 of McCarthy's top managers, who were also members of the ESOP. To encourage top performance, Mike McCarthy started a number of

Mike McCarthy (left), chairman emeritus, shakes hands with CEO Mike Bolen after signing the final papers that turned McCarthy into an employee-owned company.

stock incentive programs in which key managers could earn stock options.

Though Mike McCarthy didn't begin selling and awarding stock to employees until 1990, the decision to transition from a family-owned business to an employee-owned one came about much sooner.

"As far back as 20 years ago, Mike McCarthy had come to the conclusion that the McCarthy family members who were then in the business would not be in a position to carry the company forward," explained George Scherer. "He didn't think any of them would someday be the next CEO."[3]

"No one on his side of the family wanted to stay in the business," said Mike Bolen. "So Mike was faced with the decision to sell the company to the employees and create an employee-owned company, or sell it to somebody else, which meant the company would either be merged into a bigger organization or owned by a foreign company."[4]

Mike McCarthy and the company's other leaders realized that if McCarthy became part of another company, the company's culture, which had survived for more than 100 years, would never endure. Furthermore, explained Scherer, "Mike felt like the employees were the folks whom he'd come to the dance with, and those were the folks he wanted to inherit the business."[5]

"When the employees bought the company from the family, that helped ensure that we would continue striving to be the best builder in America," said Bolen. "We were able to keep our vision, our goals, our view of ourselves intact and not have some new owner come in and tell us how it was going to be."[6]

Employee ownership had a positive impact on employees "because their individual stake in what happens has gone up dramatically," Bolen explained. "When they were working for a salary, they got that salary whether the company was

profitable or not. Now when the company is profitable, they see a direct benefit month to month, quarter to quarter, year to year, that accrues to them, and it's very motivating."[7]

"Everybody has a long-term stake in the company rather than just a retirement plan," said Scherer. "With every employee being an owner, they're going to want to perform at their very best level for all of our customers."[8]

Mike McCarthy recalled what had triggered him to want to sell the company to the employees. "We were having a meeting with all the operating guys," he remembered, "and Mike Bolen made the comment, 'We're all just working for a paycheck here.' I went back and thought about that, and I thought, 'I don't ever want any of our people to feel like they're working for a paycheck.'"[9]

Hard-working, dedicated employees are an asset to any company, but McCarthy realized another benefit as well. "The sale to employees solves transition issues for us in terms of the stability of the company going forward," said Bolen. "Now we have a rolling succession plan, so we're not coming up to a wall wondering what's going to happen."[10] Having a succession plan in place was important to customers, underwriters, banks, and bonding companies because it created a stable environment.

The transition to employee ownership was a well-thought-out process, and the entire transaction took more than 10 years, though the actual negotiations regarding Mike McCarthy selling his remaining interest to the company took place during the last 12 months, from April 12, 2001, to April 12, 2002.

Mike McCarthy had been with the company for his entire working career. In his younger years, he had watched the business grow and very soon had become the engine of its growth. The final decision, the final letting go, was difficult for him, but he knew what had to be done.

McCarthy had been incorporated by the sons of Irish immigrants in 1907 as a brotherhood of builders. That brotherhood was enshrined in the company's title in 1926. The brotherhood (if not always the ownership and control) expanded through the years from those three Michigan farm boys to their sons and grandsons. Cousins and uncles, fathers and sons all labored together, building structures while nurturing a family corporation made up of their own families, each other, and their field forces.

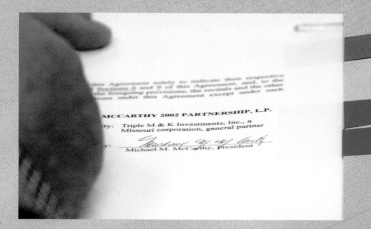

Gradually, McCarthy evolved from a family-run business to a family-like corporation. Mike McCarthy represented the last of the McCarthy bloodline in the company's management. By 2002, all of McCarthy's ownership was in nonfamily hands. Everything had changed, and yet those very changes, under Mike's watchful eye, were the fruit of what McCarthy had always been: a family business and a true brotherhood of builders.

BACK TO THE FUTURE: A MESSAGE TO MCCARTHY'S OWNERS

by

Mike Bolen

Chairman and CEO, McCarthy Building Companies, Inc.

McCARTHY—CONTINUOUS SERVICE since 1864. We have all gotten pretty used to that phrase around here, but stop for a moment and reflect on what that statement really means. It's 1864 Michigan, and being a mule skinner is an admired profession. The Civil War is still too close to call. Steam power is the newest rage. A democratic republic is still an experimental form of government. Steel buggy whips are the leading edge of technology.

Now roll it all forward. Coal. Oil. Electricity. The Industrial Revolution. Booms. Busts. Crashes. The New Deal. Two world wars and countless smaller ones. The Cold War. 9/11. Railroads. Automobiles. Airplanes. Trips to the moon. Telegraph. Telephone. Television. Telecommunications. Civil Rights. Baby Boomers. Generation X. Then Y. Wow!

It's truly amazing that any company could withstand all those external forces for so many years and survive. Add to that all the internal pressures detailed in this book and the outcome is even more remarkable. Just like America, McCarthy has seen its down times, crisis events, and major transitions. I'm certain there were many occasions when it would have been easy, maybe even smart, for McCarthy to give up, throw in the towel, and call it a good run. But every single time over nearly 145 years, somebody has stepped up, taken the lead, and said "No, not this time, not on my watch."

We at McCarthy owe our jobs and our professional futures to those leaders. Look at what they accomplished with their passion, perseverance, and integrity. That legacy is what makes us different from our competition, and it will fuel our future efforts to become the best builder in America.

That same legacy also leaves each of us with an awesome responsibility as we think about the future of the company. There are more tough times and rough circumstances coming in our future; I don't know where or when, but history says they are coming. Whenever and wherever that happens, each of us has the responsibility to be prepared to do what the McCarthys always did in the past. Step up, take the lead, and make it clear: "No, not this time, not on my watch."

If we will all commit to that responsibility and pass it on, I'll bet you a remarkable thing will happen in about 145 years. It will be time for Volume II of *The Legend of McCarthy,* and our great-great-grandchildren should really enjoy the result. Imagine the pictures, the stories, the great things to be built in the future.

We've all been left with a wonderful gift. Now it's our turn to write a little history.

Carpe diem, Partners.

NOTES TO SOURCES

Chapter One

1. *Peninsular Courier and Family Visitant*, 26 July 1866, Ann Arbor, Michigan.
2. *Peninsular Courier and Family Visitant*, 12 July 1866, Ann Arbor, Michigan.
3. Timothy McCarthy's tombstone, St. Patrick's Church Cemetery, Northfield Township, Michigan.
4. Ellen McCarthy's tombstone, St. Patrick's Church Cemetery, Northfield Township, Michigan.
5. George Pare, *History of the Diocese of Detroit*, 1701–1888, 367.
6. *Combination Atlas Map of Washtenaw County, Michigan* (Chicago: Everts & Stewart, 1874).
7. 1870 U.S. census for Northfield Township in Washtenaw County, Michigan.
8. Ibid.
9. 1880 U.S. census for Northfield Township in Washtenaw County, Michigan.
10. Ann Arbor City Directory, 1874–75.
11. Record book of Timothy McCarthy, 5 December 1879.
12. Kittie McCarthy's tombstone, St. Patrick's Church Cemetery, Northfield Township, Michigan.
13. Record book of Timothy McCarthy, 19 July 1879.
14. Record book of Timothy McCarthy, 11 August 1880.
15. Record book of Timothy McCarthy, 1 December 1879.
16. Record book of Timothy McCarthy, 20 and 21 November 1880.
17. Record book of Timothy McCarthy, October and November 1875.
18. Record book of Timothy McCarthy, October 1881.
19. Record book of Timothy McCarthy, 18 May 1877.
20. Record book of Timothy McCarthy, 19 May 1877.
21. Information provided |by Catherine O'Brien to Barbara Lopez-Lucio, 29 August 2001, Write Stuff Enterprises.
22. Record book of Timothy McCarthy, 20 March 1883.
23. Record book of Timothy McCarthy, undated entry.
24. Thomas Patrick Hennings, *From the Marshgrasses: A History of St. Patrick's of Northfield*, 1981.
25. Historical marker at St. Patrick's Church, Northfield Township, Michigan.
26. 1900 U.S. census for St. Francois County, Missouri.
27. *St. Francois Herald*, 11 December 1901.
28. Articles of Incorporation of St. Francois Real Estate Company, 19 April 1905, St. Francois County Circuit Clerk, Book 75, 166.
29. Newspaper clipping dated April 1905 on file in the Genealogy Room at the Farmington Public Library, Farmington, Missouri.
30. Mark Sullivan with Dan Rather, *Our Times* (New York: Scribner, 1996), 38.
31. 1969 Report on the Physical Growth of the City of St. Louis, St. Louis City Plan Commission, http://stlouis.missouri.org/heritage/History69/.
32. Minutes of the First Meeting of Directors, McCarthy Construction Company, 18 March 1907.
33. Ibid.
34. Minutes of the Annual Meeting of the Stockholders, McCarthy Construction Company, 26 March 1908.
35. Minutes of the Annual Meeting of the Stockholders, McCarthy Construction Company, 2 April 1910.
36. Minutes of the Annual Meeting of the Stockholders, McCarthy Lumber and

Construction Company, 22 March 1911.

37. Tom Miles, ed., "1909 Financial Statement for St. Francois County," *A Brief, Authentic History of St. Francois County, Mo.* (Farmington: *Farmington News*, 1935).

38. Marian M. Ohman, Missouri Courthouses: Scott County, http://muextension.missouri.edu, August 2001.

Chapter Two

1. 1969 Report on the Physical Growth of the City of St. Louis, St. Louis City Plan Commission.

2. "John W. McCarthy Passed Away at St. Louis Home Early Tuesday Evening," 1936 obituary, Genealogy Room, Farmington Public Library, Farmington, Missouri.

3. Polk-Gould's St. Louis Directory, 1917.

4. Polk-Gould's St. Louis Directory, 1920.

5. Polk-Gould's St. Louis Directory, 1921.

6. Polk-Gould's St. Louis Directory, 1922.

7. Polk-Gould's St. Louis Directory, 1924.

8. Polk-Gould's St. Louis Directory, 1926.

9. Polk-Gould's St. Louis Directory, 1927.

10. Ohman, Missouri Courthouses.

11. Ibid.

12. Ibid.

13. Ibid.

14. N. Collette Ellis, "Community Study of Farmington, Missouri," unpublished paper, 1934. Genealogy Room, Farmington Public Library.

15. *St. Louis Globe-Democrat,* 17 February 1933.

16. *St. Louis Globe-Democrat,* 9 October 1935.

17. *St. Louis Globe-Democrat,* 11 November 1938.

18. *St. Louis Globe-Democrat,* 27 June 1940.

19. Peggy Reynolds and Frances Fitzgerald, interview by Jeffrey L. Rodengen and Richard F. Hubbard, recording, 24 April 2001, Write Stuff Enterprises.

20. Ibid.

21. "John W. McCarthy Passed Away."

22. Ibid.

23. Ibid.

24. U.S. General Services Administration, Statement of Significance. http://w3.gsa.gov, August 2001.

Chapter Three

1. Resolution of the Board of Directors of McCarthy Construction Company, 1 August 1940.

2. Minutes of Meeting, Board of Directors, McCarthy Brothers Construction Co., 14 October 1941.

3. Ibid.

4. Ibid.

5. Ibid.

6. Ibid.

7. Ibid.

8. Partnership Agreement between John E. McCarthy and Melvin McCarthy, 27 October 1941. From Supplemental Report on Examination and Compilation, 6 November 1944.

9. Ibid.

10. Agreement between McCarthy Brothers Construction Co. and McCarthy Builders Company. From Supplemental Report on Examination and Compilation, 6 November 1944.

11. Ibid.

12. Ibid.

13. Ibid.

14. Summary Report by the Partners. From Supplemental Report on Examination and Compilation, 6 November 1944.

15. Ibid.

16. Ibid.

17. Ibid.

18. Ibid.

19. Ibid.

20. Ibid.

21. Ibid.

22. Ibid.

23. Ibid.

24. Michael M. McCarthy, interview by Jeffrey L. Rodengen, recording, 18 July 2001, Write Stuff Enterprises.

25. Ibid.

26. Ibid.

27. Ibid.

28. Summary Report by the Partners.

29. Analysis of Total Project Costs and of Job Costs for the Calendar Year 1942, 6 November 1944.

30. Ibid.

31. Ibid.

32. Summary of Gross Profit on Contracts, 31 December 1944.

33. Summary of Gross Profit or Loss on Contracts, 31 December 1945.

34. Profit and Loss Statement, 31 December 1946.

35. "St. Louis Firm Starts on $1,500,000 Camp," *St. Louis Globe-Democrat,* 15 August 1942.

36. Ibid.

37. Geoffrey C. Burt, Suzanna Walaszek, and Richard Edging, "Appendix: German POW Stonework at Fort Leonard Wood, Missouri," Construction Engineering Research Laboratories (CERL) on the World Wide Web.

38. Thomas P. "Pat" Waters Jr., interview by Richard F. Hubbard, 29 November 2001, recording, Write Stuff Enterprises.

39. McCarthy Brothers Construction Company Profit and Loss Statement, 31 December 1942.

40. McCarthy Brothers Construction Company Profit and Loss Statement, 31 December 1943.

41. McCarthy Brothers Construction Company Profit

and Loss Statement, 31 December 1944.
42. McCarthy Brothers Construction Company, Summary of Profit on Completed Contracts for Calendar Year 1946.

Chapter Four

1. Francis F. McCarthy, presentation on the history of McCarthy during the October Open Forum, videotape, early 1980s.
2. Timothy McCarthy and Mary Ellen McCarthy, "A record of work done by McCarthy Brothers and McCarthy-Pohl," 10 March 1949.
3. Timothy R. McCarthy, presentation on the history of McCarthy during the October Open Forum, videotape, early-1980s.
4. Rock Hill Quarries Company, Profit and Loss Statement, 31 December 1945.
5. Timothy R. McCarthy, presentation.
6. McCarthy Brothers Construction Company Balance Sheet, 31 December 1951.
7. McCarthy Builders, Inc., Balance Sheet, 31 December 1951.
8. Rock Hill Quarries Company, Statement of Income and Surplus, 31 December 1946.
9. Rock Hill Quarries Company, Statement of Income and Surplus, 31 December 1949.
10. Ibid.
11. Timothy R. McCarthy, presentation.
12. McCarthy-Pohl Contractors, Inc., Balance Sheet, 31 August 1949.
13. Timothy McCarthy and Mary Ellen McCarthy, "A record of work done."
14. McCarthy Brothers Construction Company, Summary of Profit on Completed Contracts for Calendar Year 1947.
15. McCarthy Brothers Construction Company,

Summary of Profit on Completed Contracts for Calendar Year 1948.
16. Timothy R. McCarthy, presentation.
17. McCarthy Brothers Construction Company, Summary of Profit, 1948.
18. Francis F. McCarthy, presentation.
19. Ibid.
20. Ibid.
21. Ibid.
22. Ibid.
23. Minutes of a Special Meeting of the Board of Directors, McCarthy Brothers Construction Company, 3 March 1949.
24. Ibid.
25. Timothy R. McCarthy, presentation.
26. McCarthy-Pohl Contractors, Inc., Profit and Loss Statement, 27 August 1950.
28. McCarthy-Pohl Contractors, Inc., Balance Sheet, 31 August 1953.
29. McCarthy-Pohl Contractors, Inc., Balance Sheet, 31 August 1958.
30. McCarthy-Pohl Contractors, Inc., Balance Sheet, 31 August 1965.
31. Timothy R. McCarthy, presentation.
32. Minutes of a Special Meeting and Annual Meeting of the Board of Directors, McCarthy Brothers Construction Company, 20 December 1949.
33. Timothy R. McCarthy, presentation.
34. Timothy McCarthy and Mary Ellen McCarthy, "A record of work done."
35. Ibid.
36. McCarthy Brothers Construction Company, Summary of Profit on Completed Contracts for Calendar Year 1949.
37. McCarthy Brothers Construction Company, Summary of Profit on Completed Contracts for Calendar Year 1950.

38. McCarthy Brothers Construction Company, Summary of Loss on Completed Contracts for Calendar Year 1951.
39. Timothy R. McCarthy, interview by Richard F. Hubbard, recording, 8 October 2001, Write Stuff Enterprises.
40. Timothy R. McCarthy, presentation.
41. Ibid.
42. Ibid.
43. Ibid.
44. McCarthy Brothers Construction Company, Summary of Profit, 1950.
45. Timothy McCarthy and Mary Ellen McCarthy, "A record of work done."
46. *St. Louis Globe-Democrat*, 2 April 1952.
47. Minutes of McCarthy Brothers Construction Company Special Meeting of the Stockholders, 30 January 1956.
48. McCarthy Brothers Construction Company, Statement of Gross Income, 31 December 1953.
49. Timothy R. McCarthy, presentation.
50. *St. Louis Globe-Democrat*, 21 July 1958.
51. McCarthy Brothers Construction Company, Statement of Gross Income, 31 December 1956.
52. McCarthy Brothers Construction Company, Statement of Income and Retained Earnings, 31 December 1960.
53. Francis F. McCarthy, presentation.
54. Ibid.
55. Ibid.

Chapter Five

1. "Thin Shell Scallops Roof a Unique House of Worship," *Building Construction*, December 1962, 16–20.
2. Ibid.

3. Esley Hamilton, St. Louis Chamber Chorus: Venues, St. Louis Abbey, www.iwc.com/slcc/venues/abbey.

4. "Thin Shell Scallops Roof."

5. Francis F. McCarthy, "Construction of Shell for Chapel of Priory School," presentation to the Mid-West Concrete Industry Board, 3 December 1963, Kansas City, Missouri.

6. "Thin Shell Scallops Roof."

7. Michael F. McCarthy, interview by Jeffrey L. Rodengen, recording, 24 April 2001, Write Stuff Enterprises.

8. Francis F. McCarthy, "Construction of Shell."

9. McCarthy Brothers Construction Company, Statement of Net Loss and Retained Earnings, 31 December 1962.

10. *St. Louis Post-Dispatch Sunday Magazine*, 26 October 1980.

11. "Thin Shell Scallops Roof."

12. Fredrick J. Dobney, "River Engineers on the Middle Mississippi: A History of the St. Louis District, U.S. Army Corps of Engineers," www.wes.army.mil/export/home.

13. "Mock 'Bomb' to Signal Start of Flood Project," *St. Louis Globe-Democrat*, 12 February 1959.

14. Ibid.

15. "Flood Wall Section Nears Completion," *St. Louis Globe-Democrat*, 9 May 1962.

16. "$2,414,451 Flood Wall Contract for Riverfront," *St. Louis Globe-Democrat*, 25 November 1962.

17. "Two St. Louis Firms Get Big U.S. Contracts," *St. Louis Post-Dispatch*, 13 August 1965.

18. "Ladue Firm Gets Engineers' Contract," *St. Louis Globe-Democrat*, 16 January 1967; "Flood Wall Sewer Contract Let for $1.48 Million," *St. Louis Globe-Democrat*, 29 June 1967.

19. "Floodwall Being Secured to Bedrock," *St. Louis Post-Dispatch*, 11 December 1963.

20. Michael M. McCarthy, interview, 18 July 2001.

21. Ibid.

22. Ibid.

23. Ibid.

24. Ibid.

25. Ibid.

26. Ibid.

27. Margaret McCarthy Reynolds, interview by Jeffrey L. Rodengen, recording, 24 April 2001, Write Stuff Enterprises.

28. Ibid.

29. Michael M. McCarthy, interview, 18 July 2001.

30. Margaret McCarthy Reynolds, interview.

31. Ibid.

32. Reynolds and Fitzgerald, interview.

33. Ibid.

34. Ibid.

35. Ibid.

36. Michael M. McCarthy, interview, 17 July 2001.

37. Thomas Waters Jr., interview.

38. Minutes of Special Meeting of Board of Directors, McCarthy Brothers Construction Company, 17 July 1964.

39. Minutes of Regular Meeting of the Board of Directors, McCarthy Brothers Construction Company, 21 December 1964.

40. Ibid.

41. Minutes of Regular Meeting of the Board of Directors, McCarthy Brothers Construction Company, 20 December 1965.

42. George Monaghan Weddle, *St. Louis Globe-Democrat*, 10 October 1965.

43. Francis F. McCarthy, presentation.

44. Ibid.

45. Michael M. McCarthy, interview, 18 July 2001.

46. Ibid.

47. Ibid.

48. Ibid.

49. Ibid.

Chapter Six

1. Minutes of a Special Meeting of the Board of Directors, McCarthy Brothers Construction Company, 3 January 1966.

2. Francis F. McCarthy's notes from meeting of 15 February 1963.

3. Minutes, Board of Directors, McCarthy Brothers Construction Company, 3 January 1966.

4. Profit-Sharing Plan for the Employees of McCarthy Brothers Construction Company, Article II(a), 30 December 1966.

5. Minutes of the Annual Meeting of the Board of Directors, McCarthy Brothers Construction Company, 18 December 1967.

6. Sue Stewart, interview by Richard F. Hubbard, recording, 24 April 2001, Write Stuff Enterprises.

7. Jim Ulkus, interview by Richard F. Hubbard, recording, 19 July 2001, Write Stuff Enterprises.

8. Jim Faust, interview by Richard F. Hubbard, recording, 13 June 2001, Write Stuff Enterprises.

9. Barb Saey, interview by Richard F. Hubbard, recording, 19 July 2001, Write Stuff Enterprises.

10. Tom Dollar, interview by Jeffrey L. Rodengen, recording, 24 April 2001, Write Stuff Enterprises.

11. Ibid.

12. Ibid.

13. Ibid.

14. Ibid.

15. Michael Hurst, interview by Richard F. Hubbard, recording, 14 June 2001, Write Stuff Enterprises.

16. Ulkus, interview.

17. Dan Cummings, interview by Richard F. Hubbard, recording, 13 June 2001, Write Stuff Enterprises.
18. Dollar, interview, 24 April 2001.
19. Mississippi River Pollution Abatement Project of the Metropolitan St. Louis Sewer District, Nomination for 1972 American Society of Civil Engineers Outstanding Civil Engineering Achievement Award, 18 January 1972.
20. Ibid.
21. Ibid.
22. Ibid.
23. Minutes of a Special Meeting of the Board of Directors, McCarthy Brothers Construction Company, 31 August 1966.
24. Minutes of the Annual Meeting of the Stockholders, McCarthy Brothers Construction Company, 21 December 1966.
25. Minutes of Special Joint Meeting of Stockholders and Directors, McCarthy Brothers Construction Company, 1 December 1966.
26. William H. Godbey, interview by Jeffrey L. Rodengen, recording, 24 April 2001, Write Stuff Enterprises.
27. Ibid.
28. Ibid.
29. Ibid.
30. Thomas L. Amberg, "New Parking Structure to Meet Growing Needs," *St. Louis Globe-Democrat*, 23 July 1969.
31. Agreement between Portable Parking Structures, Inc., and McCarthy Brothers Construction Co., 20 May 1969.
32. Ken Bonastia, interview by Richard F. Hubbard, recording, 24 April 2001, Write Stuff Enterprises.
33. Agreement, Portable Parking Structures and McCarthy Brothers Construction Company, 20 May 1969.

34. Ibid.
35. Godbey, interview.
36. Richard Vandegrift, interview by Jeffrey L. Rodengen, recording, 24 April 2001, Write Stuff Enterprises.
37. Minutes of the Annual Meeting of the Board of Directors, McCarthy Brothers Construction Company, 21 December 1970.
38. Vandegrift, interview, 24 April 2001.
39. Minutes, Board of Directors, McCarthy Brothers Construction Company, 21 December 1970.
40. Minutes of the Annual Meeting of the Board of Directors, McCarthy Brothers Construction Company, 20 December 1971.
41. Ibid.
42. Ibid.
43. Minutes of Special Meeting of Board of Directors, McCarthy Brothers Construction Company, 6 September 1968.
44. Ibid.
45. Minutes, Stockholders and Directors, 1 December 1966.
46. Minutes, Board of Directors, 6 September 1968.
47. Minutes of the Annual Meeting of the Board of Directors, McCarthy Brothers Construction Company, 16 December 1968.
48. Minutes of Annual Meeting of the Stockholders, McCarthy Brothers Construction Company, 15 December 1969.
49. McCarthy Brothers Construction Company, Statement of Income and Retained Earnings for the Year Ended December 31, 1969.
50. Minutes, Stockholders Meeting, McCarthy Brothers Construction Company, 15 December 1969.
51. Ibid.
52. Minutes, Board of Directors, McCarthy Brothers Construction Company, 21 December 1970.

53. Ibid.
54. Ibid.
55. Godbey, interview.
56. Ibid.
57. Melvin McCarthy, personal notes, undated.
58. Michael M. McCarthy, interview, 18 July 2001.
59. Data on McCarthy Supply Co., McCarthy archives, 5 February 1970.
60. Melvin McCarthy to John H. Hendren, 26 May 1970, McCarthy archives.
61. Reynolds and Fitzgerald, interview.
62. "Contract Signed For Hospital Annex," *St. Louis Post-Dispatch*, 4 January 1970.
63. McCarthy Brothers Construction Company, Financial Statements, 31 December 1970.
64. Melvin McCarthy to John H. Hendren, 26 May 1970.
65. Melvin McCarthy, "Memorandum of Closing for Agreement and Plan of Reorganization," 29 November 1971.
66. Minutes of the Annual Meeting of the Board of Directors, McCarthy Brothers Construction Company, 20 December 1971.

Chapter Seven

1. Andrew Greensfelder, interview by Jeffrey L. Rodengen, recording, 24 April 2001, Write Stuff Enterprises.
2. Hurst, interview, 14 June 2001.
3. Vandegrift, interview, 24 April 2001.
4. Ibid.
5. Ibid.
6. Michael M. McCarthy, interview, 18 July 2001.
7. Mike Bolen, interview by Jeffrey L. Rodengen, recording, 25 April 2001, Write Stuff Enterprises.
8. McCarthy Brothers Company balance sheet, 31 December 1972.

9. McCarthy Brothers Company, Statement of Income and Retained Earnings, 31 December 1972.

10. Richard Vandegrift, interview by Richard F. Hubbard, recording, 18 October 2002, Write Stuff Enterprises.

11. Michael M. McCarthy, interview 18 July 2001.

12. Ibid.

13. McBro History, 19 January 1982, unpublished.

14. Vandegrift, interview, 24 April 2001.

15. Michael M. McCarthy, interview, 18 July 2001.

16. Vandegrift, interview, 24 April 2001.

17. Michael M. McCarthy, interview, 18 July 2001.

18. Minutes of a Special Meeting of the Board of Directors, McCarthy Brothers Company, 30 April 1971.

19. Donald S. Barrie and Boyd C. Paulson, Jr., *Professional Construction Management Including CM, Design-Construct, and General Contracting*, 3rd ed. (New York: McGraw-Hill, 1992), 82.

20. Michael M. McCarthy, interview, 18 July 2001.

21. Vandegrift, interview, 24 April 2001.

22. Michael M. McCarthy, interview, 18 July 2001.

23. Vandegrift, interview, 24 April 2001.

24. Ibid.

25. Ibid.

26. McBro History, 19 January 1982.

27. Vandegrift, interview, 24 April 2001.

28. Ibid.

29. McBro History, 19 January 1982.

30. McBro Planning & Development Company, Notes to Consolidated Financial Statements, 30 March 1978.

31. McBro Planning & Development Company, Wm. H. Godbey Enterprises, Inc., and McCarthy Development Company, Notes to Combined Financial Statements, 31 December 1975.

32. Godbey, interview.

33. McBro, Godbey, and McCarthy, Notes to Combined Financial Statements, 31 December 1975.

34. Godbey, interview.

35. Gerry Murphy, interview by Richard F. Hubbard, recording, 8 October 2001, Write Stuff Enterprises.

36. Amendment of Articles of Incorporation of McCarthy Brothers Company, 14 May 1974.

37. Minutes of Joint Annual Meeting of Shareholders and Directors of McCarthy Brothers Company, 15 July 1974.

38. McCarthy Brothers Construction Company, Financial Statements, 31 December 1972.

39. McCarthy Brothers Construction Company, Financial Statements, 31 December 1973.

40. Minutes, Shareholders and Directors, 15 July 1974.

41. Ibid.

42. Ibid.

43. Ibid.

44. Ibid.

45. Timothy R. McCarthy, presentation.

46. Ted Schafers, "McCarthy Brothers Parleys Cost Control into $183 Million Construction Business," *St. Louis Globe-Democrat*, 14 December 1974.

47. Ted Schafers, "Downtown Construction Picking up Steam," *St. Louis Globe-Democrat*, 15 February 1975.

48. Ibid.

49. "Diversity and Hard Cash Lift McCarthy Firm to CM Pinnacle," *Engineering News-Record*, 26 August 1976.

50. Unanimous Consent of Directors in Lieu of Special Meeting of Board of Directors, McCarthy Brothers Company, 2 March 1976.

51. Michael M. McCarthy, interview, 18 July 2001.

52. Fitzgerald and Reynolds, interview.

53. Ibid.

54. Roger Burnet, interview by Jeffrey L. Rodengen, recording, 24 April 2001, Write Stuff Enterprises.

55. Bonastia, interview.

56. Greensfelder, interview.

57. Minutes of Special Joint Meeting of Shareholders and Directors of McCarthy Brothers Company, 28 February 1976.

58. "Tubular Design Cuts Mid-rise Framing Weight," *Engineering New-Record*, 29 April 1976.

59. Ibid.

60. Ibid.

61. "Compact Project Site Hampers Construction," *Construction Digest*, 30 March 1978, 14–18.

62. Ibid.

63. "McCarthy Reorganization," *St. Louis Globe-Democrat*, 24 September 1977.

Chapter Seven Sidebar: Roger Burnet

1. Bonastia, interview.

2. Lloyd Hansen, interview by Richard F. Hubbard, recording, 18 July 2001, Write Stuff Enterprises.

3. Tom Felton, interview by Richard F. Hubbard, recording, 19 July 2001, Write Stuff Enterprises.

4. Faust, interview.

5. Vandegrift, interview, 18 October 2002.

6. George Scherer, interview by Richard F. Hubbard, recording, 25 April 2001, Write Stuff Enterprises.

7. Vandegrift, interview, 18 October 2002.

8. Hurst, interview, 14 June 2001.

9. Scherer, interview, 25 April 2001.

10. Jim Staskiel, interview by Richard F. Hubbard, recording, 25 April 2001, Write Stuff Enterprises.
11. Vandegrift, interview, 18 October 2002.
12. Ibid.
13. Walter "Bud" Guest, interview by Richard F. Hubbard, recording, 19 July 2001, Write Stuff Enterprises.
14. Vandegrift, interview, 18 October 2002.

Chapter Eight

1. "1978 McCarthy Companies Volume Hits All-Time High," *McCurrents*, May 1979, 1.
2. "McCarthy Corporate Volume Up 35%," *McCurrents*, March 1981, 1.
3. Details of Construction Contract Operations, McCarthy Brothers Construction Company, 31 March 1979.
4. Timothy R. McCarthy, interview.
5. Robert Knochenhauer, interview by Richard F. Hubbard, recording, 7 November 2002, Write Stuff Enterprises.
6. Murphy, interview.
7. Ibid.
8. Ibid.
9. Ibid.
10. Ibid.
11. Ibid.
12. Minutes of Special Meeting of Board of Directors of TGK Construction Co., Inc., 5 February 1980.
13. "TGK Constructors, Inc. Is Now 'McCarthy Western,'" *McCurrents*, April 1983, 7.
14. Staskiel, interview.
15. Bolen, interview, 25 April 2001.
16. Knochenhauer, interview.
17. "McCarthy Brothers Opens Offices in Atlanta, Phoenix, Saudi," *McCurrents*, November 1979, 2.
18. Ibid.
19. Consent to Corporate Action in Lieu of Special Meeting of Shareholders of McCarthy Brothers Company, 2 February 1979.
20. "McMerit Opens in Houston," *McCurrents*, October 1981, 1.
21. Ibid.
22. Bo Calbert, interview by Richard F. Hubbard, tape recording, 9 January 2002, Write Stuff Enterprises.
23. Ibid.
24. Ibid.
25. Dollar, interview, 24 April 2001.
26. Details of Consolidated Financial Statements, McCarthy Brothers Company, 31 March 1982.
27. Vandegrift, interview, 24 April 2001.
28. "McBro Opens Office in Baltimore," *McCurrents*, March 1981, 1.
29. "Fourth Branch Office for McBro," *McCurrents*, April 1982, 1.
30. Guest, interview.
31. Jerri Stroud, "McCarthy Brothers," *St. Louis Post-Dispatch*, 1 March 1982.
32. Vandegrift, interview, 24 April 2001.
33. Details of Consolidated Financial Statements, 31 March 1982.
34. "McBro to Open Tampa Office This Summer," *McCurrents*, April 1983, 1.
35. "11 Area Contractors on ENR List of Top Firms in Nation," *St. Louis Globe-Democrat*, 5 May 1982.
36. Stroud, "McCarthy Brothers."
37. John Heidbreder, interview by Richard F. Hubbard, recording, 18 July 2001, Write Stuff Enterprises.
38. Details of Consolidated Financial Statements, 31 March 1982.
39. Steve Jennemann, interview by Richard F. Hubbard, recording, 19 July 2001, Write Stuff Enterprises.
40. Details of Consolidated Financial Statements, 31 March 1982.
41. "'Cadillac' of Parking Structures for Fords, Chevys, Toyotas, Etc." *McCurrents*, November 1979.
42. Kris Anderson, interview by Jeffrey L. Rodengen, recording, 25 April 2001, Write Stuff Enterprises.
43. "'Cadillac' of Parking Structures."
44. Dollar, interview, 24 April 2001.
45. Michael M. McCarthy, interview, 18 July 2001.
46. "Cautious Demolition Keys Project's Success at St. Louis Viaduct," *Construction Digest*, West Edition, 14 September 1978, 44–50.
47. Ibid.
48. Ibid.
49. Ibid.
50. "12th St. Viaduct to be Finished 5 Mo. Early," *St. Louis Globe-Democrat*, 29 September 1979.
51. "New Projects Are Announced," *McCurrents*, May 1979, 1–3.
52. Details of Construction Contract Operations, TGK Constructors, Inc., 31 March 1982.
53. Ibid.
54. Linda Osborn, interview by Richard F. Hubbard, recording, 7 February 2002, Write Stuff Enterprises.
55. Frank Pasztor, interview by Richard F. Hubbard, recording, 28 January 2001, Write Stuff Enterprises.
56. Unanimous Consent of Sole Shareholder and Directors in Lieu of Annual Meeting of Shareholders and Directors, McCarthy Building Companies, 18 June 1984.
57. Unanimous Consent of Sole Shareholder and Directors in Lieu of Annual Meeting of Shareholders and Directors, McCarthy Building Companies, 19 December 1983.
58. Stroud, "McCarthy Brothers."

Chapter Nine

1. Thomas Waters, Jr., interview.
2. "The Desert Superstate," *Time,* 22 May 1978, 34–46.
3. "Where the Constructors Strike it Rich," *Business Week,* 23 August 1976, 47–56.
4. Thomas Waters, Jr., interview.
5. Mike Krueger, interview by Richard F. Hubbard, recording, 14 June 2001, Write Stuff Enterprises.
6. Ibid.
7. Ibid.
8. Ibid.
9. Ibid.
10. Ibid.
11. Ibid.
12. "Mecca," *Columbia Encyclopedia,* 6th ed. (New York: Columbia University Press, 2001).
13. Krueger, interview.
14. Bolen, interview, 25 April 2001.
15. El-Sayed El-Refai to F. Abou El-Ghar, 26 December 1983, McCarthy archives.
16. Anderson, interview.
17. El-Sayed El-Refai, 26 December 1983.
18. Memorandum Agreement between McCarthy Brothers International and Dr. El-Sayed El-Refai, 21 February 1984, McCarthy archives.
19. Labor and Material Services Agreement between McCarthy Brothers International, Inc. and Osman El-Refai & Company, 30 May 1984, McCarthy archives.
20. Chuck Avery, interview by Richard F. Hubbard, 14 June 2001, recording, Write Stuff Enterprises.
21. Stephen L. Karp to Thomas Feldmann, 24 July 1984, McCarthy archives.
22. Thomas Waters Jr., interview.
23. Labor and Material Services Agreement, 30 May 1984.
24. Gamal El-Refai to Mike Krueger, 10 September 1984, McCarthy archives.
25. George Scherer to Osman El-Refai, 24 October 1984, McCarthy archives.
26. Ibid.
27. Osman El-Refai to Roger Burnet, 25 October 1984, McCarthy archives.
28. Osman El-Refai to George Scherer, 31 October 1984, McCarthy archives.
29. Ibid.
30. Ibid.
31. George Scherer to Osman El-Refai, 1 November 1984.
32. Osman El-Refai to George Scherer, 14 January 1985, McCarthy archives.
33. George Scherer to Pat Waters, 17 January 1985, McCarthy archives.
34. Pat Waters to Osman El-Refai, 18 February 1985, McCarthy archives.
35. Bolen, interview, 25 April 2001.
36. Pat Waters to Osman El-Refai, 18 February 1985.
37. Ibid.
38. Ibid.
39. Osman El-Refai to Pat Waters, 27 February 1985, McCarthy archives.
40. Roger Burnet, Memorandum, 4 March 1985, McCarthy archives.
41. LFathi Abou El-Ghar to Pat Waters, 1 July 1985, McCarthy archives.
42. Osman El-Refai to McCarthy International, 2 July 1985, McCarthy archives.
43. Mike Krueger to Fathi Abou El-Ghar, 4 July 1985, McCarthy archives.
44. Osman El-Refai to McCarthy International, 2 July 1985.
45. Gamil Shehata to Pat Waters, 9 September 1985, McCarthy archives.
46. George Scherer to Roger Burnet et al., 5 November 1986, McCarthy archives.
47. Roger Burnet to Osman El-Refai, 15 August 1985, McCarthy archives.
48. Osman El-Refai to Roger Burnet, undated, McCarthy archives.
49. Roger Burnet to Osman El-Refai, 21 August 1985, McCarthy archives.
50. Burnet, interview.
51. Mike McCarthy to the Cairo Governorate, 17 September 1985, McCarthy archives.
52. Mike Krueger to Banque du Caire, 19 September 1985, McCarthy archives.
53. Mike McCarthy to the Cairo Governorate, 27 September 1985, McCarthy archives.
54. Avery, interview.
55. Karen L. Koman, "Risk-Taking Leads to Trouble on the Nile," *St. Louis Post-Dispatch,* 6 February 1989.
56. Cairo Governorate to Mike McCarthy, 11 October 1985, McCarthy archives.
57. Thomas Waters Jr., interview.
58. Bolen, interview, 25 April 2001.
59. Avery, interview.
60. Bolen, interview, 25 April 2001.
61. Avery, interview.
62. Pat Waters and George Scherer to the Governorate of Cairo, 11 January 1986, McCarthy archives.
63. Ibid.
64. Ibid.
65. Bolen, interview, 25 April 2001.
66. Scherer, interview, 25 April 2001.
67. Bolen, interview, 25 April 2001.
68. Roger Burnet to the Governor of Cairo, 3 February 1986, McCarthy archives.
69. Ibid.
70. Mike Krueger and George Scherer to the Governor of Cairo, 11 February 1986, McCarthy archives.
71. Ibid.
72. Mike Krueger and George Scherer to Fahti Abou El-Ghar, 17 February 1986, McCarthy archives.

73. Roger Burnet to the Governor of Cairo, 7 March 1986, McCarthy archives.
74. Roger Burnet to the Governor of Cairo, 24 September 1986, McCarthy archives.
75. George Scherer, memorandum, 18 June 1986, McCarthy archives.
76. Roger Burnet to the Governor of Cairo, 17 October 1986, McCarthy archives.
77. George Scherer to Mike McCarthy, Roger Burnet, Pat Waters, and Gary Wiethuchter. 5 November 1986, McCarthy archives.
78. Pat Waters to George Scherer, 9 December 1986, McCarthy archives.
79. Roger Burnet to the Governor of Cairo, 19 February 1987, McCarthy archives.
80. Karen L. Koman, "Idea Man: Master Builder Mike McCarthy," *St. Louis Post-Dispatch*, 6 February 1989.

Chapter Ten

1. McCarthy Brothers Construction Company, Statement of Income and Retained Earnings, 31 December 1971.
2. McCarthy Building Companies, Consolidated Statement of Operations and Retained Earnings, 31 March 1985.
3. Charlotte-Anne Lucas, "Charles Keating Known for Conservative Values and Business Gambles," *Orange County Register*, 16 April 1989.
4. Hurst, interview, 14 June 2001.
5. Ibid.
6. Ibid.
7. Ibid.
8. Ibid.
9. Michael M. McCarthy, interview, 18 July 2001.
10. Hurst, interview, 14 June 2001.
11. George Scherer to Tim Peterson, 6 July 1992, McCarthy archives.

12. Michael M. McCarthy, interview, 18 July 2001.
13. Jennemann, interview.
14. Guest, interview.
15. Ibid.
16. Burnet, interview.
17. Ibid.
18. Michael M. McCarthy, interview, 18 July 2001.
19. Calbert, interview.
20. Ibid.
21. Michael M. McCarthy, interview, 18 July 2001.
22. Divisional Statement of Operations, McCarthy Building Companies, 31 March 1986.
23. Dollar, interview, 24 April 2001.
24. Ibid.
25. Michael M. McCarthy, interview, 18 July 2001.
26. L. Allen Klope, "Alton's New Span to Be 'Cable Stay' Type," *Telegraph*, 14 May 1987.
27. David Goodyear and Ralph Salamie, "The New Clark Bridge: Saddle-Draped Cables," *Civil Engineering-ASCE*, August 1994, 46–49.
28. Ibid.
29. Sanford Schmidt, "Super Bridge," *Telegraph*, 11 November 1997.
30. Mary Brase, "Clark Bridge Film Nears Completion," *Telegraph*, 5 July 1994.
31. Mary Brase, "Missing Link Is Hoisted into Place on New Span," *Telegraph*, 8 May 1993.
32. Mary Base, "Coming Attraction," *Telegraph*, 16 May 1993.
33. Tom Dollar, interview by Richard F. Hubbard, recording, 24 October 2002, Write Stuff Enterprises.
34. Jack M. Farmer, "Strike May Delay Opening of Bridge," *Telegraph*, 28 August 1993.
35. Dollar, interview, 24 October 2002.
36. Jack M. Farmer, "New Bridge to Open Jan. 5," *Telegraph*, 14 December 1993.
37. Paul A. Brinkmann, "Shining Moment—New Clark Bridge," *Telegraph*, 30 November 1997.

38. Burnet, interview.
39. Faust, interview.
40. Calbert, interview.
41. Faust, interview.
42. McCarthy Building Companies and Subsidiaries, Divisional Statement of Operations, 31 March 1986.
43. Ibid.
44. Michael M. McCarthy, interview, 18 July 2001.
45. Bolen, interview, 25 April 2001.
46. Karl Kloster, interview by Richard F. Hubbard, recording, 18 July 2001, Write Stuff Enterprises.
47. Michael M. McCarthy, interview, 18 July 2001.
48. Ibid.
49. Ibid.
50. Ibid.
51. Ibid.
52. Irrevocable Stock Power, McCarthy Brothers Company, 30 October 1986.
53. George Scherer to Dennis Flatness, 25 June 1990, McCarthy archives.
54. Scherer, interview, 25 April 2001.
55. McCarthy Building Companies and Subsidiaries, Divisional Statement of Operations, 31 March 1987.
56. McCarthy Building Companies and Subsidiaries, Divisional Statement of Operations, 31 March 1990.
57. Bolen, interview, 25 April 2001.
58. Carter Chappell, interview by Richard F. Hubbard, recording, 6 February 2002, Write Stuff Enterprises.
59. McCarthy Building Companies and Subsidiaries, Divisional Statement of Operations, 31 March 1990.
60. George Scherer to Dennis Flatness, 25 June 1990.
61. Jack Grone, "McCarthy Everywhere You Look," *St. Louis Business Journal*, 4 February 1991.

62. Ibid.
63. Ibid.
64. Michael M. McCarthy, interview by Richard F. Hubbard, tape recording, 16 October 2002, Write Stuff Enterprises.
65. Ibid.
66. Ibid.
67. Ibid.
68. Ibid.
69. McCarthy Building Companies and Subsidiaries, Notes to Consolidated Financial Statements, 31 March 1991.
70. Bolen, interview, 24 April 2001.
71. Anderson, interview.
72. George Scherer to Timothy Peterson, 6 July 1992, McCarthy archives.
73. Lydia Dawson, interview by Richard F. Hubbard, recording, 22 January 2002, Write Stuff Enterprises.
74. Ibid.
75. Gary Akin, interview by Richard F. Hubbard, recording, 18 January 2002, Write Stuff Enterprises.
76. George Scherer to Timothy Peterson, 6 July 1992.

Chapter Eleven

1. "News Briefs: Executive News," *McCurrents*, March 1996.
2. "Strategic Plan Update: FY 2000," *McCurrents*, June 1999.
3. Mike Hurst, "Planning . . . Strategically," *McCurrents*, December 1999.
4. Michael M. McCarthy, interview, 16 October 2002.
5. Bolen, interview by Richard F. Hubbard, recording, 14 October 2002, Write Stuff Enterprises.
6. Calbert, interview.
7. Chappell, interview, 6 February 2002.
8. Larry Glynn, "Mr. Tim—His Integrity Permeates McCarthy," *McCurrents*, July 1996.
9. Ibid.

10. Kevin Lasater, "Rich Vandegrift—Mr. Healthcare & So Much More!" *McCurrents*, January 1999.
11. Vandegrift, interview, 18 October 2002.
12. Michael M. McCarthy, interview, 18 July 2001.
13. "Burnet Hands Off to Hurst," *McCurrents*, October 1995.
14. Michael M. McCarthy, interview, 18 July 2001.
15. Ibid.
16. Carter Chappell, "Just Who Is Mike Bolen?" *McCurrents*, March 2000.
17. Michael M. McCarthy, interview, 18 July 2001.
18. Michael M. McCarthy, interview, 16 October 2002.
19. Dollar, interview, 24 October 2002.
20. Rich Henry, interview by Melody Maysonet, tape recording, 19 December 2002, Write Stuff Enterprises.
21. Ibid.
22. Dan Petry, interview by Melody Maysonet, recording, 5 December 2002, Write Stuff Enterprises.
23. "Ask Chairman Mike," *McCurrents*, October 1995.
24. Michael M. McCarthy, interview, 18 July 2001.
25. Ibid.
26. Ibid.
27. Ibid.
28. Ibid.
29. Ibid.
30. Ibid.
31. Hurst, interview, 14 June 2001.
32. Michael Hurst, interview by Richard F. Hubbard, recording, 21 October 2002, Write Stuff Enterprises.
33. Hurst, interview, 14 June 2001.
34. Dennis Tucker, interview by Richard F. Hubbard, recording, 16 January 2002, Write Stuff Enterprises.
35. Ibid.
36. Jennemann, interview.
37. Cummings, interview.

38. Neil Bauer, interview by Richard F. Hubbard, recording, 14 June 2001, Write Stuff Enterprises.
39. Mike Bollinger, "McCarthy—the Relationship Builder," *McCurrents*, September 1999.
40. Ibid.
41. Gary Amsinger, interview by Richard F. Hubbard, recording, 15 October 2002, Write Stuff Enterprises.
42. Jennemann, interview.
43. Amsinger, interview.
44. Ibid.
45. McCarthy Web site, www.mccarthy.com, March 2002.
46. Amsinger, interview.
47. Anderson, interview.
48. Russ Wenzel, interview by Richard F. Hubbard, recording, 19 July 2001, Write Stuff Enterprises.
49. Michael M. McCarthy, interview, 18 July 2001.
50. Bonastia, interview.
51. Michael M. McCarthy, interview, 18 July 2001.
52. Calbert, interview.
53. "News Briefs," *McCurrents*, January 1994.
54. Information provided by Michael M. McCarthy, February 2003.
55. Henry, interview, 19 December 2002.
56. "Communique," *McCurrents*, June 1999.
57. Kevin Kuntz, interview by Jeffrey L. Rodengen, recording, 25 April 2001, Write Stuff Enterprises.
58. Bolen, interview, 25 April 2001.
59. Henry, interview, 19 December 2002.
60. Michael M. McCarthy, interview, 18 July 2001.
61. Saey, interview.
62. Hansen, interview.
63. Safetyville flyer, published by Safety Center Inc., 2002.
64. Dawson, interview.
65. Ibid.

66. Laura Mickelson, "Building a Positive Image for McCarthy," *McCurrents*, July 1996.
67. Anderson, interview.
68. McCarthy Building Companies and Subsidiaries, Notes to Consolidated Financial Statements, 31 March 1991.
69. Murphy, interview.
70. "News Briefs," *McCurrents*, July 1996.
71. Scherer, interview, 25 April 2001.
72. "News Briefs," *McCurrents*, January 1999.
73. Anderson, interview.
74. Faust, interview.
75. Bolen, interview, 25 April 2001.
76. Avery, interview.
77. Ibid.
78. Ibid.
79. Kuntz, interview.
80. Chuck Avery, "National MEP Director Program," *McCurrents*, October 1995.
81. "National Teams—A Vehicle of Change," *McCurrents*, March 1996.
82. Avery, interview.
83. Michael McSorley, interview by Richard F. Hubbard, recording, 18 July 2001, Write Stuff Enterprises.
84. Michael Oster, interview by Richard F. Hubbard, recording, 1 November 2002, Write Stuff Enterprises.
85. Ibid.
86. Ibid.
87. "News Briefs," *McCurrents*, March 1996.
88. Anderson, interview.
89. Rob Langhoff, interview by Richard F. Hubbard, recording, 10 January 2002, Write Stuff Enterprises.
90. McCarthy Compass Services, brochure, McCarthy archives.
91. Anderson, interview.
92. Ibid.
93. Kloster, interview.
94. Kuntz, interview.
95. Bolen, interview, 14 October 2002.
96. Ibid.
97. Rich Henry, interview by Richard F. Hubbard, recording, 25 October 2002, Write Stuff Enterprises.
98. Ibid.
99. Ibid.
100. Ibid.
101. Bolen, interview, 25 April 2001.
102. Michael M. McCarthy, interview, 18 July 2001.
103. McCarthy. Markets and Services, http://mccarthy.com.
104. Kloster, interview.
105. Ibid.
106. Ibid.
107. Dennis Bryan, interview by Richard F. Hubbard, recording, 14 June 2001, Write Stuff Enterprises.
108. "Strategic Plan Update—FY 2000," *McCurrents*, June 1999.
109. Rich Corey, interview by Richard F. Hubbard, tape recording, 19 July 2001, Write Stuff Enterprises.
110. Felton, interview.
111. Kloster, interview.
112. Guest, interview.
113. Bryan, interview.
114. Case study for St. Louis University Museum of Art.
115. "Texas Satellite Office Relocates," *McCurrents*, October 1995.
116. Mary Petry, "Divisional Office Opens in Dallas," *McCurrents*, September 1998.
117. Dollar, interview, 24 April 2001.
118. Bolen, interview, 25 April 2001.
119. Mike McWay, interview by Richard F. Hubbard, recording, 14 January 2002, Write Stuff Enterprises.
120. Akin, interview.
121. Ibid.
122. Chappell, interview, 6 February 2002.
123. Steve Mynsberge, interview by Richard F. Hubbard, recording, 6 February 2002, Write Stuff Enterprises.
124. Bolen, interview, 14 October 2002.
125. Carter Chappell, interview by Richard F. Hubbard, recording, 22 October 2002, Write Stuff Enterprises.
126. Ibid.
127. Ibid.
128. Ibid.
129. Ibid.
130. Bolen, interview, 14 October 2002.
131. Chappell, interview, 6 February 2002.
132. Ibid.
133. Dennis Katovsich, interview by Richard F. Hubbard, recording, 5 February 2002, Write Stuff Enterprises.
134. Pasztor, interview.
135. Chappell, interview, 6 February 2002.
136. Mike Lipton, interview by Richard F. Hubbard, recording, 28 January 2002, Write Stuff Enterprises.
137. Ibid.
138. David Parkes, "New California Region," *McCurrents*, June 1999.
139. Bolen, interview, 14 October 2002.
140. Henry, interview, 19 December 2002.
141. Rod Thayer, interview by Richard F. Hubbard, recording, 16 January 2002, Write Stuff Enterprises.
142. Frances Choun, interview by Richard F. Hubbard, recording, 24 January 2002, Write Stuff Enterprises.
143. Lipton, interview.
144. Calbert, interview.
145. Knochenhauer, interview.
146. Calbert, interview.
147. Murphy, interview.
148. Laurie Happ, interview by Richard F. Hubbard, recording, 9 January 2002, Write Stuff Enterprises.
149. Joe Lauer, interview by Richard F. Hubbard,

recording, 11 January 2002, Write Stuff Enterprises.

150. Michael M. McCarthy, interview, 16 October 2002.

151. Ibid; "The Roger Burnet Award," *McCurrents,* May 1997.

152. Bolen, interview, 14 October 2002.

153. Ibid.

154. Michael M. McCarthy, interview, 18 July 2001.

**Chapter Eleven Sidebar:
Traveling Managers**

1. Greg Montgomery, interview by Melody Maysonet, recording, 9 December 2002, Write Stuff Enterprises.

2. Bill Schuttler, interview by Melody Maysonet, recording, 13 December 2002, Write Stuff Enterprises.

3. Harl Buckallew, interview by Melody Maysonet, recording, 9 December 2002, Write Stuff Enterprises.

4. Schuttler, interview.

5. Petry, interview.

6. Schuttler, interview.

7. Buckallew, interview.

Epilogue

1. Margaret Jackson, "McCarthy Passes the Torch," *St. Louis Business Journal,* 19 April 2002.

2. Michael M. McCarthy, interview, 16 October 2002.

3. George Scherer, interview by Richard F. Hubbard, recording, 21 October 2002, Write Stuff Enterprises.

4. Bolen, interview, 14 October 2002.

5. George Scherer, interview, 21 October 2002.

6. Bolen, interview, 14 October 2002.

7. Ibid.

8. Scherer, interview, 21 October 2002.

9. Michael M. McCarthy, interview, 16 October 2002.

10. Bolen, interview, 14 October 2002.

INDEX

Page numbers in italics indicate photographs.